Work with Me

English for Early-Childhood Teachers and Youth Workers

6., überarbeitete Auflage

Dr. Michaela Kählau
Dr. Ulrike Kamende
Lisa Klockmann
Christina Meisterburg
John Stephen Payne
Julie Anne Payne

unter Mitarbeit von Wolfgang Dohrmann

Verlag Handwerk und Technik · Hamburg

How to Work with Me

Liebe Studierende,

Work with Me soll Ihnen dabei helfen, Ihre Englischkenntnisse berufsbezogen weiterzuqualifizieren. Es bietet Ihnen die Chance, Ihre B1-Sprachkenntnisse auf B2-Niveau zu steigern. Sie werden direkt angesprochen, Ihren persönlichen Lernerfolg selbst zu steuern, daher können Sie das Werk auch im Selbststudium nutzen.

In **Work with Me** werden Themen verwendet, die der Erzieherausbildung sowie der Ausbildung der Heilerziehungspflege entspringen: Situationen des sozialpädagogischen wie sozialpflegerischen Alltags werden praxisnah und fachlich aktuell dargestellt. Die hier vorgestellte Klientel befindet sich in allen Altersbereichen (vom Krippenkind bis zum Erwachsenen) und schließt Menschen mit besonderem Förderbedarf ein. Eine Vielfalt an Texten bietet die Möglichkeit, gemeinsam mit der Lehrkraft eine Auswahl zu treffen, die Ihnen und Ihrer Lerngruppe angemessen ist.

Die zwölf sogenannten **Modules** sind als geschlossene Einheiten konzipiert und verzichten auf eine lineare Abfolge. Manche Texte in den Modules sind schwieriger als andere: Um einen für Sie angemessenen Text zu finden und für Ihren persönlichen Lernerfolg zu nutzen, sind die Fachtexte nach Niveaustufen [B1, B2] gekennzeichnet. So können Sie im Selbststudium Module Ihrer besonderen Interessenlage zur Auffrischung der Englischkenntnisse wählen. Ein **Literature Project** zu einem Roman mit sozialpädagogischem Hintergrund rundet das Buch inhaltlich ab.

Die zahlreichen **Aufgaben** zu den Fachtexten sind so gestaltet, dass sie einerseits den Fortschritt in Ihrem Fachwissen und andererseits den Spaß am Englischen fördern: Wortschatzarbeit *(Working with Words, Working with the Text)*, eine Vielzahl an Sprechanlässen *(Discussion, Mediation, Translation)*, spielerische Elemente *(Role Play)*, handlungsorientierte Projekte *(Project, Internet Research)*, Vorschläge zu Gruppenarbeiten *(Group Work)* und kreative Präsentationsmethoden *(Creative Task)* werden angeboten. Zur Unterscheidung des Schwierigkeitsgrads sind auch die Aufgaben gekennzeichnet: von einem Sternchen (★ = unteres B1-Niveau) bis zu vier Sternchen (★★★★ = oberes B2-Niveau). Das Symbol KMK vor Aufgaben bedeutet, dass hier besonders die Kompetenzen für das KMK-Fremdsprachenzertifikat (dies sind *Reception, Production, Interaction, Mediation*) geübt werden. Im Übrigen bereiten die Aufgaben generell auf die Fachhochschulreifeprüfung im Fach Englisch vor.
Blau im Text hervorgehobene Vokabeln werden in den Vokabellisten erklärt.

Das Symbol zeigt an, dass dieser Text als mp3-Datei erhältlich ist.

Der Grammatikteil **Working with Grammar** inklusive Übungen (und Lösungen!) dient Ihnen dazu, eventuelle Lücken zu schließen. Im Anhang steht Ihnen unter anderem das umfangreiche **Alphabetical Vocabulary** als Nachschlagewerk zur Verfügung. Zur Unterstützung bei Talking/Listening/Reading/Writing und mehr dient der Methodenteil **Working with Me (Methods and Skills)**.

Eine anregende Lernzeit mit großem Lernerfolg wünschen

Autoren und Verlag

Contents

Work with me ISBN 978-3-582-77856-7

Zu diesem Werk sind Audio-Dateien zum Download (Best.-Nr. DA0901059) und ein Lehrerhandbuch (Best.-Nr. E16511) erhältlich.

ISBN 978-3-582-77856-7 Best.-Nr. 1651 6., überarbeitete Auflage

---

Verlag Handwerk und Technik GmbH,
Lademannbogen 135, 22339 Hamburg; Postfach 63 05 00, 22331 Hamburg – 2025
E-Mail: info@handwerk-technik.de – Internet: www.handwerk-technik.de

Satz und Layout: Olaf Schlierf Type & Design, 29331 Lachendorf
Umschlagmotiv: iStockphoto, Berlin: Bild 1 (Sasiistock); Bild 4 (dszc)
Shutterstock Images LLC, New York, USA: Bild 3 (NadyaEugene); Bild 5 (Elizaveta Galitckaia)
stock.adobe.com: Bild 2 (Robert Kneschke)
Druck: BDZ GmbH – Buchdruck-Zentrum, 54595 Prüm

Module 1

English and Its Influence on Our Daily Lives

In this module you will have the opportunity to learn

- why it is important to study English (in school)
- in which ways English is influencing our daily lives
- the definition and grammatical rules of a language called "Denglish"
- about the influence of German on English
- about tips for your Recognition Year

Introduction

My English is not the yellow from the egg but it goes.

★ **Discussion**

1. Look at the pictures and describe what you see. Here are some words which might be helpful:

   literal translation pun

2. In which countries would you have to speak English? Have you ever had to speak English abroad?

3. Have you ever encountered a professional situation at work where you needed your English skills?

★★ 4. **Internet Research**

   a) English is spoken differently in various countries. These differences may occur in grammar, pronunciation and spelling. What varieties of English are there? In which exact ways do they differ from one another? Create a poster explaining one or more of these differences in groups and present it in class.

   b) Watch some clips from different English speaking countries. Try to imitate the different accents.

TEXT 1: Looking at Your English Skills [B1]

You have been learning English for some time now, right? You have done grammar exercises, vocabulary tests, and maybe even role plays in class. But here's the important question: how good is your English really?

German students are often quite good at English because of school lessons, streaming videos, social media, and song words they have repeated many times. But knowing words is not the same as using them. Can you order food in English without feeling nervous? Could you have a conversation with an English speaker... or would you forget your verbs? Let's look at what students do well and what is difficult for them.

Many students start learning English in elementary school, and it is a mandatory subject for many years. By high school, most German students understand English grammar, reading, and writing well. However, speaking and pronunciation can be harder if they don't practice a lot outside of school.

One strength is grammar, as German and English have similar language roots. This makes it easier for German students to understand certain grammar rules. Also, German students know many English words because some words in German and English are similar. Popular culture, like English movies and music, also helps German students improve.

However, there are some challenges. German students may find it hard to pronounce some English sounds, like the "th" sound, which doesn't exist in German.

In general, German students have strong English skills compared to students in many other countries. This is thanks to school education and exposure to English in culture.

(256 words)

★ 1. **Working with Words**
Translate the following words into German:

Pronunciation – Similar – Language roots – Exposure

★★ 2. **Working With the Text**
- a) Why do German students usually have good English skills?
- b) At what age do many German students start learning English?
- c) By the time they reach high school, which English skills are German students typically good at?
- d) Compared to students in other countries, how strong are German students' English skills?

Work with me ISBN 978-3-582-77856-7

TEXT 2: Keep On Talking [B1]

Have you ever forgotten a word in the middle of an English sentence and just used the German one instead? You're not the only one – and believe it or not, that's actually a strategy! Many learners already use smart tricks to keep talking, even when they don't know or can't remember a word. In this text, you'll learn more about these easy strategies and how they can help you speak more freely.

If you are in the middle of a conversation with a friend and don't want to use your phone to translate a single word that has slipped your mind, you can use a few easy strategies. These strategies can be applied to any language.

The first strategy is called gap-filling. A gap in this context is the word you can't remember or simply don't know. You can fill this gap by using the German word. If you are speaking to someone who also speaks German, or a bit of German, this is an easy way to keep the conversation going. Keeping the conversation going is often the reason people use this strategy.

Literal translations are translations that do not consider the grammar or context of the target language. These can be quite funny for those who understand the language the literal translation comes from. However, people who are not fluent in both languages might not be able to understand this humour.
For the next strategy, you need to have a bit of vocabulary ready.
Paraphrasing means that you describe the word or words that have slipped your mind or are unfamiliar to you so that the person you are talking to can understand what you mean. They will probably then provide the word you are looking for.
Paraphrasing is used in many fun language games you might know, like "I spy with my little eye" and "Taboo."

(309 words)

Working With the Text

★★ 1. Which of the strategies mentioned above use language mixing?

★★ 2. Which strategy do you think is the easiest? Which is the hardest to use? Why?

INFO 1: Language Mixing

*The text "Keep On Talking" mentions two strategies that **involve** language mixing.*
A mixture of German and English is called Denglish or Denglisch.
*Did you know that there are even official rules for Denglisch, particularly for how English words are **incorporated** into the German language?*

INFO 2: The Grammatical Rules of Denglish

1. Verbs

   To become *Denglish*, English verbs are conjugated as if they are German verbs, with the infinitival suffix **-en**, and the past tense prefix **-ge** (although, strangely, the English past tense suffix **-ed** often remains!)

   Ich muss den Computer **neu booten**, weil die Software **gecrashed** ist.
   → I had to *reboot* the computer because the software *crashed*.

   Hast du schon die neueste Mozillaversion **gedownloadet**?
   → Have you already *downloaded* the newest version of Mozilla?

   Here are verbs which German has adopted from English, and has also made into verbal nouns:
   (to) chill = *chillen or das Chillen*
   (to) rock = *rocken or das Rocken, das Abrocken*
   (to) skate *skaten or das Skaten*

2. Nouns

   When English nouns are integrated into the German language, we spell them – as we do our own nouns – with a capital letter (*Superstar, Pop, Beauty, Style, Band*). But remember that nouns, verbs or adjectives are not capitalised in English!

3. Adjectives

   When we borrow adjectives we change the suffix:
   groovy = *groovig* trashy = *trashig*

   But sometimes an English word is accepted without change:
   easy – cool – happy

4. Hybrid Combinations

   You will also often notice a combination of English and German words in which one component keeps its original form, while the other is simply translated. Examples:

   Live-**Sendung** Hardware-**Hersteller** **Drogen**-Dealer **Musik**-Contest

5. Literal Translations

   The trend of direct translation is going even further. Literal translations of popular English expressions are slowly but increasingly replacing German words and idioms. Some well-known examples:

   Das macht Sinn! (*That makes sense*)
   Oh, Hölle! (*Oh, hell*)
   Nicht wirklich (*Not really*)

Work with me ISBN 978-3-582-77856-7

★★ 1. **Working with the Text**

a) How are English verbs integrated into the German language?

b) What happens when we borrow adjectives?

★★ 2. **Working with Words**

a) We have learned that English nouns are always capitalized in German. Which words are always capitalized in English?

b) Complete the chart below by filling in as many English nouns, adjectives and verbs as possible which we also use in German.

Nouns	Verbs	Adjectives
Fan	relaxen	hot
Star	surfen	...
...	dissen	...

c) Reflect upon your own language. Have you ever used English loanwords in German? If yes, in which situations have you used them?

3. **Creative Tasks**

★★★ KMK
a) **Magazine Project**
Work with a partner and take a look at the adverts in magazines. Then try to answer these questions:
- In which types of advertisements are Anglicisms used?
- Could these words be replaced by German words?
- Which function do they have within the ad?

★★★★ KMK
b) **Advertisement**
Create your own magazine or TV advert for a product of your choice. Use as many Anglicisms as you can and present your results in class.

Aren't you glad to be learning English?!

In his book Nothing For Ungood", American author John Madison writes about cultural differences between Germany and the United States of America. In one of the chapters he focuses on language and states that it is impossible for an American to learn the German language. His main argument: the German language has 16 different possibilities of expressing the article "the".
See for youself:

German					English
Nominativ	der	die	das	die (Plural)	the
Genitiv	des	der	des	der	the
Dativ	dem	der	dem	den	the
Akkusativ	den	die	das	die	the

(from: Nothing For Ungood by John Madison)

Info 3: A Global Language

As English is so widely spoken, it is often referred to as a ***global language*** *or a* ***lingua franca****: this is a Latin expression to describe any language widely used beyond the population of its native speakers. Although English is not an official language in most countries, it is currently the language most often taught as a* ***second language*** *around the world.*

Text 3: Is English Taking Over the World? [B1]

In his book "English as a Global Language", **David Crystal**, a famous linguist, academic and author, explains WHY so many people around the world learn and speak English. Here are his top five reasons:

1. English is the main language of popular music, advertising, satellite broadcasting, home computers, video games, and even of international illegal activities such as pornography and drugs.
2. Most technological, scientific and academic information in the world is expressed in English. It is the leading language of academic conferences. In most parts of the world the only way people can understand e.g. Dante or Goethe is through English translation.
3. The USA's leading economic position for international business and trade forces those who wish to establish an international market to use English. It is the leading language of international business and international tourism.
4. English is also the language of international air traffic control, and is further developing its role in international maritime, policing and emergency services.
5. It is sometimes thought that English has achieved its worldwide status because of its basic linguistic features. People have said that it is a more logical or more beautiful language than others, that it is easier to pronounce, simpler in grammatical structure, or larger in vocabulary. Of course, this way of thinking is not objective because there are no objective standards for beauty or of grammatical logic.

(193 words)

★ 1. **Working with the Text**
Do you agree with Crystal's 1–5 order? In what order of importance would you put his reasons?

★★ 2. **Written Discussion**
List your *own* top five reasons for learning English and explain why English plays an important role in your life.

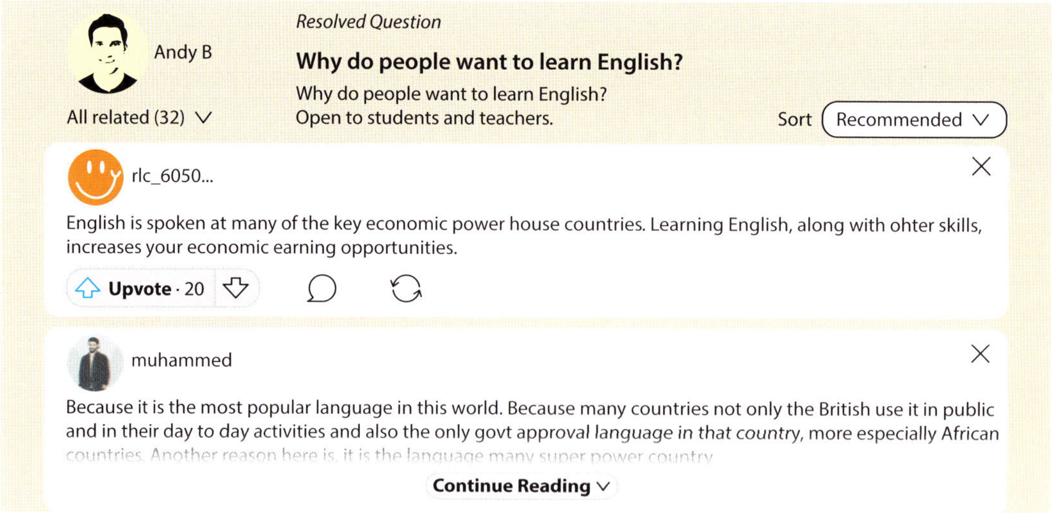

Work with me ISBN 978-3-582-77856-7

TEXT 4: An Interview with Abby: Getting to Know Someone Who Speaks Two Languages on a Daily Basis [B1]

Abby lives in Nairobi, the capital of Kenya. Nairobi is situated in the east of Africa. Abby is 41 years old and works with disabled children. In her free time, she creates artwork using old CDs and other recyclable materials.

Read this interview with Abby and find out what her language life is like in Africa.

Interviewer: *Where were you born, Abby?*
Abby: I was born in Nairobi.
Interviewer: *Where were your parents born?*
Abby: Both of them were born in England.
Interviewer: *When did your parents come to Nairobi?*
Abby: Both my parents came here in the 1970s.
Interviewer: *What was your family language when you were a child?*
Abby: It was always English.
Interviewer: *Which other languages do you speak?*
Abby: I speak Swahili. It is one of the national languages. There are 68 different languages spoken in Kenya.
Interviewer: *Which language did you speak at school?*
Abby: We spoke English. Swahili is one of the national languages, but there are so many dialects that English is the main language. Nairobi was actually a British colony, so there are still a lot of English speakers here.
Interviewer: *In which situations do you speak Swahili?*
Abby: Well, for example in a taxi. It's funny – usually they think I'm a tourist because I am white and I look British, but then I speak Swahili and they are sometimes surprised. I've heard people talk about me in Swahili, not knowing that I can understand them – oops! Sometimes I also speak Swahili at the shops. The more rural you go, the fewer people speak English.
Interviewer: *Do you have conversations where you mix both languages?*
Abby: Yes, I have friends who are fluent in both languages, and then we mix. Also, if I'm missing a certain word, or if a word is easier or shorter in one language, I switch. For example, if you say something like medicine – "dawa" – I always use the Swahili word. I guess it's because I've just grown up saying it.
Interviewer: *Are there words that you don't have in English or can't express as accurately?*
Abby: Yes, sometimes there are sayings where a direct translation would sound very strange.
Interviewer: *Which language is on your phone?*
Abby: English. I find writing in Swahili a bit more difficult. I just learned it by speaking; I have never really had to write it.
Interviewer: *Would you say that most of your friends are English speakers?*
Abby: Yes, mostly English, but they also have their own dialects. Swahili is the main one.
Interviewer: *What is the language of government and politics?*
Abby: English and Swahili.
Interviewer: *Thank you, Abby!*

(357 words)

★★ 1. **Working with the Text**
a) Where does Abby live, and what is her job?
b) Why is English the main language spoken at schools in Nairobi?

★★ 2. **Discussion**
Do you know anybody who speaks two or more languages? How do they mix them when speaking?

Text 5: Don't We All Speak English Anyway? [B1]

In addition to those native speakers who speak English as a mother tongue, there are another estimated 400 million people who use English as their second language. They live in countries in which this language has a special status. The governments in, for example, Ghana and Nigeria, have settled on English as the main language to carry on the affairs of government, education, commerce, media and the legal system. In such countries people have to start learning English at an early age.

English is either an official or semi-official language and has a special status or function in over 70 of the world's territories. Among them are American Samoa, the Federated States of Micronesia, Singapore and India.

However, although these countries adopt English officially, educational opportunities may be limited and only a small fraction of the population may be given the opportunity to learn it. India is an example of this. It is estimated that perhaps a third of the population has some competence in English and between 5 and 10 % are fluent (i. e. 50–100 million). This suggests that use of the English language in India exceeds that of the English-speaking population of Britain.

English is also used in countries where it has no official status, but where it is learned as a foreign language in schools and institutes of higher education, such as in Germany, France and Spain. People there have an enormous motivation to learn English because it has become the dominant language of communication. It is the official language of airports and the chief maritime language. It is the language of international business and academic conferences, of diplomacy, of sport, of scientists writing papers and of people writing e-mails or storing information in electronic retrieval systems.

(292 words)

★★ 1. **Working with the Text**

Decide which of these statements are true or false. Correct the false statements.

a) An estimated 40 million people use English as their second language, meaning that they must learn English at an early age.
b) English is an official or semi-official language, or has some special status or function in over 90 of the world's territories, among them Singapore and India.
c) Everyone in these territories has the opportunity of learning English.
d) English is rarely used in countries where it is learned as a foreign language.
e) People all over the world want to learn English because it has become the dominant language of modern communication

★★★ 2. **Working with Words**

Explain these words in English.

a) mother tongue
b) (to) adapt
c) foreign language
d) territory
e) retrieval system

Work with me ISBN 978-3-582-77856-7

TEXT 6: The Role of English in Youth Cultures [B2]

Anglicisms Seen from a Younger Point of View
Do you know the meaning of the words **nollie**, **grind**, **double-sets** or **nosegrab**? Perhaps **EBM**, **FMV** or **E3**? What about **rock**, **pop**, **lyrics** and **location**? Although you most certainly will have heard of the latter four words – for they have become part of our common music vocabulary – some of the first four may sound foreign to you, depending on your interests and your involvement with a youth subculture.

A youth subculture is a group of people with a culture (whether distinct or hidden) which differentiates them from a larger culture. According to subculture theorists, members of a subculture often signal their membership by making distinctive and symbolic choices in, for example, clothing styles, hairstyles and footwear. However, elements such as common interests, dialects and slang, music genres and gathering places can also be an important factor. Youth subcultures offer participants an identity outside of that ascribed by social institutions such as family, work, home and school. As youth subcultures are often defined or distinguishable by slang and dialects, they offer an interesting basis for language research. Due to a development which is described as the globalization of youth subcultures, this research has most recently been focusing on Anglicisms and the role that they play within the specific youth language used by young speakers of different cultural and subcultural groups.

Although there are many different youth languages and types of youthful slang, some basic things always remain similar:

- The popularity of English vocabulary or English-sounding vocabulary continues. This fashion has been traced back to the rise of pop culture icons, first American, then British in the Sixties.
- Different youth cultures borrow their vocabulary from the country in which their subculture has been founded. This is usually America or Great Britain and so most specific terms will be English.
- English vocabulary is often used when no German term exists for what is being referred to. This is often the case when it comes to particular music styles or special sports, such as skateboarding and biking. English terms will then usually be integrated into the German language, for example: Rocker, Hippie, Prolo, Skater, Biker, Climber.
- Certain Anglicisms within different youth languages and slang are often used to label a social group with a specific social image, for example Punker. This is especially evident in youth magazines.

(388 words)

★★ 1. **Working with Words**
Translate the following words into German.

band – blog – live – make-up – fan – track

★★★ 2. **Working with Words**
Explain the difference in content and image between the two word pairs written below. Which word would you use in which context?
a) Star – Künstler/-in
b) Drink – Getränk
c) Sound – Klang
d) shoppen – einkaufen gehen

3. **Discussion**
★★★★ Think about the children, teenagers, and parents you know or work with. Do they speak differently? What words or types of language do they use? Make a chart or mind map. Try to sort the words into groups like slang, English words (Anglicisms), special words, and normal (standard) language.

4. **Web Quest**
★★ Search the Internet and try to find other pseudo-anglicisms as well as their real English counterparts.

Info 4: Wannabe – The Wide World of Pseudo-Anglicisms

*Some German words look and sound just like English words, but they often do not actually exist in English, or have a different meaning. Such words are quite popular in Germany. As they pretend to be something they are not, we call them **pseudo-anglicisms**. Here are some examples:*

Pseudo-Anglicism	Meaning	Correct English	German
Basecap	Basiskappe	baseball cap	Schirmmütze
beachen	stranden	to play beach volleyball	Strandvolleyball spielen
Beamer	Cricket: a ball bowled directly at a batsman's head or upper body without bouncing (regarded as unsporting); Technical: a vehicle made by BMW	video projector, data projector, digital projector, projector	Videoprojektor, Datenprojektor, digitaler Projektor, Projektor
Body	Körper	bodice, body suit	Dessous-Einteiler
Bodybag	Leichensack	fanny pack (AmE); bumbag (BrE)	Gürteltasche
catchen	fangen	wrestling	Ringen
Handy	handlich, praktisch, geschickt, *handyman* = Handwerker, aber: *Handy Talkie* = tragbares Funkgerät	cell(ular) phone [AmE.]; mobile phone [BrE]	Mobiltelefon
Oldtimer	Alteingesessene/r (korrekt: *old-timer*)	vintage car, classic car	Autoveteran, Automobil
Twen	(von *twenty* = zwanzig)	young adult, twenty-something	Mittzwanziger

Work with me ISBN 978-3-582-77856-7

Text 7: Tips for Your Practical Recognition Year

Discussing your topics in English

Sovia lives in Germany and is studying to become a kindergarten teacher. Today, she is meeting up with her friend Anna. Anna is from Australia and works as an English teacher. Sovia is feeling anxious and overwhelmed because her Practical Recognition Year is coming up. She decides to talk to Anna about her feelings. Since Anna doesn't speak much German, Sovia has to try to explain her situation and her feelings in English.

(78 words)

★★ **Task:**

Look at the picture of Anna and Sovia and write a short dialogue between them in English. Use the following words to help you:

stressed, anxious, hard work, long hours, new people, work-life-balance, income, health

Mrs Boehm is the head of a kindergarten in Dortmund. Here are some of her tips for your Recognition Year:

Tip 1: Be Open to New Experiences

During your Recognition Year, you can work in different areas of childcare. This will help you gain valuable experience. Stay curious and be willing to try new things to better understand the role of an educator.

Tip 2: Work Closely with Your Mentor

You will have a mentor who will support you during this year. Take advantage of their experience by working closely with them. They can help you learn new methods and give you useful feedback to improve your skills.

Tip 3: Reflect on Your Work Regularly

Reflection is important in education. Take time to think about your experiences and how you can improve. Ask yourself questions like: "What went well?" and "What did I learn?" You can also discuss your reflections with your mentor to get more ideas.

Tip 4: Be Professional and Committed
Always act professionally by being on time, showing interest in your work and in the children, and following the rules. This shows that you are reliable and helps you build good relationships. Show initiative by taking responsibility and looking for new challenges.

Tip 5: Use Learning Opportunities
The Recognition Year is a great time to continue learning. Attend seminars, read professional books, or take online courses to improve your skills and knowledge. This can help you with your future career.

★★ 1. **Working with Words**
Explain the following terms in English:

to gain – to improve – punctual

★★ 2. **Working with the Text**
a) Look at the five tips. Which tip do you think is the most important? Rearrange the tips in order of importance to you (1 = most important, 5 = least important).
b) Which of the tips do you think you can follow during your Recognition Year? Explain why.

★★ 3. **Writing**
Write a short message to your friend. Tell them about your current situation with your Practical Recognition Year (RY). You can include the following information:
- Do you already know where you will do your RY?
- What are your concerns or worries about the RY?
- What are you looking forward to during your RY?

Me
Hi Liza,
you were asking about my Practical Recognition Year, well..

Work with me ISBN 978-3-582-77856-7

Vocabulary Module 1 English and Its Influence on Our Daily Lives

Introduction

(to) influence	[ˈɪnfluənts]	beeinflussen
literal translation	[ˈlɪtərəl trænsˈleɪʃən]	wörtliche Übersetzung
pun	[pʌn]	Wortspiel
(to) encounter	[ɪnˈkaʊntər]	begegnen, begegnet
pronunciation	[prəˌnʌntsiˈeɪʃən]	Aussprache [ling]
varieties	[vəˈraɪətis]	(hier: sprachliche) Unterschiede

Text 1: Looking at Your English Skills

elementary school	[ˌɛlɪˈmɛntəri skuːl]	Grundschule
exposure	[ɪkˈspəʊʒə]	Kontakt; das Ausgesetztsein

Text 2: Keep on Talking

context	[ˈkɒntɛkst]	Zusammenhang
target	[ˈtɑːgɪt]	Ziel
(to) provide sth.	[prəˈvaɪd]	etw. bereitstellen, liefern

Info 1 Language Mixing

(to) involve sth.	[ɪnˈvɒlv]	etw. beinhalten, mit etw. verbunden sein
(to) incorporate	[ɪnˈkɔːpəreɪt]	einbauen, enthalten

Info 2: The Grammatical Rules of Denglish

(to) conjugate	[ˈkɒndʒʊgeɪt]	konjugieren
idiom	[ˈɪdiəm]	Redensart

Info 3: A Global Language

global language	[ˈgləʊbəl ˈlæŋgwɪdʒ]	Weltsprache
second language	[ˈsəkənd ˈlæŋgwɪdʒ]	Zweitsprache

Text 3: Is English Taking Over the World?

linguist	[ˈlɪŋgwɪst]	Sprachwissenschaftler/-in
satellite broadcasting	[ˈsætəlaɪtˈbrɔːdkaːstɪŋ]	Funkwesen, Rundfunk über Satellit
(to) establish	[ɪˈstæblɪʃ]	etablieren, aufbauen
linguistic features	[lɪnˈgwɪstɪkˈfiːtʃərz]	sprachliche Merkmale

Text 4: An Interview with Abby

daily basis	[ˈdeɪli ˈbeɪsɪs]	täglich
(to) be situated	[biː ˈsɪtʃueɪtɪd]	gelegen sein
(to) switch	[swɪtʃ]	wechseln

Text 5: Don't We All Speak English Anyway?

mother tongue	[ˈmʌðər ˈtʌŋ]	Muttersprache
(to) estimate	[ˈestɪmeɪt]	schätzen
fluent	[ˈfluːənt]	hier: fließend sprechen
(to) suggest	[səˈdʒɛst]	hier: gibt Anzeichen für
(to) exceed	[ɪˈksiːd]	überschreiten
enormous	[ɪˈnɔːməs]	riesig
electronic retrieval systems	[ɪˌlekˈtrɒnɪk rɪˈtriːvəl ˈsɪstəmz]	elektronisches Datenabfragesystem

Text 6: The Role of English in Youth Cultures

latter	[ˈlætər]	letztere
(to) differentiate	[ˌdɪfəˈrentʃieɪt]	differenzieren
ascribed to sth.	[əˈskraɪbd]	einer Sache zugeschrieben sein
distinguishable	[dɪˈstɪŋgwɪʃəbəl]	erkennbar, unterscheidbar
(to) trace back	[treɪs bæk]	zurückführen auf

Info 4: Wannabe

(to) pretend	[prɪˈtənd]	so tun als ob
disguise	[dɪsˈgaɪz]	Verkleidung
counterpart	[ˈkaʊntəpɒːt]	Gegenpart

Tips for Your Practical Recognition Year

Recognition Year	[rɛkəgˈnɪʃən jɪə]	Anerkennungsjahr
childcare	[ˈtʃaɪldˌkeə]	Kinderbetreuung
(to) gain sth.	[geɪn]	etw. erlangen, etw. gewinnen
educator	[ˈɛdʒʊkeɪtə]	Erzieher/-in
committed	[kəˈmɪtɪd]	pflichtbewusst
reliable	[rɪˈlaɪəbəl]	zuverlässig
(to) attend	[əˈtɛnd]	besuchen, teilnehmen

Module 2

Child Development

In this unit you will have the opportunity to learn about

- how babies and children develop
- babies' needs
- activities to develop different skills and brain development
- resilience and how to promote it
- the anti-bias approach in education

Introduction

Baby's Words

by Frank Greg

Although I am small and cannot say a word
These thoughts of my family I wish could be heard …

I feel all your love and the kind things you do.
I get so excited that I smile and coo.
A soapy warm bath or the comb through my hair
All your soft whispers that tell me you care.
Then wrapped in your arms it is safe and secure
Protected with tenderness that is perfect and pure.
And if ever I'm messy, hungry, or cold
With just a small whimper I'm quickly consoled.
You kiss and caress to stop me from weeping
Then patiently wait till I'm comfortably sleeping.
You make my life joyous, full of colours and fun
When I see you each morning your face is my sun.
So, if you aren't certain your gestures are felt
Look deep in my eyes and I'm sure you will melt.
They say I'll grow fast like the blink of an eye
But do not be sad at the time that goes by.
Because I'll remember all you've given and shared
To get me through life completely prepared.
I'll be the great one who stands out in the crowd
Your hearts will be happy I'll make you so proud.
I thank you so much for all that you do
And never forget that I love you, too.

(238 words)

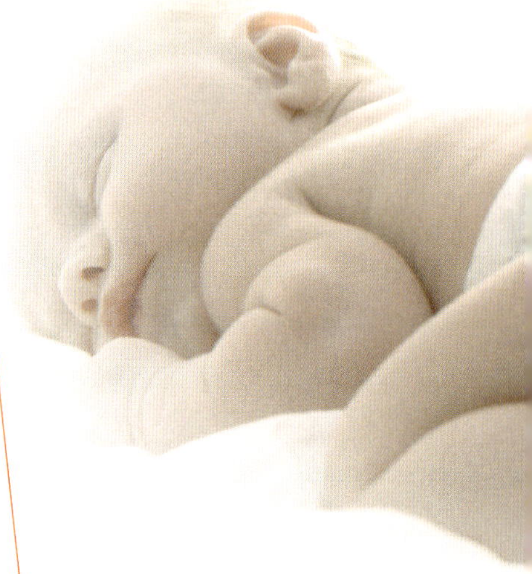

Work with me ISBN 978-3-582-77856-7

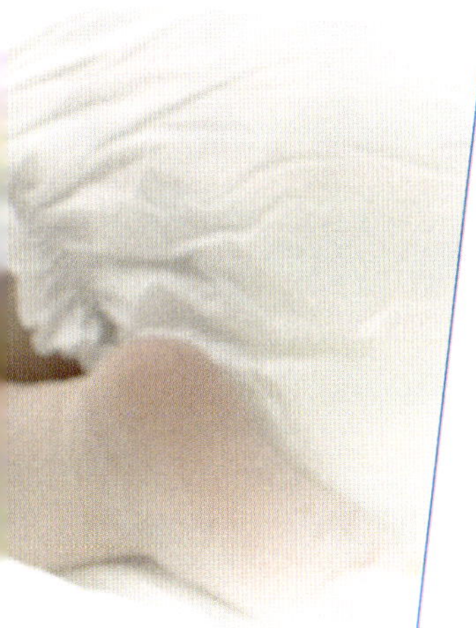

The Joy of Raising a Baby

by Karl and Joanna Fuchs

We're glad you joined our family,
Yet some things make us wonder;
How can a little package like you
Have a voice that's loud as thunder?
You are so small and oh so cute,
But you are never very shy,
For whenever you want something,
You just open your mouth and cry.
First you moved on hands and knees,
Then you were up on your feet.
We're chasing you all around the house,
We're tired; we need a retreat!
Some food is on the table,
Some food is on the floor,
Seems the only place food didn't go
Is in the baby we adore.
Diapers here and diapers there,
Stinky ... smelly ... whew!
Diapers would have done us in,
If we didn't love you as we do.
We're glad you joined our family,
You're a unique and wonderful treasure.
So, despite the work of raising you,
Being your parents is a total pleasure!

(154 words)

Working with the Text

⋆ 1. Write down the needs of a baby according to each poem.

⋆⋆ 2. The poem "Baby's Words" gives some hints about what a child needs in order to grow up to be a useful member of society. What should parents do, in order to give their child this stability?

⋆⋆ 3. The poem "The Joy of Raising a Baby" describes how a child develops.
   a) What stages of child development are mentioned?
   b) Which less attractive aspects of child-rearing are referred to?

Text 1: Child Development Chart [B1]

Age 1	
Physical Development Has control of eye muscles, lifts head when on stomach, control of head and arm movements, purposive grasping, rolls over, control of trunk and hands, sits without support, crawls at about 1 year, control of legs and feet, stands, uses his thumb and forefinger, creeps up some stairs, walks, makes lines on paper with a crayon.	**Social Development** Shows generalized tension, smiles at a face, enjoys being cuddled, emotionally attached to mother, protests at separation from mother. Shows anger, affection, fear of strangers, curiosity, exploration, fear of bathing/being bathed.
Emotional Development Makes basic distinctions in vision, hearing, smelling, tasting, touch, temperature, perception of pain, colour perception, visual exploration and oral exploration. Localizes sounds.	**Intellectual Development** Cries, coos, grunts and babbling. Utters most vowels and about half of the consonants; says 1 or 2 words and imitates sounds to responds to simple commands.
Age 2	
Physical Development Walks well, goes up and down steps alone, runs, seats self on chair. Becomes independent in toileting, uses spoon and fork, turns pages singly, kicks ball, attempts to dress self, builds tower of 6 cubes.	**Social Development** Solitary play, dependent on adult guidance, plays with dolls, refers to self by name. Socially very immature, little concept of others as „people". May respond to simple direction.
Emotional Development Very self-centered, just beginning a sense of personal identity and belongings. Possessive, often negative, often frustrated, no ability to choose between alternatives. Enjoys physical affection, becoming independent, more responsive to humour than to discipline or reason.	**Intellectual Development** Says words, phrases and simple sentences, knows about 300 words, understands simple directions, identifies simple pictures, likes to look at books, short attention span.
Age 3	
Physical Development Runs well, marches, stands on one foot briefly, rides tricycle, feeds self well, puts on shoes and stockings, unbuttons and buttons, builds tower of 10 cubes.	**Social Development** Parallel play, enjoys being with others, takes turns, knows if he/she is a boy or girl, enjoys group activities requiring no rules, likes to „help" in small ways, responds to verbal guidance.
Emotional Development Easy-going attitude, more secure, greater sense of personal identity, beginning to be adventuresome, enjoys music.	**Intellectual Development** Says short sentences, knows about 900 words, great growth in communication, tells simple stories. Wants to understand environment, answers questions, imaginative, may recite few nursery rhymes.
Age 4	
Physical Development Skips on one foot, draws „Man", cuts with scissors (not well), can wash and dry face, dresses self, can jump, throws ball overhand.	**Social Development** Cooperative play, enjoys other children's company, highly social, may play loosely organized group games like tag, is talkative.
Emotional Development Seems sure of himself/herself, often negative, seems to be testing himself/herself out, needs controlled freedom.	**Intellectual Development** Uses complete sentences, knows about 1500 words, asks endless questions, learns to generalize, highly imaginative, can draw recognizable simple objects.
Age 5	
Physical Development Hops and skips, dresses without help, good balance and smoother muscle action, skates, rides wagon and scooter, prints simple letters, ties shoes.	**Social Development** Highly cooperative play, has special „friends", highly organized, enjoys simple table games, eager to carry out some responsibility.
Emotional Development Self-assured, stable, home-centered, likes to associate with mother, capable of some self-criticism, enjoys responsibility. Likes to follow the rules.	**Intellectual Development** Knows about 2100 words, tells long tales, carries out direction well, reads own name, counts to 10, asks meaning of words, knows colours, beginning to know difference between fact and fiction, interested in environment.

(Source: CDI Child Development Institute) (471 words)

Work with me ISBN 978-3-582-77856-7

Info 1

What is child development? Child development refers to how a child becomes able to do more complex things as he/she gets older. Development is different to growth. Growth only refers to the child getting bigger in size.

Info 2

Emotional Development *is about feelings and understanding oneself. Being able to feel sorry for someone and to express yourself are examples of skills that children learn.*
Intellectual Development *is about the way in which children learn to think, handle information and solve problems. Understanding and using symbols are examples of intellectual skills.*
Physical Development *is about how to master physical movements. Running, jumping, climbing and drawing are examples of physical skills.*
Social Development *is about relationships, the way children play and work with others. Being able to play with others is an example of social development skills.*

Info 3

Toddlers is the word used to describe children from the time they walk until they are around three years old.

Working with the Text

⋆ 1. Cut up your copy of the age development table and mix up the pieces. Work at putting them back together correctly.

⋆ 2. Which of the following statements are true?
   a) Most toddlers are out of nappies by eighteen months.
   b) Most two-year-olds can share toys.
   c) At the age of three, most toddlers can draw a face.

⋆⋆ 3. Name three skills that most babies have learnt by nine months.

⋆⋆⋆ 4. **Creative Task**
   Reply to these letters.
   a) "Our four-year-old son is friendly and outgoing. But sometimes he squabbles over a toy with a friend and then he will resort to tears. I am worried that this kind of behaviour is controlling. Should I try to correct him?"
   b) "I am worried that my thirteen-month-old baby is not walking. My friend's baby walked when he was eleven months old. Should I train him to walk?"

⋆ 5. **Working with Language**
KMK Match the underlined words in the development chart on page 16 to these German translations.

Identität	springt auf einem Bein	kurze Aufmerksamkeitsspanne	Einzelspiel/ spielt alleine	genießt Gruppenspiele, die keine Regel fordern
ist sich sicherer	gesprächig	fähig sein zu	kann ein paar Reime aufsagen	genießt Verantwortung

6. **Group Work**
   Divide the class into groups. Each group is responsible for a particular age.
   ⋆ a) Think of toys which promote the development of children at the age you are responsible for. Name at least 8–10 toys which are important.
   ⋆⋆ b) Read through the development chart and write down five activities to develop skills for the stage that you have chosen.

★★★ c) Read the box below. Think of more things that
- most children can do,
- half of the children can do,
- a few children can do.

Write down five things for each aspect.

Example: Children Aged Three Years

Mastered Skills (most children can do):
▶ Jumps with both feet ▶ Brushes teeth with help ▶ Washes and dries own hands ▶ Draws a vertical line ▶ Recites own name ▶ Draws a circle ▶ Carries on a simple conversation ▶ Describes how two objects are used ▶ Names two actions (e.g. skipping, jumping)

Emerging Skills (half of the children can do)
▶ Uses pronouns (I, me, you) ▶ Understands descriptions (big, soft) ▶ Draws a circle ▶ Balances on one foot ▶ Puts on a T-shirt ▶ Uses prepositions (on, in, over) ▶ Stacks eight blocks

Advanced Skills (a few children can do)
▶ Starts to recognize letters of the alphabet ▶ Uses two adjectives ▶ Draws a cross ▶ Is toilet-trained during the day ▶ Balances on each foot for three seconds ▶ Gets dressed without help ▶ Expresses a wide range of emotions ▶ Draws a stick figure ▶ Speaks clearly most of the time

★★★★ 7. **Group Work**
Think of other ways to support the development of children aged 0–3 years and create a mind map like below. Do the same for children aged 4–7 years. After completion choose one age group and present your ideas to the class.

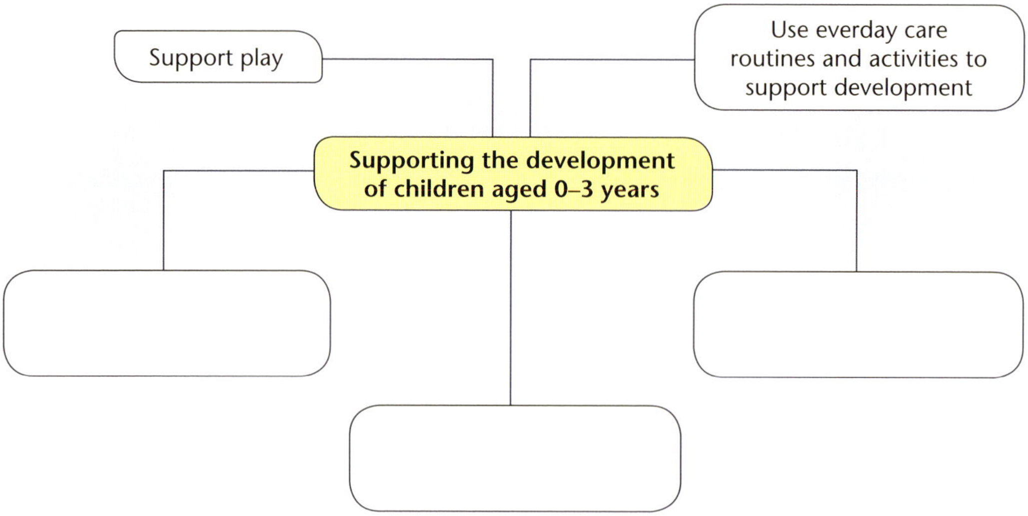

Work with me ISBN 978-3-582-77856-7

Text 2: The Developing Brain [B2]

Psychologist Jean Piaget described **play** as the serious business of all childhood learning. The brains of young infants all learn to acquire knowledge in a similar way. Children begin learning through touch, imitation, exploration, discovery, movement and play. At times during brain development, 250,000 neurons are added every minute! An amazing rate. At birth, almost all the neurons the brain will ever have are present. However, the brain continues to grow for a few years after birth.

"How does the brain continue to grow, if the brain has most of the neurons it will get when a child is born?" The answer is in glial cells. Glia continue to divide and multiply. The neurons in the brain also make many new connections after birth. Neurons communicate by sending electro-chemical signals to one another. With all new learning, the neurons respond by reaching out to their neighbours in a process connecting those cells which were not linked to other brain cells before. A fine-tuning of a child's talents occurs between three and six years of age. These are the years during which re-wiring takes place in the frontal lobes.

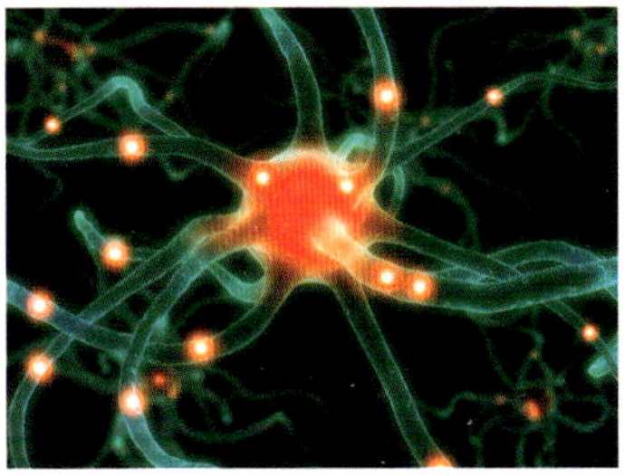

Learning-Brain Plasticity

Albert Einstein said, "Learning is experiencing. Everything else is just information," suggesting that we must "experience" learning by utilizing our twenty or more (not just five) sensory systems. In addition to being genetically programmed, brain growth and development are also influenced by neural plasticity. Once born, the human brain is incredibly sensitive to external stimuli. Therefore all early experiences and stimuli play a part in shaping the new brain, which constantly modifies connections by creating linkages between neurons, where all our knowledge and skills are stored. The more frequently those neurons are linked together and work together, the greater is the chance that life-long learning will take place. We have to use our sensory systems before new information enters into permanent memory. Educators promote effective learning by combining multi-sensory experiences and multi-modal teaching. The architecture of each human brain is changed as a result of all those newly acquired skills and competencies. By the process of neural plasticity the number of these functional neural pathways will be determined by the learning experiences one has.

Conclusion

Recognizing that early exposure to a wide range of learning experiences has a tremendous impact on the brain, we must take a closer look at the critical role which early cognitive development should play in pre-school, child-care programmes and in primary education. These years are not just the "developmental years". They are the years most critical for the development and growth of necessary skills for life-long learning, from nursery school through to college-level and beyond. The neural networks the brain forms in infancy have the capacity to learn the most complex material and generate the most advanced ideas at a later stage. That capacity to learn, as long as we choose to continue stimulating the mind, is limitless and endless. The human brain is the perfect example of the use-it-or-lose-it principle.

(497 words)

(adapted from: Dr. Mark Rosenzweig / Kenneth A. Wesson, Education Consultant)

Info 4: The Two Hemispheres

*Each hemisphere of the brain is dominant for different behaviours. The **left side** of the brain is the seat of language, it processes in a logical and sequential order. The **right side** is more visual and processes intuitively, holistically and randomly.*
Most people seem to have a dominant side. Of course, these are generalizations and in normal people the two hemispheres work together, are connected and share information.

Info 5

- ***Neural plasticity:** Does it mean the brain is made of plastic? No, this refers to the brain's ability to alter itself – physically, chemically and structurally as it responds to experiences and to the environment.*
- *At birth, a baby's brain already has 100,000,000,000 cells. This is about the number of stars in the Milky Way.*
- *Brain development takes place prenatally.*
- *By the age of two years, the child's brain is about 80 % of the adult size.*
- *At age five or six, the brain has reached 90–95 % of its adult volume and is four times its birth size.*
- *A toddler's brain has twice as many connections among its 100 billion neurons as the brain of a fully-matured adult.*
- *Scientists have used advanced scanning methods to study the changes that occur in the adolescent brain. Much to their surprise, they have discovered that the brain continues to develop and grow well into the teenage years. Here is possibly one other reason why teenagers might rebel.*

1. **Working with the Text**
   - ★ a) Why do you think 'play is the serious business' in life of children as Jean Piaget says?
   - ★ b) The neurons in the brain make many new connections. What else helps the brain grow? Name two things.
   - ★★ c) Why is it important to support young children as they develop?
   - ★★★ d) What can professional educators do to support children's brain development? Think about experiences you have had.

2. ★★★ **Comment**
   Here are two myths about babies:
   a) A newborn is not capable of interacting right away.
   b) It takes a while for a baby to see or hear.
   Comment on these in your own words.

3. ★★ **Working with Words**
   KMK Explain these expressions – underlined in the text – in English in your own words.

acquire knowledge	respond	genetically programmed	incredibly sensitive
fully-matured adult	not linked to other brain cells	constantly modifies the connections	tremendous impact

Work with me ISBN 978-3-582-77856-7

4. **Group Work**

★★★ a) According to Text 2 play is essential to a child's (brain) development. Everything is learned through play. Agree on one game which children usually play and name three skills that are involved and say how they might be linked to the areas of development (physical, intellectual, social/emotional and language development). Present your results to the class. Use different presentation methods, such as mind maps, diagrams, posters.

★★★★ b) Create a list entitled *"BETTER BRAINS FOR BABIES"* with ten things families should do to support their child´s brain development. The following keywords should be used: bonding, nutrition, alcohol, breast feeding, reading stories, music, environment, toys. For example:
1. Brain development starts prenatally. Do not drink alcohol during pregnancy.
Use the text and Internet to obtain more information.

Teaching Methods

Take a look at the different teaching methods used in kindergarten classrooms (in order to promote child development):

Cooperative Learning
Cooperative learning is a teaching method that groups students in pairs or small groups where they are challenged to complete a task. Successful completion of a task is determined by how well the pair or group work together. This teaching method promotes peer-to-peer respect and develops understanding of each other's interests, skills and needs. Furthermore, it encourages students to take control over their own learning experience by providing ample opportunity for them to express and share their personal concerns, feelings and thoughts. Group tasks in cooperative learning are structured to involve the entire group and can't be completed by only one person. The teacher should monitor group activity and intervene when necessary to clarify instructions and demonstrate good team behaviour.

Hands-On Approach
The hands-on approach is a teaching method that encourages students to learn by doing and by example. Using props helps students to learn about abstract concepts, develop critical thinking and solve problems. Teaching students about basic mathematics concepts such as addition and subtraction, for example, might involve the use of board games. Computers also play a role in hands-on learning when students are encouraged to learn a concept through an education game or in an interactive multimedia format. Again, students are encouraged to be actively involved in their own education.

Conference Learning
Conference learning is a teaching method that gives a teacher one-on-one time with each student. This works best while the other students are engaged in an activity or play time. The teacher should meet each student to discuss their difficulties, successes, and interests. These mini-conferences provide a teacher with a better understanding of a student's strengths and interests, which will help tailor lessons, activities and homework to help students thrive. Conferences should happen periodically throughout the year to keep individuals on task and get progress reports which provide information on how to proceed. Furthermore, conferences can take place while children are learning if a teacher individually asks them engaging questions about their work, encouraging them to talk about their approach to the task.

The Play Method
An ideal kindergarten classroom is a safe environment that provides ample opportunity for children to play, which in turn develops confidence and social skills. The first step to play as a teaching method is observa-

Work with me ISBN 978-3-582-77856-7

tion – then the teacher can structure the play. Teachers should do so without dominating or directing the play, but by sharing the experience with the children and presenting ideas and materials that will help extend the play into a learning experience. If children at play are having an imaginary tea party, for example, the teacher should knock on the door and ask to join, sit at the table and drink imaginary tea. The play is extended when the teacher asks questions about what's being served, introduces new vocabulary and adds ideas.

1. **Working with the Text**
   ★ a) Set up a ranking of the teaching methods, giving reasons for your decision.
   ★★ b) Discuss your ranking with your classmates; make changes in your ranking if necessary.

2. **Internet Research**
   ★★★ a) Search the Internet for other teaching methods used in nursery schools, list them, and write down an explanation for each of them.
   ★ b) Exhibit your findings in the classroom and record likes or dislikes for the methods your classmates found.

3. **Group Work**
   ★ a) Listen to/ watch videos and clips (maybe on YouTube) about different teaching concepts, e.g. Waldorf, Reggio, Montessori.
   ★★ b) Construct mind-maps of the teaching concepts you have just got to know and explain them to your classmates.
   ★★★ c) Think up a situation in a nursery school, e.g. snack-time, and prepare a roleplay according to the different teaching concepts. Record your roleplay and let your classmates match the video to the corresponding concept by giving reasons for their choice.

Social and Emotional Development

Here are some pictures illustrating the typical social and emotional behaviour the pre-schoolers show in the nursery school you're working at:

★★★ **Project/Creative Task**

As you want the children to perform much better in the social and emotional aspects of their development, you plan a project on this matter. Outline the individual steps of the project in detail and give reasons for your choice of each step (methodical and didactical planning).

Work with me ISBN 978-3-582-77856-7

TEXT 3: Resilience and Child Development [B2]

"If you can keep your head about you when all are losing theirs"
Rudyard Kipling

What do most parents want for their children? High on their list are: happiness, success in school, satisfaction with their lives and solid friendships. In order to reach these goals, children need inner strength to deal competently with the many challenges and demands they meet. We call this capacity to cope and feel competent **resilience**.

Psychological resilience refers to an individual's capacity to withstand stressors. Psychological stressors or "risk factors" are often considered to be experiences of major acute or chronic stress such as the death of a close relative, chronic illness, sexual, physical or emotional abuse, fear, unemployment and community violence. Some studies have consistently documented that between half and two-thirds of children growing up in families with risk factors (for example, mental illness, alcoholism and abuse) do overcome the odds.

One of the characteristics of resilient children is that they take realistic credit for their successes. Children who are emotionally resilient are those who are optimistic and more likely to bounce back when faced with hardship or difficulty – be it the divorce or separation of their parents, the death of someone close or personal injury. Resilient children are aware of their weaknesses and vulnerabilities but they also recognize their strong points and talents. They have developed effective interpersonal skills with peers and adults. They focus on the aspects of their lives over which they have control rather than those over which they have little or no influence.

Research on resilience gives educators a blueprint for creating (nursery) schools where all children and students can thrive socially and academically. Research suggests that institutions which can satisfy basic human needs for support, respect and belonging, also foster a solid motivation for learning.

(283 words)

Three Main Factors Helping to Build Resilience

Being empathetic. In a relationship with children, empathy is the capacity of teaching professionals and parents to see the world through the children's eyes. Empathy does not imply that you agree with everything children do, but rather that you have an ability to understand their point of view.

Communicating effectively and listening actively. Communication is not simply how we speak to others. It involves actively listening to children, understanding and avoiding interrupting them, by not telling them how they should be feeling.

Treating children in ways which help them feel special and appreciated. A basic rule for building resilience is the presence of at least one adult (hopefully several) who believe in the value of the child. Such adults need not necessarily be parents. In their interactions with children they help them to feel special. It is vital that children can identify themselves with such adults and draw strength from them.

(153 words)
(Source: FamilyTLC.net)

1. **Working with the Text**

★ a) Answer the following questions.
- What are the characteristics of resilient children? Write them down.
- What are the main stressors mentioned in the text? List them.
- How should nursery schools and schools be organized to promote resilience?

★★★ b) Think of two more ways of building resilience.

★★★★ c) Think of three ways of building resilience in children with special needs.

★★★ d) Under the headings "FAMILY" and "OUTSIDE THE FAMILY" list at least two resilience-building measures for each.

★★ 2. **Working with Words**

KMK Match the underlined words from the text with these synonyms.

a) to encourage
b) to flourish
c) targets
d) stable
e) difficult obstacles
f) are conscious

★★★★ 3. **Mediation**

KMK You are asked to address a further education course for your colleagues and for some professionals from abroad. Therefore you have to
a) sum up the main parts of the text and
b) translate the main parts into German.

Resilience and Non-Resilience-Promoting Actions

Situation A

The baby boy is in the crib, lying on his back screaming and kicking. You do not know what is wrong. He just keeps screaming and kicking.

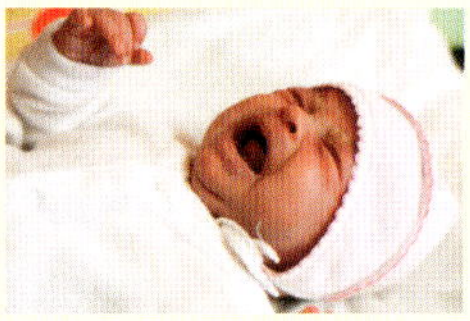

You promote resilience if you pick him up and begin to comfort him while finding out if he is wet, too cold or too hot, needs patting on his back to remove wind or mainly needs comforting. You help him calm down if he feels loved and cared for. Then he can begin to calm himself down.

You do not promote resilience if you look at him, decide to change his diaper and then tell him to stop crying. If he does not stop crying, it is wrong to walk away and let him "cry it out". This interaction does not promote resilience as the baby needs more than a change of diapers. He needs to be held and comforted so that he knows he is loved and cared for. Only then can he begin to calm down.

Work with me ISBN 978-3-582-77856-7

★★★ 4. **Group Work**
Get together in a group and read the situations below.
How would you as early-childhood teachers respond in these situations? Write them down.

Situation B

The two-year-old toddler is in a supermarket with you. He sees some candy, grabs it and starts to eat it. When you try to take it away from him, he shouts, „No! Mine, mine!"

- You promote resilience if you ...
- You do not promote resilience if you ...

Situation C

Pam, 11 months old, is crawling on the floor and finds a dirty rag. She picks it up and begins to bite it and suck it. The nursery school teacher sees this and knows that the rag is so dirty that it may cause an infection in the child.

- You promote resilience if you ...
- You do not promote resilience if you ...

Situation D

A nine-year-old girl has walked out of the flat even though her mother told her not to go out. The mother only realised much later that she had gone.

- You promote resilience if you ...
- You do not promote resilience if you ...

Situation E

Cengiz is a two-and-a-half year old boy. He is supposed to be eating because he needs food to grow. But he refuses to eat and when urged to, he throws himself on the floor and screams and kicks in a real temper tantrum.

- You promote resilience if you ...
- You do not promote resilience if you ...

Text 4: The Anti-Bias Approach [B2]

Children are aware of differences between people in colour, language, gender and physical ability at a very early age. Numerous research studies about the process of identity and development conclude that children learn by observing differences and similarities and by absorbing the spoken and unspoken messages attached to them. Example: a four-year-old boy, wanting to take over the wheel of a pretend bus, tells the girl already driving it: "Girls can't be bus drivers."

The anti-bias curriculum is an excellent multicultural learning resource for early-childhood educators and school teachers.

The specific goals of this curriculum are:
- to foster a confident self-identity in each child
- to provide empathic interaction with people from diverse backgrounds
- to promote critical thinking about bias
- to encourage children to stand up for themselves and for others, in the face of bias

The Anti-Bias Curriculum – Strategies for Implementation

The following is a list of strategies which can be used to create a rich educational context for the exploration of issues around gender, ethnicity and physical ability. This list was modified from work by Louise Derman-Sparks, the founder of the anti-bias approach and curriculum.
- The educational environment should be welcoming, aesthetically pleasing, but most importantly it should make all children and families feel included and comfortable.
- It is vital to display attractive pictures of all the children, families and staff in your class. If the class is ethnically homogeneous, include pictures and images of children, adults and families from the other ethnic groups in the community.
- Ensure that the images and pictures reflect people's current daily lives, both in work settings and with their families during leisure activities.
- Make sure you have a balance of people representing different ethnic and ability groups, particularly of those with special needs.
- Include a balance of images and pictures of both women and men shown doing "jobs at home" and "jobs outside the home." Stay away from images showing women and men doing stereotypical gender activities.
- Include images of elderly people from various backgrounds doing a range of activities.

Visit youTube and have a look at the following video about the Anti-Bias Curriculum:
https://www.youtube.com/watch?v=NPKXKEWfSzQ

(349 words)

(Sources: Anti-Bias Curriculum - Tools For Empowering Young Children, by Louise Derman-Sparks, 1989; Teachingforchange.org)

Work with me ISBN 978-3-582-77856-7

1. **Creative Task**

★★★ a) Books function as role models. Give examples of stereotypes in gender and of people with different skincolour displayed in children's books:
- Make up your own checklist to evaluate children's books that address disability as a part of diversity (e.g. do the children's books reflect diversity of gender roles, ethnical and cultural backgrounds?)
- Can you find anti-bias versions of children's books in your library?

★★ b) Evaluating the nursery school and classroom environment means that teaching professionals must take a critical look at all their materials, asking themselves what messages about diversity the children get from them.
What kind of toys should there be in a nursery school in line with the anti-bias curriculum? Find at least five examples for each word and list them:
- role-play corner: kaftan ...
- cuddle corner: different coloured dolls ...
- kitchen area: different spices ...

2. **Creative Task/Group Work**
Ramon, an early-childhood teacher, has been planning to do a project called "OURSELVES". He has decided first to encourage the children to look at a mirror and then to paint pictures of themselves. Many of the children in his nursery school are Asian and Turkish. The children who are involved are between 3 and 5 years old. He would like to invite the parents to join in, too.
Get together in groups.

★ a) List the materials and equipment etc. which you think Ramon may need for this project.

★★ b) Think of three guidelines for avoiding stereotypes.

★★ c) Write down how Ramon can involve the parents.

d) Describe the project in its single stages.

★★★★ 3. **Project**
Go through your school or your nursery school, gathering evidence and taking photos of pieces of work which students or children have created. After that have a look at the photos and discuss the following questions:
a) What kind of things do you see?
b) What do they depict or reveal?
c) Is every single student or child represented?
d) Is there any one-sideness?
e) What has to be added so that every student/child can identify with their place of learning?

★ 4. **Internet Research**
Have a look at the webpage www.kinderwelten.net and find out more about the anti-bias concept. What are the learning goals of the concept?

★★★ 5. **Mediation**
KMK Imagine you have visitors from a nursery school in Denmark who want to know more about the aims of the anti-bias curriculum. Translate the main points into English, so that you can tell your colleagues more about it.

Work with me ISBN 978-3-582-77856-7

Vocabulary Module 2 Child Development

Introduction		
(to) coo	[kuː]	gurren
(to) console	[kən'səʊl]	jem. trösten
caress, (to) caress	[kə'res]	Liebkosung, liebkosen
Text 1: Child Development Chart		
grasping, (to) grasp	['graːspɪŋ]	Greifbewegung, etw. fassen
attention span	[ə'tentʃən spæn]	Aufmerksamkeitsspanne
responsive	[rɪ'spɒntsɪv]	ansprechbar, reagierend
stockings (AmE)	['stɒkɪŋz]	Socken
growth	[grəʊθ]	das Wachstum
(to) recite	[rɪ'saɪt]	auswendig aufsagen
(to) tag	[tæg]	ticken
hops and skips	[hɒps ænd skɪps]	hüpft und springt
self-assured	[ˌselfə'ʃɔːd]	selbstsicher
mastered skills	['maːstərd 'skɪlz]	"Meisterfertigkeiten"
emerging skills	[ɪ'mɜːdʒɪŋ 'skɪlz]	neu entstehende, junge Fertigkeiten
Text 2: Brain Development		
Glial cells (neuroglia or simply glia for "glue")		Gliazellen (Schutzzelle eines Neurons): Die Gliazellen sind eine Grundeinheit des Nervengewebes. Sie dienen der Erregungsbildung/-leitung
frontal lobe	['frʌntəl ləʊb]	Frontallappen, Stirnlappen: eine Gehirnregion, zuständig für die Steuerung der Motorik sowie für kognitive Funktionen
stimuli	['stɪmjʊlaɪ]	Anregung, Reiz
linkages	['lɪŋkɪdʒɪz]	Verknüpfung, Verbindung
acquired	[ə'kwaɪərd]	angeeignet, erlangt, erworben
determined	[dɪ'tɜːmɪnd]	festgelegt, entschlossen
(to) occur	[ə'kɜːr]	sich ereignen, eintreten
Teaching Methods		
completion	[kəm'pliːʃən]	Vervollständigung
(to be) determined to do something	[dɪ'tɜːmɪnd tuː duː 'sʌmθɪŋ]	entschlossen sein, etwas zu tun
ample	['æmpl]	reichlich, umfänglich
props (short for "properties")	[prɒps]	Requisiten
(to be) engaged in doing something	[ɪn'geɪdʒd ɪn 'du(ː)ɪŋ 'sʌmθɪŋ]	mit etwas beschäftigt sein
(to) tailor to	['teɪlə tuː]	zuschneiden auf
(to) thrive	[θraɪv]	aufblühen, Erfolg haben
(to) extend	[ɪks'tɛnd]	erweitern, verlängern
Text 3: Resilience and Child Development		
resilience	[rɪ'zɪliəns]	Resilienz: die Fähigkeit von Menschen, erfolgreich mit belastenden Lebenssituationen umzugehen und sich trotz widrigster Lebensumstände zu gesunden Erwachsen zu entwickeln. auch: Elastizität, Strapazierfähigkeit
odds	[ɒdz]	hier: Widrigkeiten
(to) bounce back	[baʊnts bæk]	rasch wieder auf die Beine kommen
blueprint	['bluːprɪnt]	Bauplan, Entwurf, aber auch technische Zeichnung
(to) imply	[ɪm'plaɪ]	hier: beinhalten
rag	[ræg]	Lappen, auch: Fetzen
temper tantrum	['tempər 'tæntrəm]	Wutanfall
Text 4: The Anti-Bias Approach		
bias	['baɪəs]	Einseitigkeit (Syn.: one-sideness, prejudice)
diversity	[daɪ'vɜːsɪti]	Vielfältigkeit

Work with me ISBN 978-3-582-77856-7

Module 3

Observation

In this module you will have the opportunity to learn about

- different methods of observation
- what is important to observe
- talking to parents about their child's development
- learning stories

Introduction

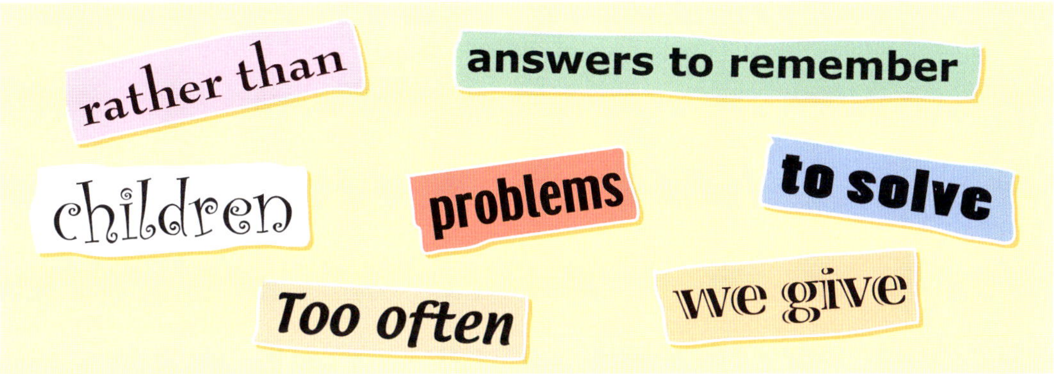

★★ 1. **Comment**
Put the snippets of the sentence into the right order and discuss in class what do you think this statement means.

★ 2. **Discussion**
"Who are you going to believe, me or your lying eyes?" (Groucho Marx)
To observe people you need your eyes. What can you see in this image – both women?
a) Why do you think some people see only one person when looking at this picture?
b) Why is it important to see both? (Think of observing in nursery school.)

Info 1: Observation Charts

Observations serve many purposes for early-childhood teachers. Children can be studied without interruption and the complex detail of their play followed, providing detailed insight into their knowledge and ability.

Observation Charts

Child's Name: Robert			Child's Age: 3;5 years		Observer: Josephine
Kind of Observation: participating observation					Date: 31st March 20..
Event	**Time**	**Activity of Child**	**Social Group**	**Language Used**	**Comment**
1	11:02	Playing with the garage	Robert and adult	"At the other nursery school they have a garage but not like this one"	Robert was smiling and pointing at the toy and made good eye contact with the adult.
2	11:05	Playing with the garage	Robert, Meg and adult	R: "I need this" snatching car from Meg M: "I need this" R: "I had it first"	Meg had the car first but when she let go of it Robert picked it up and began to play with it.
3	11:11	Finding some more cars at the suggestion of the adult	Robert, Meg and adult	R: "You can have this car, I don't want to play cars, I want to play trains"	Robert having spotted the other children playing with the trains handed Meg the car. He went off to join in with the children playing with the train track.
4	...				

1. **Working with the Text**
   Read the observation chart and answer the following questions.
   - ★ a) Do you think it is important to fill in an observation chart every six months? Explain your answer.
   - ★★ b) Do you think this observation chart helps you to understand the child better? Give your reasons.
   - ★ c) Suggest what other aspects of child development should be observed and recorded by early-childhood teachers in nursery schools. Write them down.
   - ★★★★ d) Think of ten good questions an attentive observer should consider. For example: What does the child see, hear or feel?
2. **Discussion/Group Work**
   - ★★ a) After working with the observation chart discuss in your group which aspects of observation are important and which are less important. Give reasons.
   - ★★★ b) Discuss the following methods: do you think it is good practice to sit near a child and make notes? Or do you think it is better to interact with a child first and then fill in the chart soon after observing it? Find arguments for and against each method.
3. ★★★★ **Project**
   Only for those who are doing their practical work experience this semester in a nursery school
   - a) Choose a child in your nursery school who you think is suitable to observe.
   - b) Fill in the observation chart shown above.
   - c) Write a conclusion about what you have observed.
   - d) In the following school week present the chart in class and tell the others what conclusion you have reached.

Work with me ISBN 978-3-582-77856-7

TEXT 1: Observation of Beatrix [B1]

A fifteen-minute planned observation of Beatrix was undertaken. Her interests, her interaction with others and her general level of development were the focuses of the observation.

Beatrix is a little girl who is intellectually, socially and emotionally mature for her age of three-and-a-quarter years. She enjoys co-operative play, is happy to make suggestions and is also willing to adopt styles of play suggested by others. She negotiates in such a way that she appears confident but not bossy.

She understands co-operation and competition. She clearly grasps the concept of fairness in a game, the importance of taking turns and the need for rules. Although she did not win the game Beatrix shared the winner's joy and smiled at him.

When she and Susan started to play with the small doll's house, Andi put on a monkey hand-puppet. He moved forward and rather boisterously waved the puppet in her face. Without getting angry she pushed the puppet away and said good-humouredly "get off".

Then Beatrix and Susan went through to the attic to do some drawing. She appeared totally absorbed in whatever activity she chose to do during my observations. I got the impression that she makes a conscious decision to do something and then does it wholeheartedly. Her ability to complete a task unaided or unprompted impressed me. For example, when the girls left the playhouse they did so because they had to "write a letter to our mummies". The change of activity was part of the game, not just 'flitting' from one thing to another.

(256 words)

(from: The Foundation Stage Forum, Great Britain)

Working with the Text

★★ KMK 1. This observation is about Beatrix's emotional, social and intellectual development. Fill in the chart with items which you think are important.

Observation Beatrix 3;3

Social Development	Emotional Development	Intellectual Development
takes turns	…	

★★★ 2. Read the observation carefully, come to a conclusion and write it down. Has Beatrix reached her expected stage of development? To justify your conclusion, point out exactly what Beatrix did. You may need to have a look at development charts.

★★ 3. What advantages will Beatrix have in the next stage of her development?

Group Work

★★ a) If you were responsible for Beatrix, which play activities would you suggest to her? Give reasons.

★★★ b) Present the results of your discussions to the class. Display your results (e. g. poster, mind map, cards).

Text 2: Sharing Observations with Parents – A Guide for Educators [B1]

Observing children is an important part of early childhood education. Through observations, teachers can understand a child's development and help meet their individual needs. It is also essential to share these observations with parents, ensuring a positive and respectful communication process.

Case Studies on Observation

Case Study 1:
Shiba, 2.5 years old

Shiba is two and a half years old. She has been potty trained for a few months and speaks very well for her age. During free play, Shiba sat with another child and had a conversation about her weekend. She described in detail how she went to the park with her family and used many different words, even talking about the sky and what she saw.

Case Study 2:
Tim, 5.5 years old

Tim is a five-and-a-half-year-old boy who is very creative. He enjoys drawing and making up stories. However, during a group activity, Tim had trouble focusing on the task because it didn't interest him. While the other children were making crafts, Tim wanted to paint freely instead of following the instructions.

Preparing for Parent Meetings

Before meeting with parents, it's important to prepare carefully. The teacher should think about the child's strengths and note any significant progress. These meetings are an opportunity to provide positive feedback and work together with the parents to support the child's development. Here's how Anna prepares for her meetings with Shiba's and Tim's parents:

1. Focus on the child's strengths: For Shiba, Anna will highlight her strong language skills and suggest ways to continue supporting her vocabulary growth at home. For Tim, she will emphasize his creativity and discuss strategies to help him stay focused during activities that may not be as interesting to him.

2. Involve the parents: Anna asks the parents about their own observations at home. Shiba's parents mention that she enjoys telling stories at home, and Tim's parents say that they also notice his concentration issues.

3. Offer practical advice: Anna suggests that Shiba's parents continue to encourage her by reading books together and talking about daily activities. For Tim, Anna recommends using small, clear tasks to help him focus when needed.

Work with me ISBN 978-3-582-77856-7

Involving Parents in the Observation Process

A strong partnership with parents is essential for a child's development. Parents can also share their own observations from home, giving teachers a more complete picture of the child's behaviour and progress. For example, Shiba's parents report that she loves telling stories at home, and Tim's parents note that he has similar issues with concentration during activities that don't interest him. For sharing observations with parents, it is important that all parents are encouraged and supported to feel confident about their involvement in their child´s learning. A model can be that it provides for a continuous two-way flow of information from nursery school to home and from home to nursery school. How can you as an educator make sure that parents share observations from home.

1. **Working with the Text**
   - ★★ a) Case Study 1, Shiba: What is your conclusion of this observation?
   - ★★ b) Case Study 2, Tim: What is your conclusion of this observation?

★★★ 2. **Role Playing Exercise: Parent-Teacher Meeting**
In pairs, take turns role-playing a parentteacher meeting. One of you will be the teacher (sharing observations from Shiba's or Tim's case), and the other will be the parent. Focus on discussing the child's strengths and any areas for development. Consider how to involve parents in the conversation and provide practical advice for supporting the child at home.

★★★ 3. **Creative Task: Design a Parent Communication Tool**
Imagine that your daycare centre is not using any digital communication tools. Design a simple tool (e.g., a template for a weekly report or an app feature) that teachers could use to share observations with parents. Describe what information would be included? And how would you ensure that the communication remains positive and constructive?

Work with me ISBN 978-3-582-77856-7

Learning Stories

Text 3: What is a Learning Story? [B2]

A learning story is a story of a child's progress. Early-childhood teachers document what they have observed, heard and seen when a child has been busy interacting with others in a group or has been playing alone. The contents of the folder should show evidence of the child's learning and development.

This evidence can be in the form of:

- written observations
- photographs of the child participating in different activities
- examples of their 'work', for example, a picture they have drawn
- notes teachers have made and any other relevant information

Early-education teachers discuss with each other and with parents what they have seen, and then plan for further learning. A learning story not only captures what is happening in a simple but effective way, but can be the beginning for further planning to extend a child's interests and strengths.

What is a good learning story? Think how ordinary stories work. They usually take place over time, sometimes days or months, but the time can be, for example, as in a fairy tale: *"A long time ago a child was born to a rich woman who sadly became very ill. On her fourth birthday …"*

Not every minute detail is recorded, just the main, important events. Good stories give details about the context and background and also present personal feelings and opinions to engage the reader.

When we compare the genre of a learning story with case studies or other forms of report-writing, we find they are less clinical

and less concerned with keeping subjective interpretations off the record. The learning story can be used with other teachers, parents and children as a basis for interesting conversations. Parents too can be involved in writing learning stories. Interviews and dialogues with children can be included. Learning stories can be quite short pieces or several episodes linked together.

After they have been written the early-childhood teacher finally comments on the child's progress and suggests plans for future work.

Are there right or wrong ways to write a learning story? Other people will read the account, so maybe we should take a positive rather than a negative approach when we describe children. Stories should surely tell what they can do rather than what they cannot do! By describing strengths and interests educators can look for positive ways forward. A learning story considers the context of the child, the location and the people involved as all play a part in learning.

(410 words)
(adapted from: Susan Hill, Learning Stories, 2004)

Work with me ISBN 978-3-582-77856-7

Working with the Text

★ 1. Find arguments for using learning stories instead of observation charts.
★ 2. Write down four criteria of a good story.
★★ 3. What do you think is the most important advantage of using learning stories?
★★ 4. What advice would you give a new colleague to help her write a learning story?
★★ 5. Do you agree that a child's weaknesses should be left out of a learning story? Explain your answer.
★ 6. Complete these sentences.
   a) You start a learning story with …
   b) You can use…
   c) Drawings …
   d) It is not necessary …
   d) The strengths of a child …

★ 7. **Working with Words**
Explain in your own words:

capturing what is happening – engage the reader – the context of the child

★★★ 8. **Translation**
KMK Summarize the main aspects of Text 3 and translate them into German.

Example of Paolo's Learning Story

Name: *Paolo*
Age: *13 months*
Date: *12th May 20..*
Context for Learning: *Physical development*

What Has Paolo Been Doing?
Paolo is thirteen months old and at a nursery school. During the past four weeks staff member Maria has been observing the development of his mobility. He has progressed from pulling himself up on furniture to walking along it, using objects for support when moving across spaces. To encourage him further, Teresa and other members of staff have been walking with him and holding on to both of his hands. He has become quite confident doing this.

Yesterday Teresa introduced Paolo to the walker in the outdoor area where he would have more space to explore. Paolo was very excited by this new toy and began exploring the bricks in the base. After a time Teresa noticed that he was trying to pull himself up on the handle and so she supported his efforts. By gently moving the walker forward she tried to start him walking – and when he began to move she encouraged him enthusiastically. Paolo spent a long time outside today practising this new skill, while Teresa ensured that he was able to move freely in an uncluttered space.

Physical Development and Use of Movement
Paolo makes strong and purposeful movements often moving from the position in which they are placed.

How Did the Adults Support Paolo's Learning?
By providing Paolo with quality time and adequate space to learn in.

Next Steps
Support his independent walking by encouraging him to take steps between two people.

★★ KMK 1. **Role Play I**

Work with a partner. One of you plays the role of an early-years teacher, the other can be Paolo's mother or father.

a) Write a dialogue between you and the parent. You have been asked to give information about Paolo's development. To prepare for the conversation use the learning story.
b) Think of two things the parent can do to support Paolo.
c) Tell the parent what you, Paolo's teacher, think are the next steps to support him. Try to think of one more activity which is not in "Next Steps".
★★★★ d) Act the dialogue out (without looking at what you have written down if possible).

★★★ 2. **Role Play II**

A team meeting is scheduled at four o'clock in the afternoon between you, Maria and Teresa.

a) Read through the different roles and think about what you would say during the team meeting.
b) Act the meeting out.

Your Role:
Imagine you are new in the team with Maria and Teresa. It is your first team meeting and they would like to discuss Paolo's development with you. During the last weeks you have observed how they have been working and you have also read Maria's learning story about Paolo.
You do not agree with how they are teaching Paolo to walk. You would prefer that Paolo walk by himself and not be supported by Teresa. You have learned during your training that children develop in their own time. You have read Emmi Pikler's idea that babies do "not need help or teaching to reach their milestones in life" but rather support.

Maria:
You have observed Paolo for a few weeks and wrote his learning story. You are very happy about Paolo's development and proud that your team has helped him to walk. You think it is a good thing for Paolo because now he can see and explore other things. He is more independent. During your observation you saw Paolo pulling himself up and liked the idea that your colleague Teresa helped him by giving him the walker and pushing it forward. You are not sure if Paolo would have walked so quickly if Teresa hadn't supported him.

Teresa:
You are also very proud of Paolo's development. You have supported him with his first steps in walking and you would like to give him more help because you think his grandmother is not able to do so (and you worry that she coddles him).

INFO 2: Emmi Pikler (1902–1984)

Pikler, a Hungarian paediatrician, established innovative theories on infant care and child development. They were successfully tested during her work as director of a home for children in Budapest.
Her key principles are:

- *Pay full attention – especially when involved in caring activities.*
- *Slow down.*
- *Build trust and your relationship during caring activities.*
- *Give babies room to move around. Never put them into a position which they cannot get into by themselves (freedom of movement).*
- *Allow babies uninterrupted time for play.*
- *Babies send out signals all the time. Tune in carefully to them.*
- *They do not need teaching but rather support to teach themselves.*

★★★ 3. **Evaluation of Module 3 Observation**

a) What kind of observation method did you learn to use during your practical work experience?
b) Compare that method to one of those mentioned in this module.
c) Draw a chart and write down the key points of each method.
d) Which method would you prefer to use in nursery school? Explain why.
e) Write down at least three things you have learnt about observation and tell a partner.

Work with me ISBN 978-3-582-77856-7

VOCABULARY MODULE 3 Observation

Text 1: Observation of Beatrix		
maturity; (to be) mature	[mə'tʃʊərɪtɪ; mə'tʃʊər]	Reife/Laufzeit; reif, durchdacht
bossy	['bɒsi]	rechthaberisch, herrisch
competition	[ˌkɒmpə'tɪʃən]	Wettbewerb
boisterously	['bɔɪstərəsli]	heftig, ungestüm, wild
absorbed	[əb'zɔːbd]	absorbiert, vertieft, auch: aufgesaugt, gedämpft
conscious	['kɒntʃəs]	bewusst
wholeheartedly	[ˌhəʊl'hɑːtɪdli]	mit ganzem Herzen, ernsthaft
ability	[ə'bɪlɪti]	Fähigkeit
unaided	[ˌʌn'eɪdɪd]	ohne fremde Hilfe
Text 2: Sharing Observations with Parents		
ensuring	[ɪn'ʃɔːrɪŋ]	sicherstellend, garantierend
potty trained	['pɒti treɪnd]	meint, dass das Kind sauber/trocken ist/ keine Windeln mehr trägt
(to) make up stories	['meɪkɪŋ ʌp 'stɔːriz]	Geschichten erfinden
significant	[sɪg'nɪfɪkənt]	signifikant, auch bedeutend, erheblich
(to) provide	[tuː prə'vaɪd]	zur Verfügung stellen
(to) emphasize	['ɛmfəsaɪz]	hervorheben
Text 3: What is a Learning Story?		
contents	['kɒn'tɛnts]	Inhalt
(to) capture	['kæptʃər]	aufbringen, erfassen, auch: erobern, einfangen
genre	['ʒɒnrə]	Gattung, Genre
approach	[ə'prəʊtʃ]	Herangehensweise, auch Anfahrt, Vorstoß
Example of Paolo's Learning Story		
bricks	[brɪks]	Ziegel, hier: Bausteine
uncluttered	[ən'klʌtərd]	ordentlich
walker	['wɔːkər]	Gehwagen
(to) coddle	['kɒdl]	verzärteln

Module 4

English as a Second Language in Nursery School

In this module you will have the opportunity

- to consider different points of view about the best age to start learning a second language
- to think about the "window of opportunity" hypothesis
- to reflect on how you started to learn English as a second language
- to discuss different methods of teaching a second language in nursery school
- to compare various theories of teaching English
- to develop your own ideas for teaching English to very young children

Introduction

"Boys and girls should already be learning English in nursery school"

That is the opinion of the former Lower Saxony Minister of Cultural Affairs Bernd Busemann. "There they should learn the basics," said the Minister. "However, learning should be fun and play-based."

Discussion

★★ 1. What does Mr Busemann mean by "fun" and "play-based"?

★★ 2. Do you agree with him that children should begin learning English in nursery school? Give reasons for your opinion.

★★★ 3. How would that affect you as an early-childhood teacher, if you were working in a nursery school?

Work with me ISBN 978-3-582-77856-7

Text 1: Sooner or Later? [B2]

In an increasingly globalized world, it is more and more important to be able to speak foreign languages to get a good job, to use the Internet or to study and to work or travel abroad. To improve language skills in the future, government must invest more in language-teaching in nursery and primary schools. But at what age should children begin to learn a foreign language?

Until recently, children in most countries began learning foreign languages in secondary school between the ages of eleven and thirteen years. However, research has shown that this is the worst possible time to start. With the beginning of puberty, experts argue, children become more self-conscious. They become increasingly unwilling to experiment with language and to make the mistakes which are necessary for learning. At this age, changes in the developing brain also make learning languages more difficult. As a result, a "window of opportunity" for learning languages during childhood – open at its widest between the age of five and ten – closes.

Consequently, more and more countries - for example, Germany - are deciding that foreign language-learning should begin in nursery school on a voluntary basis. So the trend nowadays in Europe is to teach foreign languages earlier rather than later.

Research has shown that there are several **reasons** why children can benefit from learning foreign languages during their early years:

- Young children are highly receptive to language in general. They are also sensitive to certain aspects of language-learning, especially pronunciation.
- Young children are curious, highly motivated and uninhibited language-learners. They learn by imitation and experimentation rather than by consciously analysing grammar.
- Some parents worry that a foreign language will inhibit their child's learning of their own language. It is a fact, though, that children who learn foreign languages develop a better awareness of their own. Consciously or subconsciously they compare different languages, thereby gaining a greater sensitivity for learning basic structures and patterns.

- In similar fashion, younger learners have a greater "tolerance of ambiguity" in languages. At the beginning of secondary school, usually when they are about eleven years old, children find it harder to accept the fact that, for example, word order in another language might be different. They are less open to rules which differ from their mother-tongue. Younger children are much more willing to accept those differences and say, "Oh well, that's the way it is".
- There is evidence that children who learn foreign languages develop better problem-solving skills and reach higher standards in other subjects.
- Children who start at a young age have a longer time to learn. It has often been shown that their listening skills later are more advanced, as they are more used to the language and the sounds of its words.
- Children who learn languages also develop intercultural skills and grow up with greater tolerance for and interest in other languages and cultures. Early language-learning could even help to promote international cooperation.

Despite all the good news, a report from the British Council warns that an early start alone does not guarantee success with foreign language-learning. Proper learning conditions are essential if children are to be motivated. Teachers must have good knowledge of the language and be trained in the special teaching methods suitable for children of nursery and primary school age. "Whereas older children are ready to analyse grammar, younger children learn best intuitively – through games, songs, stories, rhymes, role play and simple conversation."

Language-teaching at nursery and primary level must concentrate on "input" more than "output". Children, as all learners, can understand a new language much earlier than they can speak it. Young children's enjoyment of experimenting with language and their positive attitudes should not be spoiled by tests and marks. Finally, language-teaching in secondary school should build on the work done at the nursery and primary level, instead of starting again from the beginning. Liaison between primary and secondary teachers of foreign languages is therefore vital.

(659 words)
(Adapted from: Spotlight 5/2003)

Working with the Text

★★ 1. Decide which of these statements are true or false. Correct the false ones.
   a) In our more and more continuously globalized world it is not important to speak foreign languages.
   b) At the age of eleven years children are eager to experiment with language and to make the mistakes that are necessary for learning it.
   c) Young learners should learn a foreign language by using games, songs and rhymes.
   d) Everybody who learns a foreign language at a young age is successful in speaking the language fluently.

★★ 2. Explain these words in English in your own words.

   a) window of opportunity
   b) pronunciation
   c) uninhibited
   d) ambiguity
   e) learning conditions

★★ 3. Sum up the pros and cons of learning a second language in nursery school from Text 1.

Work with me ISBN 978-3-582-77856-7

Text 2: The Window of Opportunity [B2]

Just a Hypothesis?

The Window of Opportunity: Sensitive Phases

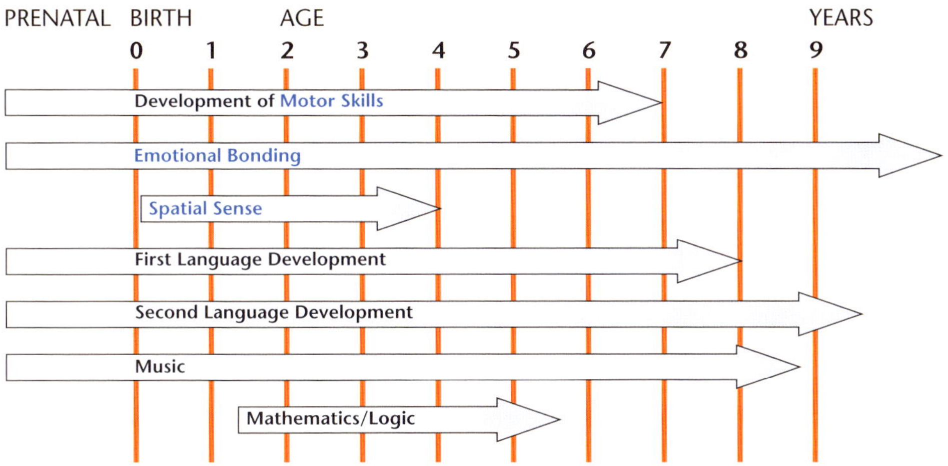

(Source: Fokus 10/1996)

The "window of opportunity" theory is part of a long-standing debate in language learning. The question is, to what extent is the ability to learn a second language biologically linked to age? The "window" hypothesis claims that there is an ideal time to learn a second language and if language input does not occur until after this time, then the individual will never achieve a full command of the second language - especially of its grammatical systems.

The evidence however that there is a window of opportunity is limited because it is based mainly on theoretical arguments taken from biological research. Nonetheless this hypothesis is widely accepted. Some writers use the term "critical" while others say it is a "sensitive" period – as shown by the diagram. The length of the period also varies greatly in different accounts.

In second language learning the strongest evidence for the "window of opportunity" comes from the study of accent, where most older beginners do not reach a native-like level. However, under certain conditions, a native-like accent has been observed. So one might suggest that accent is affected by multiple factors, such as the personality and motivation of the learner, rather than by the constraints of a critical developmental period. Certainly, older learners of a second language, despite making more rapid progress in the initial stages, rarely achieve the native-like fluency which younger learners show. David Singleton, a professor of Applied Linguistics, states that in learning a second language, "younger is better" in the long run. But he also points out that there are many exceptions, noting that five percent of adult bilinguals master a second language, even though they begin learning it when they are well into adulthood – long after any critical period has presumably come to a close.

Paul Robertson, founder of a linguistic journal, observed that other factors – such as personal motivation, the quality of teaching inputs, the quality of the learning environment, the linguistic ability of learners and, not least, their time-commitment – may be even more significant than age in successful second language learning.

(348 words)

Working with the Text

★★ 1. Answer the following questions.
   a) What does the "window of opportunity" refer to?
   b) What happens after the "window" is closed?
   c) What evidence is this thesis based on?
   d) What does Singleton say about the "window of opportunity"?
   e) What other factors may be important for learning a second language?

★★★ 2. Complete your list of pros and cons of learning a second language in nursery school (see Text 1) with the arguments from Text 2. Find at least two more arguments for and against learning a second language in nursery school. Present them to the class.

My Own English-Learning Experiences

Group Work: How Did I Learn English as a Second Language?

★ 1. First answer these questions for yourself.
- When did you start learning English?
- How did you start learning it?
- Did you like the way you where taught? Why or why not?
- Describe any experiences you have had teaching or observing English being taught in nursery school during your training.
- Do you think that you have the ability to teach English in nursery school? What makes you think so? What is required to teach it?

★★ 2. Then discuss your answers in your group. Analyse your answers and use them to draw up a set of statistics for each question. Example:

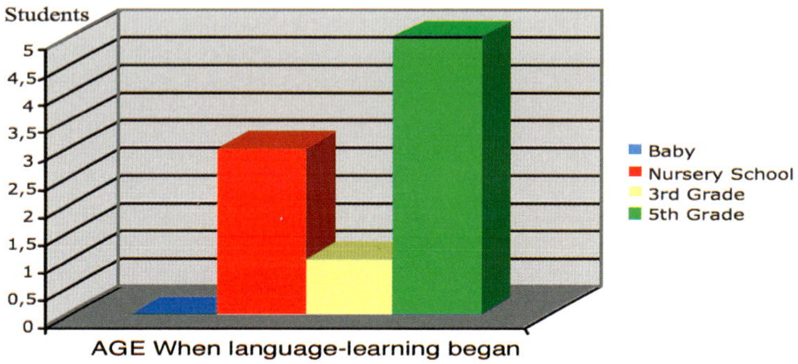

★★★ 3. Present the statistics for your group, perhaps in the form of a graph, to the class. Then draw up a set of statistics from the findings of the entire class.

★★★ 4. Compare the pros and cons list of learning a second language with your statistics. Write down the correlations you can find.

★★★★ 5. **Mediation**
KMK Situation: The headmistress in your nursery school is thinking about introducing English into the curriculum and would like to read the above articles. Translate the main ideas of Text 1 and 2 into German for her to consider.

Work with me ISBN 978-3-582-77856-7

Project: Integrating English as a Second Language in Nursery School

Your team has decided to develop a concept to integrate English as a second language into your nursery curriculum. Before you start you need to get more information on teaching theories and methods, schemes of work and ideas for involving and co-operating with parents.

Note for the Teacher:

- You can either have the students work through the different contents together so that they all have the same information, then start a project in which each group can develop one individual concept for learning a second language in nursery school.
- Or you can make the students choose one of the main topics and be the expert group. Then all have to work together closely and share their information to develop one individual concept as a class.

Methods of Teaching a Foreign Language

★★★ 1. **Internet Research**

KMK There are many ways of teaching a foreign language in nursery school in Germany. Search the Internet and gather information about the methods shown in the table. Answer the questions and complete the grid. Most of the pages will be in German, so your task is to translate the important information into English.

	Immersionsmethode	Angebotsmodell	Sandwichtechnik
How is it done?	...	...	...
What do the children learn?	...	...	...
What do early-childhood teachers need?	...	...	...

★★★ 2. **Discussion**

Discuss the different methods in class. Explain which one you would choose and give reasons for your decision.

Teaching English in Nursery School

★★★ 1. **Internet Research**

KMK There already exist a number of courses for teaching English in nursery school in Germany. Gather information about them on the Internet. Example:

Abrakadabra www.spielsprachschule.de
Kindersprachclub www.kindersprachclub.de

Make sure you collect information about the methods used, the age of the children, the frequency of tuition and how much the parents have to pay for it. Most of the pages will be written in German, so your task is to translate the important information into English.

★★★ 2. Present the different courses in class, describing their methods and schemes of work. Which is your favourite? Rank them in order of preference and explain your decision.

How to Work with Children

No matter which method you choose, always consider the following rules when teaching English in nursery school:

Golden Rules for Teaching English in the Nursery School

- Children will understand little or nothing at the beginning, so your lessons must be visual, physical and active.
- Present the lesson/unit in your own way, so that you feel comfortable and relaxed.
- Use short sentences combined with gestures.
- Speak slowly and clearly.
- Use a lot of repetition.
- Change your activities frequently – about every 10 minutes.
- Children enjoy simple finger rhymes, activity songs and short stories with lots of illustrations.
- Plan to finish each lesson with a story, song or rhyme.

1. **Working with the Text**
   ★ a) What do "visual", "physical" and "active" mean in this context?
   ★★ b) Explain why those rules are important.
   ★★ c) Plan one lesson to teach English according to the golden rules.

★★ 2. **Creative Task: Flashcards**
   Flashcards are very useful to show to children when you are introducing new vocabulary, giving them instructions, reading them a story or teaching them a song. If learners can see a word, they also have a better opportunity to adapt it.
   - Collect at least 20 English words or phrases you could easily teach to children in nursery school.
   - Put one word or phrase on one side of a flashcard and a picture which describes it on the other.

dance		**clap your hands**		**lift your leg**	
sit down		**turn around**		**jump**	

Work with me ISBN 978-3-582-77856-7

Learning by Playing

Children should absorb English with all their senses. They should be brought into contact with language in a very easy and unconstrained way. The aim is for children to learn by having a lot of fun. Topics should be chosen which are interesting and easy to understand.

Info 1: Teaching English with Games

Games help and encourage children to sustain their interest in the foreign language. Games also help early-childhood teachers to create contexts in which the language is useful and meaningful. Children want to take part and in order to do so they want to understand what others are saying or doing.

The need for "meaningfulness" in language-learning has been accepted for some years. A useful test of whether language is indeed meaningful to children is to watch how positively they respond to the content. If they are amused, angered, intrigued or surprised, the content is clearly meaningful to them. Thus the meaning of the language they listen to and speak will be more vividly experienced and therefore better remembered.
If it is accepted that games can provide an intense and meaningful practice of language, then they must be regarded as crucial to a nursery school teacher's repertoire.

Info 2: Teaching English with Songs and Rhymes

Songs and rhymes provide a fun and active learning framework for developing phonemic awareness (the ability to hear sounds in English and distinguish between them). The use of songs and rhymes improves this awareness and helps the children to succeed in reading later on.

INFO 3: Teaching English by Telling Stories or Fairy Tales

People have told stories for as long as there has been language, and the art of story-telling has a long tradition. Wherever and whenever a story is told, people come together to listen. To listen to a story is a good opportunity to dive into the world of fantasy. Everybody can create their own images and thereby re-invent the story in the light of their own experiences.
Telling a story can act as a bridge between people. Children especially love a good story and of course they love people who are good storytellers. To become a good storyteller and to make sure your audience enjoys your story, you should use the following suggestions.

How to Tell a Story

- *Create a dramatic atmosphere with mystic symbols (for example, use candles, flowers).*
- *Take your time. Tell the story when you are ready!*
- *Keep eye contact with your audience.*
- *Make use of dramatic pauses and give your audience time to follow the plot.*
- *Use gestures and mimes but make sure you are still being yourself. Do not just pretend that you are the storyteller. Be the storyteller!*
- *Trust in the story. The plot will carry everyone along if you have images, places and characters in mind. So believe in what you are telling!*
- *Practise telling your story as if you have an audience. Find a good sitting position where you feel comfortable and are able to use your voice in an appropriate way.*
- *Whether your words are like toads and snakes or pearls and gems is your responsibility!*
- *... And remember: the more stories you tell, the better you will become!*

(Source: Sabine Lutkat, Berlin)

Working with the Text

★★ 1. Explain why these suggestions are important for being a good storyteller.

★★★ 2. Pick one story or fairy tale and practise telling it by using the suggestions. Then tell your story to your classmates.

Methods to Use when Working with Stories or Fairy Tales

- *Have the children paint pictures after the story has been told.*
- *Make the children retell the story in their own words.*
- *Use appropriate music and create a dance.*
- *Let the characters "speak" by using speech bubbles.*
- *...*

(Source: Sabine Lutkat, Berlin)

★ 3. Find at least two more methods of working with a story or fairy tale.

★★★ 4. How can you tell a story or fairy tale to children in English? What do you have to bear in mind?

Project

★ 1. Which topics can be taught in nursery school? Name as many as you can think of.

★★ 2. Here are some ways of teaching English in a play-based way. Can you think of more ways to teach English in a play-based way? Complete the list.

games – songs – rhymes – telling stories or fairy tales

★★★ 3. Choose one topic (e.g. animals) and plan at least five lessons around it to teach in your nursery school. Consider your aims and remember what you have learnt about methods, golden rules and different teaching styles. Create the games you need, choose the appropriate songs and rhymes and include other ways of teaching you might have found.

Work with me ISBN 978-3-582-77856-7

★★★★ 4. Situation: you are having another team meeting in your nursery school. Present your lesson plans in a suitable way to your team (= your classmates). Decide together which idea is the best.

★★★★ 5. Choose one of the lessons and present it to your class, pretending they are the children you want to teach.

TEXT 3: Working with Parents [B1]

Interview with Opal Dunn, an expert for early English-teaching

How Can Parents Help Their Children to Make a Good Start in English?
One thing they can do is to point out to children all the English words they already know. They should also teach them some "survival English" like *Hello, I don't understand, Say it again, Please and Thank you*. The first stages have to be right. If children lose their motivation, it takes them weeks to get it back.

What Else Can Parents Do?
Every night they could sit down for five minutes and say, *"Let's have some English time."* It might be at the dinner table, naming all the things they are going to eat in English. They should do a little switch to English and then switch back to German. English could be like a game, having fun together.

Should Parents Try to Help a Child to Read in English?
For children who can already read in their own language the transfer to English is very quick. Parents have to make sure that the child knows the text well *orally* before he or she tries to read it. Otherwise, they will use language "decoding" skills from German to read in English and that will get them reading with a German accent.

Should Parents Be Worried if They Think Their English Pronunciation is not Good?
No, parents should not be too worried about their pronunciation. Parents should use the foreign language if they can communicate reasonably well and encourage their children, backing it up with videos and cassettes.

Should a Parent Correct a Child's Mistakes?
It is very demotivating for children to be told they have made a mistake. Parents should not say, *"You have made a mistake"*, because the child is going to stop taking risks and so much of language-learning depends on risk-taking. It is much better to "reflect" back what the child has said as the conversation continues but in the correct form. If the child goes on making the mistake, the parent could perhaps say *"Listen, I say it like this" or "This is the way to say it"*.

What Sort of Expectations Should Parents Have?
Parents should at first expect a "silent period" before the "output" comes, exactly as is the case when the child learns its first language. Parents may however be impatient, wanting to hear their child speak some English immediately. If they teach a child a few rhymes, that is the way to crack the silent period. It gives the child a great feeling of success if he or she can say things. Parents should also try to talk to the teacher to find out what she or he has been teaching and how, so that they can support the learning. But the most important thing is to enjoy the language with your child, to motivate and to praise.

(470 words)
(From: Spotlight 5/2003)

★★ 1. **Working with the Text**

Answer the following questions.

a) What are the first words parents can teach their children?
b) How can parents introduce English to their children?
c) What does Opal Dunn think about parental pronunciation? Do you agree with her?
d) What kind of methods for backing up language learning does Opal Dunn suggest?
d) Explain the meaning of "survival English" in the first paragraph.
f) Do you think "survival English" would encourage children to learn English? Give reasons for your opinion.

2. **Group Work: Parent-Teacher Conference**

Situation: You want to organize a parent-teacher conference to inform parents about teaching English in the nursery school.

★★ a) Plan an agenda for the evening. Which information do you want to put across? How do you want to communicate it? Make sure your presentation is interesting and informative.
★★ b) Make a list of possible questions and worries the parents might have. Think about how you can convince the parents to let their children participate in the programme.
★★★ c) Create a role play for this parent-teacher evening. Act it out.

★★ 3. **Evaluation of the Project/Creative Task**

a) Make a list of what you have learned during the project from page 43 ff. What information are you still lacking? Talk about it in class.
b) Write a letter to yourself about what you liked/disliked about this project. Note down the things which you definitely want to remember because they are important for your job.
c) Write down key words to give your opinion about the project. Use the words to create an elfin poem (see appendix).

KMK 4. **Role Play**

★★★ Be a guest in an international talk show! Choose one of the role cards below and act in a talk show filmed by a classmate and presented to the whole class later on.

A) Mr Müller from Germany
You work in a residential home for children and teenagers. You're against teaching English as a 2nd language in nursery school.

B) Mrs Robertson from Sweden
You're the director of a bilingual nursery school and you're really happy with the language skills of the children.

C) Mrs Ortega from Spain
You're an expert in migration. You value the English language highly as it gives you the opportunity to talk to many migrants and refugees but you also see the necessity of having to learn the language of the new country of residence as soon as possible.

D) Mrs Dimitrova from Bulgaria
You're a language teacher in a primary school. You are concerned about the poor language skills of the children.

E) Mr Walker
You are the moderator.

Work with me ISBN 978-3-582-77856-7

Vocabulary Module 4 English as a Second Language in Nursery School

Text 1: Sooner or Later?		
increasingly	[ɪn'kri:sɪŋli]	zunehmend
self-conscious	[ˌself-'kɒnʃəs]	hier: gehemmt, sonst: selbstbewusst
window of opportunity	['wɪndəʊ ʌv ɒpə'tju:nəti]	Fenster der Möglichkeiten; beschreibt einen Zeitraum, in dem etwas geschehen soll, andernfalls geht die Gelegenheit vorbei
voluntary basis	['vɒləntəri'beɪsɪs]	freiwillige Basis
receptive	[rɪ'septɪv]	aufnahmefähig
pronunciation	[prəˌnʌntsi'eɪʃən]	Aussprache
uninhibited	[ˌʌnɪn'hɪbɪtɪd]	ungehemmt
consciously	['kɒntʃəsli]	absichtlich, bewusst
tolerance of ambiguity	['tɒlərənts ʌv æmbɪ'gju:ɪti]	Ambiguitätstoleranz; die Fähigkeit, Widersprüchlichkeiten oder Informationen, die schwer verständlich oder inakzeptabel erscheinen, wahrzunehmen und nicht negativ oder vorbehaltlos positiv zu bewerten
evidence	['evɪdənts]	Beweise/-e
listening skills	['lɪsənɪŋ 'skɪlz]	Hörverstehen
essential	[ɪ'sentʃəl]	notwendig, entscheidend
intuitively	[ɪntju:ɪtɪvli]	instinktiv, intuitiv
(to) spoil	[spɔɪl]	hier: den Spaß verderben; auch: verwöhnen; zerstören
liaison	[li'eɪzɒn]	hier: Zusammenarbeit
vital	['vaɪtəl]	entscheidend, grundlegend
Text 2: The Window of Opportunity		
motor skills	['məʊtər 'skɪlz]	motorische Fähigkeiten
emotional bonding	[ɪ'məʊʃənəl 'bɒndɪŋ]	emotionale Bindung
spatial sense	['speɪʃəl 'sents]	räumliches Vorstellungsvermögen
extent	[ɪk'stent]	Ausmaß, Umfang
native-like	['neɪtɪv-laɪk]	hier: wie ein Muttersprachler
constraint	[kən'streɪnt]	Bedingung
initial	[ɪ'nɪʃəl]	anfänglich
exception	[ɪk'sepʃən]	Ausnahme
time-commitment	['taɪm-kə'mɪtmənt]	zeitlicher Einsatz
Teaching English in Nursery School		
frequency of tuition	['fri:kwəntsi ʌv tju:'iʃən]	Regelmäßigkeit des Unterrichts
How to Work with Children		
repetition	[ˌrepɪ'tɪʃən]	Wiederholung
Learning by Playing		
unconstrained	[ʌnkən'streɪnd]	locker, zwanglos
(to) sustain	[sə'steɪn]	aufrecht erhalten
intrigued	['ɪntri:gd]	fasziniert, interessiert
vividly	['vɪvɪdli]	plastisch, lebhaft
crucial	['kru:ʃəl]	ausschlaggebend, entscheidend
phonemic awareness	['fəʊ'ni:mɪk ə'weənəs]	phonemisches Bewusstsein
appropriate	[ə'prəʊpriət]	angebracht, angemessen
(to) reinvent	[ˌrɪ:-ɪn'vent]	neu erfinden
plot	[plɒt]	Geschichte
Text 3: Working with Parents		
language decoding skills	['læŋgwɪʤ di:'kəʊdɪŋ 'skɪlz]	(Sprach-) Entschlüsselungsmechanismen
orally	['ɔ:rəl̩i]	mündlich
(to) back up	[bæk 'ʌp]	unterstützen
(to) crack	[kræk]	unterbrechen, aufbrechen
(to) praise	[preɪz]	loben
(to) convince	[kən'vɪnts]	Überzeugen

MODULE 5

Healthy Living

In this unit you will have the opportunity to learn about

- a healthy lifestyle
- how to stay calm and relaxed
- obesity
- different dietary and food requirements
- how to prevent sunburn

Introduction

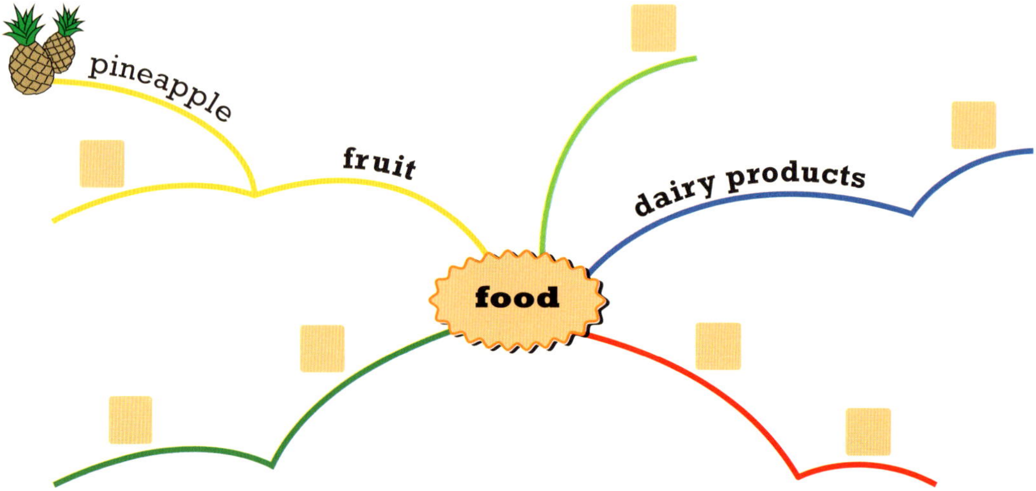

1. Copy and complete this mind map with a partner.
   Use the words you know or look words up in the dictionary.

2. Fill in another mind map. Choose one of these words for the center:

   health (in general) – movement – illness

Work with me ISBN 978-3-582-77856-7

Text 1: Moms and Dads Get Moving, Too [B1]

Adults should follow medical recommendations for daily physical activity – **30 minutes or more** – not just for improved health and reduced disease risk, but also to get energy, lift spirits and increase productivity. You will benefit even if you don't spend your workday sitting around.

For example: park further away from your workplace, take the stairs instead of elevators and pace while on the phone. Your goal should be ten thousand steps every day.

Walk or bike your child to school. If you live too far to walk, do not park too near, so that you have to walk part of the way.

Make time for exercise and show your children that it's a priority. Have a friend look after your children or join a health club with facilities and programmes which keep children moving while you work out.

What Are the Keys to Getting Children Active?

Keep a diary of your children's day. Monitor if they are less active than they could be:

- **Outdoor time:** Children are far more active outside than they are inside, so shoo them out the door for part of every day.
- **Sufficient safe space to move in:** Play areas must be free of traffic, scary dogs and broken glass. There should be enough room to run, chase, jump and throw, providing quality playtime. For some parents the backyard may be fine, but others will have to make a conscious effort to get their kids to a good play space.
- **Different activities:** Children have to try lots of different things to discover their passions. You can sign them up for team sports, swimming lessons, gymnastics or tennis, but make sure they get to explore individual activities, too. The child who picks dandelions at soccer may scramble like a mountain goat on a family hike. The adolescent who can't throw or catch may be a natural surfer.
- **Parent-child play:** It sounds obvious, but how many parents take the time? Play tag, throw the frisbee and climb up to the tree fort together. If they prefer team sports, be a coach or helper.

(351 words)

1. **Working with the Text**
   ★ a) Give at least four examples of what moms and dads can do to get moving every day.
   ★★ b) Write a diary of 60–80 words about an active family with a healthy lifestyle.

★★ 2. **Working with Words**
   Find the opposites of these words.

   a) improve – b) increase – c) team sport – d) shortfall – e) safe – f) active

Text 2: Mindfulness for children and educators [B2]

Self-Care and mindfulness – can you stay calm and relaxed during the day?

Chat with a colleague:

Simra
Hey Suse, I'm so drained, and I might call in sick tomorrow. It was so loud again today and...

Suse
I totally understand. I feel the same way. Why don't you come with me to my mindfulness class? A spot just opened up. It starts at 7:00 PM at Studio Butterfly.

Simra
Oh, thanks. I think I'll come. It can't hurt ☺

Why is Mindfulness Important for Children and educators?

Mindfulness is the practice of being fully present in the moment, noticing your thoughts, feelings, and the world around you without judgment. For children and educators, mindfulness can help to reduce stress, improve focus, and develop a positive attitude.

Mindfulness is important because it helps children and educators manage their emotions and reduce stress. For children, practicing mindfulness can improve their attention and concentration in school. It also helps them understand and control their feelings, making them more resilient and better able to handle challenges.

For educators, mindfulness is a valuable tool to stay calm and patient, even in difficult situations. It allows them to respond to children's needs with kindness and understanding. Mindful educators are also better at taking care of their own well-being, which is important for maintaining a positive and healthy environment for children.

(147 words)

Mindfulness Exercises for children and educators

Exercise 1: Breathing Buddy

Aim: To help children focus on their breathing and calm down.
Instructions:

- Ask each child to lie down and place a small stuffed animal (their "Breathing Buddy") on their stomach.
- Tell them to watch their Breathing Buddy go up and down as they breathe in and out slowly.
- Encourage them to focus on how their Breathing Buddy moves with each breath.
- Ask them to do 10 breaths with their Breathing Buddy

Exercise 2: Mindful Listening

Aim: To improve focus and awareness through listening.
Instructions:

- Gather the children in a circle and sit quietly.
- Play a sound, such as the ringing of a bell or a piece of soft music and ask the children to listen carefully until they can no longer hear the sound.
- After the sound stops, ask each child to share what they heard and how it made them feel.

Work with me ISBN 978-3-582-77856-7

Exercise 3: Gratitude Jar

Aim: To help children and educators focus on positive thoughts and emotions.
Instructions:

- Provide each child and educator with a small jar and some paper slips.
- Ask them to write down one thing they are thankful for and put it in the jar.
- Encourage them to do it every day
- Everyone can share what they wrote and reflect on the good things in their lives

★ 1. **Working with Words**
Find synonyms for the following words from the chat:

drained – spot – opened up

★★ 2. **Creative Task**
Imagine you are Simra. Write a short text message to a friend after the mindfulness class, describing how you felt and if the class helped you relax.

★★★ 3. **Role Play:**
Work in pairs. One of you plays Simra, the other plays Suse. Act out the conversation from the chat, then continue the dialogue. Talk about other ways to relax and practice self-care.

★★ 4. **Working with the Text**
a) What is mindfulness?
b) How does mindfulness benefit children in school?
c) Why is mindfulness helpful for educators?

★★★ 5. **Creative Task**
1. Choose one mindfulness exercise and
   a) try it out in small groups during class.
   b) integrate it into your daily routine with the children.
2. Reflect on the following:
   a) How has this practice affected your own sense of well-being?
   b) How has it affected the children's behaviour, the classroom environment, and your own well-being?
3. Answer these questions:
   a) Did you notice a difference in how the children handled stressful situations?
   b) How did practising mindfulness affect your reactions to challenging moments in the classroom?
   c) What was the biggest challenge in maintaining a regular mindfulness practice? How did you overcome it?

Info 1: Facts About Obesity

- *The International Association for the Study of Obesity found out that 62 percent of American women and 71 percent of American men are overweight. Among EU countries, Germany has the most overweight women and men. Among adults, the study found that 58.9 % of German women are overweight, while 75.4 % of men are carrying excess pounds.*
- *Among women, the UK came in second, with 58.5 % of the women overweight and 70 % of the men.*
- *Among men, the Czech Republic had the second highest score – higher than the men from the UK.*
- *The thinnest Europeans of both sexes live in Italy and France.*
- *One in three (or 58 million) American adults aged 20 through to 74 years are overweight.*
- *20 % of all children in Germany are obese.*
- *Globally, there are more than 1 billion overweight adults. At least 300 million of them are obese.*
- *Generally, a child is not considered obese until his/her weight is at least 10 % higher than what is recommended for his/her height and body type.*
- *Obesity most commonly begins in childhood between the ages of 5 and 6 but also during adolescence.*
- *Studies have shown that a child who is obese between the ages of 10 and 13 has an 80 % chance of becoming an obese adult.*
- *The key causes are increased consumption of energy-dense foods high in saturated fats and sugars and reduced physical activity.*
- *Being overweight and obesity are commonly assessed by using the* ***body mass index (BMI)****, which is defined as the weight in kilograms divided by the square of the height in metres (kg/m^2). A BMI over 25 kg/m^2 is defined as overweight and a BMI of over 30 kg/m^2 as obese.*
- *Obesity and being overweight pose a major risk for chronic diseases, including type 2 diabetes, cardiovascular disease, hypertension and stroke and certain forms of cancer.*

★ 1. **Working with the Text**

Do this quiz with the help of Info 1.

a) What causes obesity?
b) What are the consequences for your health if you are overweight?
c) How high is the chance of a 12-year-old child becoming an obese adult?
d) Which nation in Europe has the most obese adults?
e) How can you find out if you are overweight? What guidelines can you use?

Solutions:
to eat too much energy-dense food – causes chronic diseases like diabetes and cardiovascular diseases, strokes and certain forms of cancer – an 80 % chance to become an obese adult – Germany – BMI

2. **Creative Task**

KMK

You want to inform other people about obesity. Create a brochure.
You can use the text above and the website from the World Health Organisation (www.who.int/topics/obesity/en/). Present your brochure to the class.
You brochure should contain information on:

- the general facts about obesity and its causes
- the consequences of being overweight or obese
- the ways to help obese people and advice to give them about losing weight

Work with me ISBN 978-3-582-77856-7

★★ 3. **Mediation**

KMK

Situation: you work in a nursery school in Great Britain and a child in your group is overweight. You want to speak to the parents. The father of the child, Mr Grossmann, does not speak English but he speaks German. Mediate between him and the nursery school teacher, Mrs Lincon.

Mrs Lincon: Good morning, Mr Grossmann. I would like to talk to you about your daughter Marie and her weight problems.

You: …

Mr Grossmann: Guten Morgen. Das ist sehr interessant, ich würde gern von Ihnen ein paar Tipps haben, was wir zu Hause machen können.

You: …

Mrs Lincon: Well, I am happy to hear that. It is very important that we work together. Marie has to reduce her weight. Our nursery school provides healthy food. What about at home?

You: …

Mr Grossmann: Meine Frau und ich sind froh, dass es hier gesundes Essen gibt. Zu Hause kocht unsere Haushälterin – das Essen ist eigentlich sehr gut. Vielleicht sind es die vielen Süßigkeiten, die Marie von uns bekommt … Leider arbeiten meine Frau und ich sehr viel, sodass wir wenig Zeit für unsere Tochter haben.

You: …

Mrs Lincon: Mmm … eating a lot of sweets is one of the main reasons for obesity in children, as well as not having enough exercise. Maybe you could start by giving Marie pieces of apples, bananas and grapes for her lunch box? They are also very sweet. I know she likes them because we offer them at our nursery school as snacks in between.

Mr Grossmann: Aha! Das wusste ich nicht. Ich werde mit unserer Haushälterin und mit meiner Frau reden. Können wir sonst noch was tun?

You: …

Mrs Lincon: Another important thing is to try to get your daughter to be more active. The best way is to do something together. Start for example with one afternoon during the week and on Sundays. Try to get outdoors. Children are more active in the fresh air. Marie loves to cycle, I know. Maybe you can go on a bike-ride once a week …

You: …

Mr Grossmann: Das ist eine sehr gute Idee. Ich könnte auch mehr Bewegung brauchen – den ganzen Tag zu sitzen ist nicht gut für meinen Rücken. Vielen Dank für die Tipps.

You: …

Work with me ISBN 978-3-582-77856-7

INFO 2: Five Steps to a Healthy Lifestyle

Current research indicates a rise in the number of overweight or obese children. In response to this growing concern, governments such as the Australian government have released "physical activity recommendations" for children and young people:
Nursery schools and schools are important places to learn about a healthy lifestyle. Educational professionals should know about its importance and promote it in their work. The above recommendations consist of two parts:

- *healthy eating habits and*
- *physical activity*

Children and young people should be active every day in as many ways as possible. To promote this, teachers could introduce "energisers" throughout the day, i.e. short energetic activities that get the children moving. It is useful to have an idea of how much activity is recommended:

Age	***How Much Activity For a Day?***
2 to 5 years	*This age group needs a lot of activity because through movement they learn. One hour a day is not enough.*
5 to 12 years	*At least 60 minutes a day (and up to several hours), combining moderate and vigorous activity*
12 to 18 years	*At least 60 minutes a day, including 20 minutes or more of vigorous activity 3-4 times a week*

Moderate intensity physical activity: *a brisk walking pace, riding a bike or playing small-space activities, such as handball.*

Vigorous intensity physical activity: *exceeds a brisk walking pace. It involves moving different body parts and a range of movement patterns, such as running, jumping, climbing, dancing and skipping. This activity makes you develop a light sweat.*

60 minutes of physical activity does not have to be continuous and can be accumulated throughout the whole day, e.g. in 10 minutes between spells.

(Source: www.healthykids.nsw.gov.au)

★★★ 1. **Group Work**
Taking note of the five steps from the physical activity recommendations for children and young people, work out a programme for your nursery school to present to parents at a parent-teacher evening next month. The programme should contain information about what to put in lunch boxes - for example, fewer snacks and healthier alternatives such as pieces of fruit or vegetables like raw carrots. It should also recommend what parents can do at home.

★★ 2. **Discussion/Role Play**
a) Should we change our lifestyles to lose weight?
b) Situation: try to persuade an obese teenager who has little self-esteem why she should make an effort to lose weight. Act it out!

Work with me ISBN 978-3-582-77856-7

TEXT 3: Different Food or Dietary Requirements [B1]

Related to Culture, Ethnicity or Religious Beliefs

Food has a spiritual significance within some cultures, religions and other ethnic groups, meaning that certain foods either cannot be eaten or can only be prepared in a particular way. The importance of understanding diversity (= respect for the child's culture and family setting) extends also to children's food or diet. When there is a new child in your group it is important to find out if they have any specific dietary requirements due to their religion, so that you can meet their needs.

Religion	Dietary Requirements
Muslims	Muslims do not eat pork or any pork products. The meat must be "halal". It means that all animals must be killed according to Islamic regulations. Yoghurt and milk are eaten without the rennet. During Ramadan (an Islamic festival), adults fast between sunrise and sunset.
Buddhists	Most Buddhists are vegetarians. They respect all life and avoid killing animals.
Hindus	Hindus are mainly vegetarians. They do not eat beef because they believe that the cow is a sacred animal. Yoghurt and milk are eaten without the rennet.
Jews	Most food, but especially meat, must be "kosher" (= prepared according to Jewish dietary laws). Jews may not eat shellfish at all and may only eat fish which have fins or scales. Birds of prey, rabbit and pork are forbidden. Separate cooking utensils must be used for dairy products. Milk and meat may not be eaten together.
Rastafarians	Rastafarians are mainly vegetarians. Fruits and vegetables are important and called Ital. They do not eat pork. Yoghurt and milk is eaten without the rennet.

Vegetarian and Vegan Diets

Some people do not eat meat or certain kinds of meat. Some will not eat fish. This can be due to their religious beliefs. Some will not eat meat because they are against the killing of animals.

Vegetarians

- The lacto-ovo vegetarian will eat dairy products like milk, cheese and eggs, but will not eat meat.
- The lacto-vegetarian diet excludes eggs.

Vegans

Vegans eat nothing which comes from animals, such as eggs, cheese and honey. They will eat rice and flour but without additives made from animal products, for example, gelatine or pasta made with eggs.

Vegetarian and Vegan Alternatives to Animal Sources

Nutrient	Animal Sources	Alternatives
Protein	meat, fish, eggs, milk, cheese, yogurt	soya, peas and beans, grain, bread, potatoes, nuts, beans
Calcium	milk, cheese, yogurt	soya milk, tofu, seeds, nuts, bread, dried fruits
Iron	liver, red meat, chicken, fish	green vegetables (broccoli), dried fruits, nuts, bread, pulses
Vitamin B12	meat, fish, milk and its products	enriched products only

(Source: P. Tassoni) (426 words)

★ 1. **Working with Words**
Put the words from the chart "Vegetarian and Vegan Alternatives …" into the correct columns and find more if possible.

Fruits	Vegetables	Meat	Grain	Others

Working with the Text

★★ 2. Situation: the Timberland Nursery School is having a party for all the children and their parents. Staff member Ragna is in charge of the food. Among the families and their children are several Muslims, Hindus and vegetarian families. Ragna has to plan the food with the help of the nursery school cook.
a) What sort of food do you think the nursery school cook could suggest?
b) What sort of food might not be suitable for some of the party guests?
c) What type of party food will provide a wide range of nutrients?
d) Make a list of meals that can be served. Everyone at the party should be able to eat the food. Write down at least four ideas for meals.

★★★ 3. Situation: your nursery school enrols a child called Vandela. She is a Hindu. The other children do not know that she does not eat meat, especially beef. You want to encourage the children to take an interest in different foods. How can you achieve this? Copy and fill in this mind map with your ideas.

★★★ **Internet Research**
Find out what the term "Ital" means for Rastafarians. Explain in your own words.

Work with me ISBN 978-3-582-77856-7

The Menu for the Day

Breakfast

Toast with jam and milk

Snack

Biscuits and fresh orange juice

Lunch

Ham and potato pie
Banana with chocolate ice cream
Glass of apple juice

Teatime

Yoghurt and a biscuit
Glass of milk

★★ 1. **Working with the Text**
   a) Does this menu lack any nutrients? Have a look at the tables from Text 3 (page 57).
   b) List the nutrients this menu would provide.
   c) List those items on the menu which some children might not be able to eat. Use the information from Text 3.

★★ 2. **Creative Task**
   Imagine your work in a primary school and your task is it to make sure that the food is nutritious and it contains items which every child is allowed to eat.
   a) Improve the menue above or create your own menue for the pupils.
   b) Create a healthy lunch box for an outing.

★★ 3. **Project**
   Get together in groups of 4–6 students and prepare different meals from various cultures for your next class meeting or the school's summer celebration. Make sure that the foods contain different ingredients.

Text 4: Keeping Teeth Healthy - a Story for Children [B1]

The Toothy Toad

A long, long time ago there was a wizard who accidentally invented a rather unusual spell. Whoever the spell was used on would get perfect teeth. As he didn't know what to do with this discovery, the wizard decided to use it on one of his toads. After the spell was cast, the toad became a very smiley happy amphibian. Not only could he now eat all sorts of foods, but he also started speaking.

"I'm delighted with the change", repeated the toad, proudly, "I much prefer the consumption of candy to feeding on filthy flies".

The wizard noticed that the toad was taking little care about choosing what to eat, and he kept telling the toad,

"Look after your teeth, Mr Toad. Brush them so you don't get a toothache. And, above all, don't eat so many sweets..."

But the toad didn't pay much attention. He thought his teeth were too strong for him to have to brush them, and he liked sweets so much that he didn't even try to eat less.

One day, a tooth started decaying and, gradually, the decay spread throughout his mouth. Before long, the toad discovered that there were holes in all his teeth, and they were starting to fall out. He decided to start looking after them, but by then it was too late. And when his last tooth fell out, he lost the ability to talk.

Poor Mr Toad! If he hadn't lost that last tooth he could have told the wizard that if he gave him teeth again he would brush them every day. After all, there's nothing more disgusting than having to go back to eating bugs. Yuck!

(Source: Pedro Pablo Sacristán)

Working with the Text

★ 1. Read the story to a partner.

★★ 2. Discuss whether you'd read this story to children or not. Give reasons for your opinion.

Creative Task

★★ 3. a) Find other stories that could convince children of the necessity to take good care of their teeth.

★★★ b) Send the stories you found to a paedodontist asking her or him for evaluation.

Work with me ISBN 978-3-582-77856-7

TEXT 5: Health Newsletter: Dental Care [B1]

Tooth-Brushing at Nursery School

Glasgow had the worst record for dental decay in Scotland for young children. However, thanks to oral health improvement initiatives such as the Smile Too Programme, we are happy to report that there have been significant improvements.

At nursery, your child may be provided with the opportunity to participate in the Smile Too Programme. This means that, with your consent, your child will be able to brush their teeth in nursery as well as carry out a range of Oral Health and Nutrition related activities to promote good health.

The aim of tooth-brushing at nursery is to teach children the importance of caring for their teeth and to provide them with the opportunity to learn some basic tooth-brushing techniques. However, we realise that nursery age children are not able to effectively clean their own teeth as they do not have the ability to do this correctly. Therefore it does not replace the tooth-brushing that happens twice a day at home when an adult physically helps a child up to the age of 7 (at least) to clean their teeth effectively and thoroughly.

So what can you do?

As a parent or carer you can also get involved with the Smile Too programme and help in the following ways, by:

- Registering your child with a dentist and attending for check-ups every 6 months.
- Helping your children to brush their teeth at home with a toothpaste.
- Bringing only healthy food into nursery. Snacks should be sugar-free.
- Reducing the consumption of added sugars in your child's diet and restricting these sugars to mealtimes only.
- Encouraging your child to eat fruit and vegetables, especially as snacks.
- Asking your child about the Smile Too activities they have been involved in.

★ 1. **Working with Words**
Look at the following nouns and find the verbs or adjectives in the text:

Relation – Replacement – Involvement – Encouragement – Consumption

★ 2. Find synonyms in the text for the following words:
a) happy to report –
b) significant improvements –
c) provide –

★★ 3. Explain the following words.
a) Participate
b) Ability
c) Registering
d) Decay

★★★ 4. **Creative Tasks**
How would you brush children's teeth in nursery school? Write a short description of the procedure you would follow.

Start like this:
With the age group from one to …
After meal times I would …

★★★ 5. Write a health newsletter for parents about one of the following themes:
– What to give your child for breakfast or
– How often a day should children play outside?
The newsletter should be similar to the one above (in length as well as in structure (introduction, aim, what one can do).

Text 6: Staying Healthy in the Sun [B1]

The skin of a child is very thin and sensitive. Often it only takes fifteen minutes outside for a child to get sunburnt. This can even happen on a cloudy or cold days because ultraviolet light can be very strong in the summer time. There are two kinds of sunburn, first-degree and second-degree. First-degree sunburn is not obviously harmful. The skin is not red or painful but unseen damage has already been done. Second-degree sunburn causes skin to go red and hot and maybe blister. It is painful to the touch.

Info 3: Attention Sunburn

- *Babies less than 12 months old must be kept out of the sun altogether.*
- *Encourage your child to drink a lot of water.*
- *Remember, being in the water will not protect you from the sun.*
- *The sun is responsible for many kinds of skin cancers and for 90 percent of premature ageing.*
- *In the event of sunburn: put some cold natural yogurt or aloe vera on your child's skin. Do not use iced water to cool the skin.*

How to Prevent Sunburn

Do not let youngsters play in the sun between 11 a.m. and 3 p.m. without protection, rather encourage them to play in the shade. When the sun is high, ultraviolet light is very strong and harmful.

Generally it is very important to use a good sun cream with SPF (sun protection factor) 15 or higher. It should be put on whenever children are outside. Apply generously. Swimming makes the skin more sun-sensitive. Use a water-resistant sunscreen and always reapply it after swimming.

Do not allow your child to go into the sun without lightweight clothes on (at least a T-shirt) and possibly a hat with a wide brim which shades the face. For adults, too, it is advisable to wear sunglasses with UV-protection or lightweight clothes. Some clothing comes with UV-protection.

It is important, however, to distinguish between different types of skin – there are darker types and lighter ones. The lighter types are more sensitive. Using a high SPF sunscreen does not mean one can spend a limitless time in the sun! The SPF number indicates how long it is possible to be in the sun without burning. If one normally burns after fifteen minutes, an SPF of 15 will protect the skin for 15 times longer (i.e. three hours and fifteen minutes). After that (possibly some time before it) it is advisable to stay in the shade. Reapplying does not prolong the time in the sun.

In spite of all its dangers, the sun should not be avoided as it is such a vital source of Vitamin D. Commonsense and using the right preventive measures should keep everyone safe.

(449 words)

Work with me ISBN 978-3-582-77856-7

Working with the Text

★ 1. All of these statements are false. Correct them.
   a) The skin of a child is very robust.
   b) Second-degree sunburn causes red, hot and spotty skin which bleeds a lot.
   c) Put some warm yoghurt or ice on your child's skin.
   d) To prevent sunburn dress your child in white clothes.
   e) Using a SPF of 60 means you can spend the whole day in the sun without risk.

★★ 2. Answer these questions in full sentences.
   a) If the sun's rays are so harmful, should we not avoid being in the sun completely?
   b) What does "sun protection factor 15" mean?
   c) What are the main measures for protection against the sun, especially for children?

★★ 3. Situation: you are going on an outing to the outdoor swimming pool with a group of children. It is going to be a very hot day. Write a list of things you have to think about, in terms of sun-protection, before you start out.

★★★ 4. **Creative Task**
KMK Write a brochure for parents to inform them
- about the risks of sunburn,
- what they can do to prevent it,
- what they should put into their children's bag during summer time.

★★★ 5. **Evaluation of Module 5**

Project
What do you think you can do in your nursery school to promote healthy lifestyles? Write down your ideas and create a project.

Discussion
a) Do you live in a "healthy" neighbourhood? List four items that are important for a healthy environment (e.g. park nearby …).
b) Discuss the fact that some people still have prejudices against people with darker skin, BUT that it is still a matter of beauty for people with fair skin to suntan (i.e. darken their skin).

Vocabulary Module 5 Healthy Living

Text 1: Moms and Dads Get Moving, Too		
(to) pace	[peɪs]	Hier: hin- und hergehen
shortfall	['ʃɔːtfɔːl]	Defizit
(to) shoo them out	[ʃuː ðəm aʊt]	to shoo = jem. verscheuchen, hier = rausscheuchen
Text 2: Mindfulness for children and educators		
drained	[dreɪnd]	erschöpft
judgement	['ʤʌʤmənt]	Urteil
(to) reduce	[rɪ'djuːs]	reduzieren
(to) maintain	[meɪn'teɪn]	aufrechterhalten
stuffed	[stʌft]	gestopft/vollgestopft
(to) encourage	[ɪn'kʌrɪʤ]	ermutigen
(to) gather	['gæðə]	hier: die Kinder sammeln
gratitude	['grætɪtjuːd]	Dankbarkeit
jar	[ʤɑː]	Glas/Gefäß
Info 1: Facts About Obesity		
obesity	[əʊ'biːsɪti]	Fettleibigkeit
energy-dense foods	['enəʤi-'dents fuːds]	kalorienreiche Kost
saturated fats	['sætʃʊreɪtɪd fæts]	gesättigte Fette
(to) assess; assessed	[ə'ses, ə'sest]	bemessen; bewertet
(to) pose	[pəʊz]	etw. darstellen, auch: posieren
cardiovascular disease	[ˌkɒːdiəʊ'væskjʊlər dɪ'ziːz]	Herz- und Gefäßkrankheit
Info 2: Five Steps to a Healthy Lifestyle		
(to) make an effort	[meɪk ən 'efət]	sich bemühen
Text 3: Different Food or Dietary Requirements		
(to) extend	[ɪk'stend]	hier: erstreckt sich bis; auch: etw. aufstocken, ausbauen
dietary requirements	['daɪətəri rɪ'kwaɪəmənts]	diätische Ansprüche/Bedarfe
rennet	['renɪt]	Lab (zum Dicklegen von Milch bei der Käseherstellung)
fins or scales	[fɪnz ɔːr skeɪlz]	Flossen oder Schuppen (vom Fisch)
lacto-ovo vegetarian	[lakto-ovo ˌveʤɪ'teəriən]	Ovo-Lacto-Vegetarier
nutrient	['njuːtriənt]	Nährstoffe
grain	[greɪn]	Getreide
(to) enrol	[ɪn'rəʊl]	jem. aufnehmen (in Schule etc.)
Text 4 Keeping Teeth Healthy – A Story for Children		
(to) decay	[dɪ'keɪ]	verfaulen
paedodontist	[ˌpiːdəʊ'dɒntɪst]	Kinderzahnarzt, Kinderzahnärztin
Text 5 Health Newsletter: Dental Care		
tooth decay	[tuːθ dɪ'keɪ]	Karies
(to) carry out	['kæri aʊt]	verrichten
range	[reɪnʤ]	Umfang, Reihe
(to) promote	[prə'məʊt]	fördern
effectively	[effectively]	wirkungsvoll
thoroughly	['θʌrəli]	gründlich
Text 6: Staying Healthy in the Sun		
(to) blister	['blɪstər]	Blasen werfen
premature	['premətʃər]	verfrüht, frühreif, unreif
preventive measures	[prɪ'ventɪv 'meʒərs]	Vorsichtsmaßnahmen

Work with me ISBN 978-3-582-77856-7

Module 6

Teamwork and Cooperation with Parents

In this module you will have the opportunity to learn about

- team development
- different types of teacher parent communication
- communication techniques
- body language
- aspects of leading a team

Introduction

★★ 1. **Discussion**
Is every group a team? Which aspects characterize a team?

★★ 2. **Working with Words**
Give English definitions of every German word for "team" so that a non-German speaker would understand the differences between each one.

Text 1: The Development of a Team [B2]

A Model by Bruce Tuckman

A model for team development was published by American psychologist Dr. Bruce Tuckman in 1965. He called it the "Forming, Storming, Norming, Performing model". He added a fifth stage, called "Adjourning", to his model in 1977.

In his model Tuckman explains how a team develops in its maturity and ability and how the leader of a team should act at the different stages. At the beginning, leadership should be characterized by a directing style, moving on later from coaching to participating, then delegating, finally becoming almost detached from the team. Thus the leader's control reduces as the team acquires more authority and freedom. As the name of the model already suggests, the sequence of stages is:

Forming – Storming – Norming – Performing – Adjourning

Stage 1 Forming
The roles of individuals and their responsibilities are unclear at first. The group depends entirely on the leader for guidance and direction. People need clear targets set by the leader, who also needs to answer lots of questions about organisational matters, as well as the content of the programme. The members of the group test the tolerance of the leader and may challenge the rules of the institution.

Stage 2 Storming
The individual members vie for their position within the team. Cliques form, struggles for power take place. The group does not come up with decisions easily and compromises have to be made. The leader has to refocus the group on its tasks so that people do not get hung up on issues of relationships and emotional matters.

Stage 3 Norming
Individual roles and responsibilities are becoming clear and accepted. The team is able to make decisions on its own and takes over some leadership tasks. The working process and the achievement of goals have become important.
There is general agreement about the tasks and arrangements which have been defined. Members of the team show unity and may participate in social and fun activities. There is widespread respect by now for the leader, who by this time is mainly enabling and facilitating the working process of the team.

Stage 4 Performing
The team is now working at its best and has a high level of autonomy. Individual members are aware of their strengths and are using them for the good of the team and in the process of reaching the goal. Disagreements are resolved within the team and the members care about each other.
The team no longer needs any interference or participation from the leader, whose role is now to agree to the decisions the team has made and to delegate tasks and projects. In addition, the leadership is there to assist with personal and interpersonal development.

Stage 5 Adjourning
The team's purpose is fulfilled and the group breaks up. Individuals are moving on to new tasks. The leader has to find time for the disbanding of the group. No new tasks should be given and the wellbeing of each individual becomes the focus.

(493 words)

Work with me ISBN 978-3-582-77856-7

INFO 1: The Team and Interventions by the Leader

In order to intervene and move a team forward, it is important to diagnose the stage it has reached. There are many possible interventions a leader may then consider.

INTERVENTIONS that a Leader Should Make

	Forming	*Storming*	*Norming*	*Performing*
Overview	*Set objectives*	*Resolve conflicts*	*Facilitate processes*	*Coach*
Direction	*High*	*High*	*Low*	*Low*
Support	*Low*	*High*	*High*	*Low*
Leader Focus	*Individual tasks*	*People interactions*	*Task interactions*	*Team self-development*
Communicative Style	*Tell/push*	*Sell/consult*	*Listen/advise*	*Observe/support*
Team Interaction	*Provide links*	*Facilitate relationships*	*Facilitate team processes*	*Dynamic grouping*
Summary	Individuals	Relationships	Processes	Self-development

INFO 2: Stage Adjourning

The main reason for adding "adjourning" to the model was the consideration of the feelings of group members. This stage is not important for the process of team development. The leader should find time for the group members to say goodbye to each other but he should not really intervene.

★★ 1. **Working with the Text**
Answer the following questions in your own words.
a) What does Tuckman explain in his model?
b) Why do you think Tuckman added a fifth stage to it?
c) How should leadership be characterized as the team develops?
d) Why is it important to know what stage a team is at?
e) Give your opinion about what might happen if the leader fails to make the right intervention.
f) Give your opinion about why the leader should not intervene at the fifth stage.

★ 2. **Working with Words**
Find a way of memorising the names of the five stages.

★★ 3. **Group Work**
Discuss why it is important to divide team development into different stages. How do they help the leader to evaluate progress?

★★★ 4. **Role Play**
Situation: you are working as a social worker in a residential home for young people. They are busy working on an activity while your leadership-style might be characterized as intervening very seldom and giving minimal direction and support. Your director notices this and questions your practice.
Make up a dialogue between you and the director in which you justify your methods and explain why you are not intervening much at that stage. Practise your dialogue with a partner and perform it to your class. Let them judge whether they would dismiss you or praise your work!

★★★ KMK 5. **Mediation**
Situation: your English team colleague did not understand the description of the "Storming" stage. Explain it to him or her in your own words.

★★★★ 6. **Internet Research**
Find other models of team development (for example from Lewin or Garland/Colodny/Jones) and compare them to Tuckman's model. Outline the pros and cons of each model and come to a conclusion about which is the best one. Explain your decision.

Text 2: Communicating with Parents [B2]

Effective parent-teacher communication is essential in all educational institutions, but all too often it breaks down, leading to the parent becoming an opponent of the (early-childhood) teacher, youth worker or social worker and hindering their educational aims.
In order to achieve good communication with parents one should see them as part of a team whose aim is to raise a child. Parents will be very cooperative as long as they feel that their vital role in the education of their offspring is acknowledged.

There are different ways of getting parents to be active in the educational process. While some parents might like to become involved in social tasks, for example in organizing parties, others might prefer to take on creative work for plays or work on a parents' council. There is so much to do in an educational institution that it should not be a problem to meet the interests of parents and get them actively involved in their child's education and development. They are then much more likely to become allies rather than opponents.

Communication with parents can take place in many different ways:

- Professionals should introduce themselves to parents. A **get-together** for staff and parents might be arranged, so that everyone has the chance to get to know each other in a relaxed atmosphere. This is a pleasant way of starting off after summer holidays and the next contact will be easier to make.
- At the end of the week, notes written down in a **personal booklet** or register can be given to the parents to inform them about the development of their child or to communicate important issues. Pictures and photographs can be collected there during the week and forms can be put into them, so that they do not get lost – as so often happens to a single sheet stuffed into a bag!
- Once a month a **newsletter** can be sent out to inform parents about key dates, new projects and charity events and to ask for volunteers or support in different areas. To personalise the letter, a digital photograph of the individual child could be taken each month and scanned onto the front cover.
- **Regular meetings** can help sort out little problems before they turn into big issues.
- Details of the day's events can be talked over in passing, whenever the child is picked up by Mum or Dad.

Work with me ISBN 978-3-582-77856-7

Summing up, it is clear that successful parent-teacher relationships will only be established by frequent contact and discussion. It is vital that the parent and the teacher get to know and respect each other's opinions in order to come to an agreement about how best the individual child should be educated.

(451 words)

★★ 1. **Working with the Text**
Imagine you have been on a further education course and have collected the information above on "Communicating with Parents". Summarize the text for the weekly staff meeting.

★ 2. **Group Work**
Draw up a set of simple rules for good parent-teacher communication and explain them to your class.

★ 3. **Creative Task**
Design a poster showing how parents could get actively involved in the educational process in different institutions, for example in nursery schools, schools for children with special needs and residential homes.

★★★ 4. **Internet Research**
Most nursery schools now have a website for parents to access. Go online to find two or three such websites in an English-speaking country to see what kind of information is available and how it is presented. Make notes and discuss your findings with the class.

Creative Tasks

★★ 5. Plan a parent-teacher get-together in which everyone has the chance to get to know each other and communicate in a relaxed way.

★★★ 6. Design a monthly newsletter for parents. Decide what sort of school or institution you are referring to.

★★★★ 7. **Written Discussion**
Discuss the following statement: "Pedagogically unqualified people should stay out of the educational process in institutions."

★★★ **Mediation**

KMK 8. Everyone in the nursery school where you work does as much as they possibly can to fulfil the individual needs of the children. Nevertheless, some parents still keep complaining about the work being done. Searching the internet, you found this article below (page 70). Inform the international team in English about methods of how to communicate with parents in order to solve (potential) conflicts.

9. a) Think of a conflict situation with parents in an educational institution and prepare a role play following the ideas suggested in the text.
   b) Act out the role play and ask your classmates for feedback on how you solved the conflict.

Work with me ISBN 978-3-582-77856-7

Konfliktgespräche

„Meine Güte, schon wieder nur ein Bastel- und Spieletag für die Kinder. Fällt den Erziehern in dieser Kita wirklich nichts Besseres ein? In der Kita „Löwenzahn" im Ostend werden die Kinder viel besser gefördert. Es gibt jeden Tag ein anderes Angebot: Montags bieten die Erzieher einen Computerkurs an, dienstags kommt eine Ballettlehrerin in die Kita, mittwochs gehen die Kinder mit dem Förster in den Wald und donnerstags werden naturwissensch aftliche Experimente durchgeführt. Selbst freitags gibt es noch ein ordentliches Angebot und nicht nur eine Betreuungssituation."

Diese Beschwerde einer Mutter kommt Ihnen bekannt vor? Dann ist zeitnahes Handeln gefragt! Erfolgt eine verspätete oder gar überhaupt keine Reaktion der Fachkräfte auf solche Aussagen, streut sich die negative Meinung recht schnell, wobei sie eigentlich nur von der Angst ausgeht, dass die Förderung des eigenen Kindes nicht bestmöglich verlaufe. Es liegt also ein anspruchsbedingter Konflikt vor, der nach einer konstruktiven Konfliktbearbeitung verlangt.

Die konstruktive Konfliktbearbeitung
Eine sorgfältige Konfliktdiagnose und ein detailliertes Konfliktgespräch sind die Bestandteile der konstruktiven Konfliktbearbeitung. Sie werden im Folgenden in ihren einzelnen Schritten vorgestellt:

Die Konfliktdiagnose

1. Schritt:Zuerst ist zu klären, welche Ansprüche bestehen, wie sie in Existenz gekommen sind und wer damit in direkter Verbindung steht.
2. Schritt: Hier erfolgt die Analyse, seit wann der Konflikt schon besteht.
3. Schritt: Das Warum und die Frage nach dem Wohin stehen nun im Vordergrund der Diagnose. Die Erforschung der Ursachen für die Entstehung des Konflikts und der intendierten Ziele ist durchzuführen.
4. Schritt: Nun gilt es herauszufinden, welche Personen aktuell an der Konfliktlage beteiligt sind und in Zusammenhang mit der unzufriedenen Stimmung stehen.

Das Konfliktgespräch
Nachdem die Diagnose abgeschlossen ist, folgt das Konfliktgespräch, welches sachlich durchzuführen ist. Empfehlenswert ist eine Sammlung von Argumenten, die Sie in das Gespräch einbringen wollen. Gehen Sie aber nicht in eine Rechtfertigungshaltung, sondern führen Sie das Gespräch unter dem Aspekt, dass Sie gemeinsam mit den Eltern an einer zielführenden Lösung arbeiten möchten. Vor diesem Hintergrund ist den Sorgeberechtigten genügend Zeit für die Schilderungen ihrer Sichtweisen einzuräumen.

Trotz aller Bemühungen, eine gemeinsame Lösung zu finden, sollten Sie aber auf keinen Fall vergessen, das eigene pädagogische Konzept und seine alltägliche Ausgestaltung zu verdeutlichen. Vorteile dieses Konzepts könnten den Eltern beispielhaft vor Augen geführt werden. Innerhalb der Gesprächssituation sollten Sie stets die allgemein gültigen Gesprächsregeln aus der Kommunikationspsychologie, z.B. das Senden von Ich-Botschaften, beachten. Damit geben Sie dem Gespräch eine weitgehende entspannte und offene Atmosphäre.

Sind schließlich alle Personen mit ihren Sichtweisen zu Wort gekommen, gilt es, mögliche Lösungen mit ihren jeweiligen Vor- und Nachteilen zu sammeln. Ist dies geschehen, steht der Abschluss des Gesprächs, nämlich die Einigung auf eine Lösung an, mit der sich alle Beteiligten einverstanden erklären.

Durch diese Vorgehensweise zeigen Sie den Erziehungsberechtigten Ihre Bereitschaft für das Anstreben gemeinsamer Ziele und Ihre Offenheit für Interessen der Eltern. Auf diese Art können Sie Partner im Erziehungsprozess gewinnen, die Sie schließlich beim Durchsetzen der vereinbarten gemeinsamen Ziele zukünftig zuverlässig unterstützen werden.

Work with me ISBN 978-3-582-77856-7

Text 3: Individualized Newsletters [B1]

Susan is an early-childhood teacher who likes her job a lot. There is just one thing she has never really liked about her work: letters to parents. They tended to get lost or ignored and did not look attractive. Then she tried sending newsletters.
This is what Susan has to say about her experience:

One day my director came into nursery school with a digital camera for each teacher. At first I didn't really know how to make good use of it. But when I started thinking about my letters to parents and how they turned out most of the time, I decided to try sending out newsletters with photographs, using a computer.
I started taking photos of our children in different situations, for example, making a lantern, carving a pumpkin or playing on a climbing-frame. Well, I got some lovely pictures of them, documenting loads of steps in their development. And they loved being photographed! They felt important and it showed them I was taking an active interest in their play.
But then I came across the problem of getting the photographs from the camera onto the computer and finally into a newsletter. Believe me, I came close to giving up my project - as I was no good when it came to ICT. Besides, I couldn't find time within my working day to learn how to do it. In the end I talked about my problems in the staff meeting and my director decided to let me take part in a further education course on using digital media. Afterwards I found it so easy to attach the photographs to the newsletters I e-mailed to parents! It took me a while to get used to this new way of communicating, but now I feel so confident that I can create the newsletters in the same time I needed to write the old kind.

The response to the newsletters has been great. From the very start lots of parents gave me positive feedback on them. They liked the personalized format of receiving a photograph of their child and seeing what and how they were doing in school. Apart from that they liked getting e-mails and opening them in their own time. How much better was that than finding an old, crumpled piece of paper, covered in butter and orange juice, three weeks out of date, at the bottom of their child's bag?! Parents even contacted me to ask questions about this and that, taking more of an interest in what was happening at school and how their child was doing.

Comments and tips for improving the quality of our nursery school have even emerged from this change and volunteers for different events are much easier to find.
I won't say that my newsletters are solving all the problems in my dealings with parents, but I can sense a definite improvement in the relationship between them and me.

(497 words)

Work with me ISBN 978-3-582-77856-7

INFO 3:
Parts of an Individualized Newsletter

- *photographs*
- *headings (i.e. school, group, teacher, child)*
- *upcoming dates and events*
- *projects, steps of the curriculum*
- *needs (volunteers, material, money)*
- *greetings*

★ 1. **Working with Words**
Explain these expressions in your own words.

documenting – newsletter – further education course – development – staff meeting

★★ 2. **Group Work**
Write down some guidelines for producing individualized newsletters. What should they /should they not contain? Give reasons for your answers.

★★★ 3. **Written Discussion**

a) Which positive and negative aspects do you see in using individualized newsletters as a form of parent-teacher communication? Come to a conclusion after weighing up the pros and cons.

b) Text 3 is given in a colloquial style. Imagine you are Susan and have the task of writing a summary of what you achieved for the director. Change the above account into a formal report of no more than 150 words.

★★★ KMK 4. **Mediation**
Situation: you are Susan's colleague whose task it is to summarize the positive and negative aspects of individualized newsletters for a visiting group from Germany. Get together in a small group and tell each other the summarized contents in German.

★★ KMK 5. **Role Play**
Situation: you are an early-childhood teacher who communicates to parents using individualized newsletters. Finley's parents do not want him to be photographed at all but he has asked you several times to take a photograph of him at play. Make up a dialogue between you and Finley's parents talking the issue over. Practise your dialogue, (video-)tape it and present it to your class. Ask your classmates for feedback.

NURSERY SCHOOL

Newsletter July

Look at what we learned

Topic: NATURE
All month long we used different environments as themes throughout our lessons. We set up desert landscapes, read a book about penguins, and excavated fossils.

Topic: MINDFULNESS
The class has been learning the importance of being present in the moment, focusing on the task in front of them.

Topic: MUSICAL MATH
The children not only made a variety of musical instruments, they also learned songs to help them with mathematical numbers.

Topic: SLIME-TASTIC FUN
Bubble slime, galactic slime, edible slime… we made it all! And learned about states of matter in the process.

What´s new

GARDEN GROWTH
We would like to appreciate all the work the children have put into creating our school garden. We will be sowing seeds for some spring plants. The children are already excited about being able to watch the plants grow.

Reminders

We still need quite a lot of toilet paper rolls and shoe boxes for some upcoming projects. You're welcome to leave the donations in the big box in the entrance hall. Thank you!

Upcoming

- Summer festival: 29th July
- Autumn Break: 1st-5th October
- Nursery closed: 22nd November

Work with me ISBN 978-3-582-77856-7

TEXT 4: Communication Techniques [B1]

Linda and Emma want to become youth workers. Today they have to do a presentation on communication techniques to their class.

Emma: Hi, we want to start by showing you a poster (below) which describes good practice when having conversations with parents.

Linda: Now we have read out the poster to you, we want to show you three photographs. We don't know what these people were saying or what they really felt, but we can try to interpret their attitudes to each other simply by studying their body language.

Emma: Look at this picture here. The two of them are holding hands. Isn't that cute? They seem to be in love, being happy with one another. But take a second look. Don't you think that the woman's hand has a superior touch to it? She's holding his hand with a hard grip. It makes the woman seem to be in control with the man just being lead along. He isn't holding on to her at all. She is the boss in this relationship.

RULES FOR GOOD CONVERSATION AND LISTENING SKILLS

Listen Actively

- Be attentive – concentrate on what is being said.
- Be impartial – do not form an opinion, just listen.
- Reflect back – restating what has been said helps the speaker know that you understand.
- Summarize – bring out the main messages so that you and the speaker recognize what was important during the conversation.

Nonverbal Messages

- Posture – let your body show that you are interested by sitting up and leaning toward the speaker.
- Equal positioning – if the speaker is standing, you stand. If the speaker is sitting, you should sit as well.
- Facial expression – remember that feelings are reflected in facial expressions.
- Gestures – your body language reveals a lot about how you interpret a message, so be aware that you might be sending signals which cause the speaker to believe that you are angry, in a hurry, bored.

Express Thoughts and Feelings

- Be open and honest – collaboration between parents and professionals begins with the understanding that you trust each other with all information.
- Speak clearly – do not mumble or talk too quietly. If you do not know the word for something, describe what you mean so that you and the speaker can have a shared understanding of your concern or question.
- Communicate without being adversarial – use "I" messages. Rather than say, "You didn't explain that very well," say, "I didn't understand what you just said. Please explain it again."

Linda: Now have a look at this one of a married couple. Lovely, isn't it? One is actually reflecting the posture of the other one, as in a mirror image. Don't you think the two of them are very likely to grow old together?

Emma: Our last photograph shows a man holding his partner very tightly – as if he wants to stop her from running away. He seems to be showing off that she belongs to him. But you get the feeling she will be happy when he lets go of her and she gets her freedom back. Personally, I wouldn't give them a long time together.

Linda: After these examples, we have to go into theory a little. Body language describes the non-verbal movements we make, such as waving our hands or crossing our legs. Body language often tells us more than the words a person says. According to research carried out by Albert Mehrabian, when we show like or dislike for someone else, more than 55 % of our communication is through body language and 38 % is through tone of voice. Only 7 % is verbal. This is called **"Mehrabian's rule"**.

Emma: The ways we communicate through body language are differentiated into these aspects:

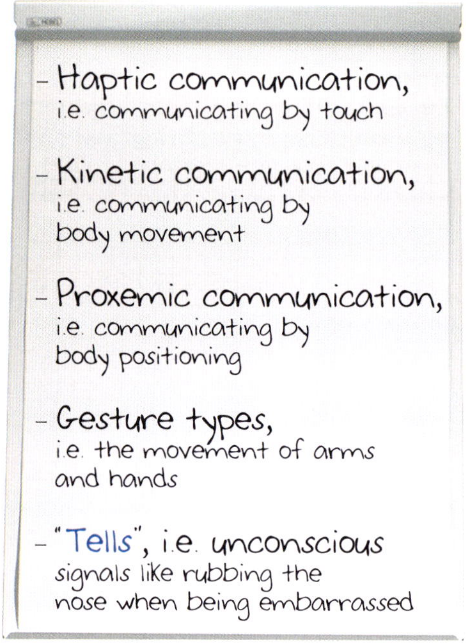

Linda: I hope you find this as interesting as we do - but be careful about interpreting body language. It is not an exact science and because signals are very often subconscious, they are hard to interpret - even for experts like Mehrabian! Anyway, you can't tell very much from one movement only. You need to look at all the gestures a person uses.

Emma: Yes, and don't go out of here telling people what they meant by scratching their chin or rubbing their ear! And don't try to control your own body language too much. Just remember the good advice in the poster for the time being.

Work with me ISBN 978-3-582-77856-7

★ 1. **Working with the Text**
List at least three aspects Emma did not mention in the poster concerning communication behaviour (e.g. tone of voice) and explain them in your own words.

★★ 2. **Role Play**
KMK
Get together in groups of four. Make up a conversation where two parents are speaking to an early-years teacher about the boy Joey, who does not want to eat vegetables at lunchtime. Discuss his eating behaviour.
The fourth member of the group should be the observer, checking that the "teacher" is sticking to the rules set out in the poster. The observer should evaluate the conversation in the end.

★ 3. **Group Work**
a) Take photographs of someone's body language expressing different attitudes. You can choose some of the attitudes mentioned in the box.
b) Get together in a small group, present your photographs to each other and let the group members guess what mood is being shown.

> aggressive – attentive – bored – closed – deceptive – defensive – dominant – emotional – evaluating – greeting – open – power ready – relaxed – romantic – submissive

4. **Internet Research**
★★★ a) Find out what meaning aspects of non-verbal communication have in other countries. Make up a list of "dos" and "don'ts" for different cultures. For example: showing the soles of your feet to people is an insult in Japan.
★★ b) Find out more about Albert Mehrabian.

★★★ 5. **Group Work**
Get together in small groups and write down the consequences of "Mehrabian's rule" for your educational work.

★★ 6. **Internet Research**
Find at least two pictures of celebrities and try to interpret their body language. Get together in small groups to discuss the pictures and to see what classmates think about your interpretations.

★★★★ 7. **Discussion**
Some people teach their babies the use of body language before they can communicate verbally, for example by patting the mouth when hungry. State whether you are in favour of this method or not and give reasons for your opinion.

Text 5: Leading a Team [B1]

Carol Jones is the director of a nursery school in Cardiff. This is an interview with her and students who want to become social workers and early-childhood teachers. The interview is about leading a team.

Sue Morgan, the teacher: Hi Carol, it's nice to have you here today for an interview. Should we start right away?
Carol Jones: Yes, fire away. I can't wait to hear your questions.
Jamie: What are the key factors of leading a team?
Carol Jones: Oh, there are many. I think the most four most important ones are these.
First of all, it is vital to set a target which people can visualize and, secondly, to show them the way to achieve it. There has to be an inspiring image of what the team can achieve or contribute. For example: "We'll have a Christmas parade with a Santa and children in costume."
At the same time, one has to make sure that the team has clear objectives for its work and that these are doable in the time available.
Thirdly, it is also important to ensure that the team has the right members with the right skills and commitment to achieve its aims.
Last but not least, there is the coaching and managing of the team. One has to see the team as a whole unit, not just as a group of separate individuals. The team members should have frequent opportunities to communicate effectively. The team leader needs to build effective links between members and to be a mediator. Conflicts should be managed creatively and productively and decision-making should be of high quality – and timely.
Lily: You stress the coaching and managing of the team as a unit. But what about the individual? Shouldn't each individual be praised for their personal commitment as well?
Carol Jones: You're right. One must not neglect individual commitment. A team leader has to ensure that everyone gets feedback on their personal performance. This feedback should not only be given by the leader but also by the team members and the team's customers, for example the parents.
Joanna: How do you make sure the team members show commitment?
Carol Jones: This is not easy but individual tasks should be clearly related to the overall aims and objectives of the organisation. Otherwise people might get confused and lose interest.
Stan: How many people should a team consist of?
Carol Jones: Judging from my experience I would say that the number of members should be the minimum needed to perform the team's tasks effectively – certainly no more than eight to ten people.
Ella: In my practical work experience I've witnessed intra-team conflict and rivalry. What can a leader do to prevent team members going down that road?
Carol Jones: It's important that the leader is positive about the organisation as a whole and positive about the team in particular. His or her role is to ensure that there is cooperation and support. In order to achieve this, the leader should be positive about the work the team does, always encouraging people to consider how they can help each other.
Nora: What can go wrong in leading a team?
Carol Jones: Most failures of team leadership occur where leaders are too dominant. And there is the opposite danger that they provide insufficient direction and support. Or they may set challenging goals, but then not provide the resources necessary for them to be achieved. Not giving feedback and forgetting to encourage reflection is a recipe for frustration within a team, resulting in low performance.
Any: What's your personal definition of "team"?
Carol Jones: I would say it is a group of individuals who share their knowledge, skills and experience in order to reach a certain goal.
Sue Morgan: Okay Carol, I think that's it. Thank you so much for coming and answering our questions.
Carol Jones: It was a pleasure for me.

(615 words)

Work with me ISBN 978-3-582-77856-7

★★ 1. **Translation**
Situation: Carol Jones (Text 5) brought along a trainee from Germany who would like to have the students' questions translated. Write down translations of them, then get together in groups of three to four students and compare your findings. Present the best ones to your classmates.

★★★ 2. **Working with the Text**
Explain in your own words what Carol Jones means by the following expressions:
- a target which people can visualize
- conflicts should be managed creatively and productively
- tasks should be clearly related to the overall aims and objectives of the organisation
- there is the danger that the team leader provides insufficient direction and support

3. **Role Play**
★★ a) Write a scenario of badly-led teamwork in an institution. Perform it with classmates in front of another group.
★★★ b) Together decide why the teamwork went wrong and what the leader could have done to make it effective.

4. **Internet Research**
★★★ a) Find out what educational qualifications you have to have to become a leader of a nursery school in Great Britain, the USA, Canada or Australia. Contrast these to their German equivalents.
★★★★ KMK b) **Discussion**
In a small group discuss the differences between these qualifications. Present the results of your discussion to your classmates.

★★★ 5. **Written Discussion**
State whether you would like to become the team leader of an institution of your choice or not. Give reasons for your decision.

TEXT 6: Staying Fit In Your Job – Stress Management [B1]

10 Stress Busters

Identifying the cause of your stress is the first thing to do to help yourself feel better. Remember – problems are solutions in disguise!

Good stress management is dependent on
- Building emotional resilience
- Feeling in control of your life
- Having a good circle of friends and family
- Developing a positive attitude

Here are ten suggestions of how one might ease stress by taking positive action:

1 Exercise
Exercise alone will not get rid of stress but it will lessen some of the emotional effects and will help you think more clearly and calmly about you problems.

2 Take Control
All problems have solutions. Your stress will worsen if you are passive and think that there is nothing you can do. Losing control is – in itself – one of the main factors in the onset of stress and having negative feelings.

3 Keep in touch with people
Strong relationships with colleagues, friends and relatives can ease your problems at work and give you a fresh perspective on them. Being with friends helps us to chill out. Laughter has been shown to be an excellent medicine and stress-buster. And you can often find a way to solve a problem just by having a chat with a mate.

4 Quality "me-time"
Everyone needs to find time for socialising, relaxing and doing exercise or sport. It is recommended that we devote at least two evenings every week to "me-time".

5 Challenging oneself
You can build your confidence by setting yourself targets and challenging yourself to achieve them, for example, by enrolling on a foreign language course or taking up a new sport. This will help you cope with your stress.

6 Beware of unhealthy habits!
Do not resort to alcohol, cigarettes, coffee or other stimulants to help with stress. Men are more likely than women to make this mistake. This is a classic avoidance strategy, particularly for men. Research shows that women are more likely to seek help from their social network. In the end, using a crutch will never solve the problem. Indeed, such behaviour, in creating new problems – e.g. alcohol or substance dependency - will only make the situation worse

7 Get active in your community
There is a lot of evidence that individuals who offer to help others by volunteering or getting involved in the community develop extra resilience. Being close to those who are experiencing bigger problems than yourself can also put your own difficulties into proper perspective. Giving is a proven way of feeling better and happier about yourself. Even if you do not have time to volunteer, doing others a small favour on a daily basis will make a difference to your mood. Helping an old lady across the road or fetching the coffees at work will be rewarded by expressions of gratitude, increasing your feelings of self-worth.

8 Don't work harder, work smarter!
This means ranking work demands and seeing which have priority. Then, you can invest more time, thought and energy into getting on with those tasks which are vital to achieving the desired overall outcome, leaving the least important ones till last.

9 Act positive!
Concentrate on the positive aspects of life and on those things for which to feel grateful. We often fail to appreciate what we have. Is your glass half full or half empty? Why not try writing down two or three examples of what went well today or things which you appreciate.

10 Accept what you cannot change
It is not always possible to make a difficult situation better. Concentrate on those things over which you have some control. If your company is failing and people are losing their jobs, what can you do about it? In such a situation, the only positive thing to do is to look for a new job.

(633 words)

★★ **Creative Task**

a) Take a look at the 10 stress busters and describe examples from your own life that show how you are turning (could turn) each of them into reality.
b) Make a video that demonstrates the best examples of the 10 stress busters and show it to your classmates. Within your class a ranking could be made.
c) Ask the director of your school whether he could put the best examples on the school's website. Be careful with privacy matters!

Work with me ISBN 978-3-582-77856-7

Vocabulary Module 6 Teamwork and Cooperation with Parents

Text 1: The Development of a Team

(to) form	[fɔːm]	formen, bilden
(to) storm	[stɔːm]	(er-) stürmen
norm	[nɔːm]	Regel, Norm
(to) perform	[pəˈfɔːm]	agieren, durchführen, funktionieren
(to) adjourn	[əˈdʒɜːn]	sich an einen anderen Ort begeben; auch: vertagen; verschieben
(to) coach	[kəʊtʃ]	einarbeiten
detached	[dɪˈtætʃt]	freistehend, getrennt, separat
guidance	[ˈgaɪdənts]	Führung, Leitung
(to) vie	[vaɪ]	konkurrieren, wetteifern
(to) enable	[ɪˈneɪbl]	befähigen
(to) facilitate	[fəˈsɪlɪteɪt]	ermöglichen; fördern, unterstützen

Info 1: The Team and Interventions by the Leader

objective	[əbˈdʒektɪv]	Ansatz, Ziel, Zielvorgabe
(to) consult	[kənˈsʌlt]	zu Rate ziehen; befragen

Text 2: Communicating with Parents

(to) hinder	[ˈhɪndər]	verhindern, behindern
offspring	[ˈɒfsprɪŋ]	Kind(er), Nachkomme(n), Nachwuchs
(to) become involved in	[bɪˈkʌm ɪnˈvɒlvd ɪn]	sich engagieren
parents' council	[ˈpeərənts kaʊntsəl]	Elternbeirat
in passing	[ɪnˈpaːsɪŋ]	zwischen Tür und Angel
(to) sum up	[ˌsʌm ˈʌp]	Zusammenfassen, das Fazit ziehen aus etw.
further education course	[ˈfɜːðər ˌedjʊˈkeɪʃən kɔːs]	Fortbildungsveranstaltung

Text 3: Individualized Newsletters

ICT	[aɪsiːˈtiː]	EDV
(to) weigh up	[ωeɪ ʌp]	abwägen

Rules for Good Conversation and Listening Skills

impartial	[ɪmˈpɒːʃəl]	neutral, vorurteilslos, unbefangen

Text 4: Communication Techniques

savvy	[ˈsævi]	praktische Fertigkeiten, Können, Intelligenz
tells	[telz]	Fachausdruck der Körpersprache: unbewusste Zeichen

Text 5: Leading a Team

do able	[ˈduːəbl]	machbar
timely	[ˈtaɪmli]	rechtzeitig, zeitgemäß
(to) neglect	[nɪˈglekt]	missachten, vernachlässigen, versäumen
rivalry	[ˈraɪvəlri]	Konkurrenz, Rivalität

Text 6: Staying fit in your job

(to) ease	[iːz]	mildern, lindern
(to) lessen	[ˈlɛsn]	verringern
(to) worsen	[ˈwɜːsn]	(sich) verschlimmern
onset	[ˈɒnsɛt]	Entstehung, Anfang
(to) resort to sth.	[rɪˈzɔːt]	zu etw. greifen
crutch	[krʌtʃ]	Krücke

Module 7
Working Abroad

In this module you will have the opportunity to learn about

- terms such as preschool and infant school
- programmes for students who wish to work abroad
- how to read advertisements for posts worldwide and how to apply for them
- taking a gap year

Introduction

What would I be called abroad? There are many names for one and the same profession …

⋆ 1. Which of these terms have you heard or used before to describe your vocational training or intended profession in Germany?

⋆ 2. Do you have any work experience abroad? If so, where have you been? Have you ever considered leaving Germany and pursuing your career elsewhere? Which country would you like to work in?

Info 1:

Early-Childhood Education

It means education in early childhood. According to the NAEYC (National Association for the Education of Young Children), it spans the time from birth to age eight. Other terms which are often used instead of early-childhood education are early-childhood learning, early care and early education.

Work with me ISBN 978-3-582-77856-7

TEXT 1: A Chat with Lydia and Doug [B1]

What a Chaos of Terms!

Selina is studying early-childhood education at a vocational college in Germany. As part of her final assessment in English, she has to make an oral report about early-childhood education systems abroad. It is now the night before her oral exam and she is still quite confused. So she is searching on the Internet. She finally finds help on a social media platform for parents who are trying to decide whether or not to send their children to preschool.

[…]

Lydia: I know there's a great play school just around the corner.

Doug: I'm looking into preschool here. It's a joint venture between teachers and parents.

Lydia: How does it work exactly?

Doug: The parents have to pitch in and prepare snacks for the kids. And every parent has to help out with the kids once a month – just with easy stuff, like supervising them during recess or playing games and singing songs.

Lydia: That sounds great.

Selina: ***[joins the conversation]***

Lydia: Hi there, Selina

Selina: Hi – I need help!

Doug: What with?

Selina: I'm in panic! I have to make a presentations about preschool and nursery school and kindergarten and infant school – or whatever – and I'm really confused! Now you've mentioned *play school* as well – what's all that about? ☹

Lydia: We Americans just love to use a whole load of different words for more or less the same concept!

Selina: So what is *preschool*?

Lydia: Preschool education is just the education for children before the beginning of statutory education, usually between the ages of two and five. It can be private, statutory or a combination of both.

Doug: To put it simply, in the US preschool is education before real school starts – which kids have to go to. It can be called preschool or play school or nursery school or daycare. It usually all boils down to the same thing but some organizations think that nursery school sounds better than play school.

Lydia: The German word kindergarten is also used in many non-English-speaking countries to describe a type of preschool education. I know this from a friend in Sweden – but in the United States, Canada and some parts of Australia, kindergarten is the term used to describe the first year of compulsory schooling.

Selina: What does that mean?

Doug: Again, that kids have to go there! Kindergarten with us, in the United States, is like real school!

Selina: Thanks, that really helps me! It all seemed so complicated! Do you guys know what it's like in the UK?

Lydia: The word kindergarten is not generally used in the UK. They call it nursery school.

Selina: Oh, and what is *nursery school*?

Lydia: A nursery school is a type of school which cares for young children, usually between the ages of 3 and 4 years. In the United Kingdom a nursery school is part of primary education. In England and Wales, nursery schools provide education for pupils in a reception class.

Selina: And what then is a *reception class*?

Lydia: It's like an American kindergarten and as it makes up the final part of the "Foundation Stage" – which goes up to the age of five – it's compulsory, children have to go there.

(525 words) [American English]

Working with Words

★★ 1. Explain these terms in English.

education – private –
to supervise –
compulsory schooling

★★ 2. Find an opposite for each word.

infant – statutory –
common – local

★★ 3. Find a synonym for these words.

qualified – young children –
generally – to have to

4. **Working with the Text**

★ a) What is preschool education?

★ b) Name other common terms for "nursery school".

★★ c) How does the term kindergarten differ in the USA, Canada and Germany?

★★ d) What is a "reception class" in the UK?

★★★ e) Situation: A woman you know from your practical work experience is moving to the USA (UK) next month. Explain the differences between German and American (British) kindergarten to her.

TEXT 2: School Exchange Programmes [B1]

First Steps Into a Foreign Environment

Mrs McCoy is a teacher at a vocational college in Dublin. In an interview she tells of her experiences with different school exchange programmes.

Interviewer (I): You fulfil a very special role in your school, Mrs *McCoy*. What is it exactly?
Mrs McCoy: I'm coordinator of our school's Erasmus+ programmes.
Interviewer: What exactly are the Erasmus+ programmes?
Mrs McCoy: They are quite different from one another: first, there is a mobility programme which allows our students to go abroad for a certain period of time. Second, there is a **partnership programme** which involves vocational colleges in various European countries. Third, there is a **programme for teachers** and other people who train early-childhood teachers during their work experiences.
I: Okay, could we concentrate on the student programme?
Mrs McCoy: Yes of course. Do you mean vocational training in Europe?
I: Yes. Who are these vocational courses for?
Mrs MC: They're for students who want to become early-childhood teachers or social workers.
I: What must students do in order to be considered for your programme?
Mrs MC: They must have good personal skills, meaning they should be able to adjust to a cultural context quite new to them. They have to be outgoing and willing to prepare themselves for the visit abroad. On top of that, they have to write an application stating why they want to do their practical work experience abroad and what they expect from their stay.
I: Do they have to hand in a letter of application only or are there other documents required as well?
Mrs MC: Well, they have to hand in their CVs and certificates showing their personal and professional achievement so far.
I: Do many students apply?

Work with me ISBN 978-3-582-77856-7

Mrs MC: Oh yes! And the ones who can't be taken are really upset, asking me why I didn't choose them.
I: And what do you tell them?
Mrs MC: The truth of course – that personal aspects are taken very much into consideration. Marks and language skills are important but are not the main criteria for my choice.
I: So when you've picked your students, what happens next?
Mrs MC: They have to take part in an induction course. The content of the course depends on the country they are going to. The students who go to Finland, for example, have to learn some basic Finnish phrases to show their respect for the people and their willingness to make contact. Apart from that, they get to learn about Finnish characteristics. Organisational matters have to be talked about, rules of how to behave are given and tasks are discussed.
I: Do you only go to Finland?
Mrs MC: No, we've got partner institutions in France, Spain and in Germany as well.

I: Does every vocational college have such an exchange programme?
Mrs MC: No, not every school – as far as I know.
I: Apart from school exchange programmes, what other choices exist for students who are willing to work abroad?
Mrs MC: Hmm, it's much easier for students to get opportunities to work abroad if their school is involved in a mobility programme. Big programmes such as Erasmus+ only work in cooperation with schools. But as an alternative, students can – and do – organise exchanges independently, say as an au pair.

See also: Erasmus+ Programme www.erasmusplus.de and www.na-bibb.de

Erasmus+: Personal and Professional Benefits

Erasmus+ is an investment in your future. You grow as a person and learn new skills – this makes you stronger and more attractive for future employers.

Personal Benefits

Intercultural Experience
- You learn about other cultures, ways of working, and lifestyles.
- You become more open-minded and understand international cooperation better.

Independence & Self-Confidence
- You organize your life in a new place and solve problems by yourself.
- This helps you become more confident and responsible.

Improve Language Skills
- You improve your English or the language of the host country.
- Good language skills help you in work and everyday life.

Personal Growth
- You become more flexible, adaptable, and mature.
- Many people say the stay abroad helps them grow a lot.

Professional Benefits

Better Job Opportunities
- International experience looks good in your CV.
- Employers like people with initiative, language skills, and experience abroad.

New Work Skills
- You learn new methods, tools, or ways of working.
- You can bring this knowledge back to your school or care institution.

Networking
- You make contacts with people and organisations in other countries.
- These contacts can help you in your future job or education.

Certificates and Recognition
- You receive the *Europass Mobility* – an official document for your time abroad.
- It helps when applying for jobs or further training.

★ 1. **Working with the Text**
   a) What does Mrs McCoy have special charge of at her school?
   b) Which criteria must students who apply fulfil?
   c) What importance do language aspects have?

★★ 2. **Discussion**
   Does your school offer a mobility programme that could help you to investigate a future career abroad? If so, which qualifications would you need in order to apply?

★★★ 3. **Internet Research**
   Which other possibilities are there for students who wish to work abroad for a limited period of time? Search the Internet, taking your own specific abilities into account.

★★★★ 4. **Creative Task/Group Work**
   Create a (virtual) mobility exchange programme of your own and design a webpage for it. Consider the following aspects:
   - Who is this programme suitable for?
   - Which qualifications must the applicants have?
   - Which countries would be involved?
   - How would the programme be organised and funded?

Text 3:
Goodbye Germany! The Trend of Working Abroad [B1]

Have you ever dreamed of packing your things and leaving your old life for a far away destination? If so, then you are not alone. Every year, approximately 155,000 Germans leave their homes behind in search of a new life abroad. Recent studies show that not only students and dreamers but more and more qualified employees, as well as people who work in positions of higher management, are happily leaving the country.

A number of surveys, including those supported by the Federal Ministry of Economics, give the following reasons for this development: About two thirds of those questioned said they hoped to get a better job and earn more money abroad. Around 40 % mentioned that the tax burden in Germany was one of the reasons for leaving the country.

Another 30 % or so claimed that too much bureaucracy at a local level motivated them to continue their lives elsewhere. A lack of tolerance and creative freedom at the workplace convinced about a quarter to move abroad.

Nearly half of those questioned said that once integrated into their new surroundings, they saw no reason to return to Germany. Another large group said they could imagine returning someday, and a small number admitted they were actively planning their return.

Note: These numbers are based on earlier surveys. Newer studies (e.g. IAB 2024–2025) show similar trends, though exact percentages may vary slightly.

(230 words)

Work with me ISBN 978-3-582-77856-7

★ 1. **Working with the Text**

True or False?

a) Over 100,000 people leave Germany every year and emigrate to different countries.

b) One of the reasons for this development is the tax burden on Germans.

c) Of all the people questioned, less than ten percent wished to return home.

d) Family and friends remained crucial factors when deciding whether to stay or return.

★★ 2. **Discussion**

a) Have you ever seen TV programmes on the subject of emigration? If so, what difficulties are often mentioned?

b) Weigh up the pros and cons of leaving the country. Think of your own situation and reflect upon your personal and professional future.

Applying for a Job Abroad

Here are some helpful hints for those who would like to work abroad.

1. Consider the country you want to work in and research thoroughly. Each country has different employment laws and regulations you must follow. In addition, research the country's culture and language requirements. Remember, you will also be living in this country, so you want to make sure you will fit in and be comfortable.

2. Apply for a visa and/or work permit. A work permit is usually required by a foreign country for you to be able to work in that country. Many countries also require you to have a visa to travel and live in that country. You should apply for any visas or work permits you need before you apply for a position.

3. Peruse work-abroad websites and websites about short-term work abroad programs such as teaching, summer-jobbing or working as an Au Pair. (Source: Kristi Gray, eHow)

Additional Links

www.rausvonzuhaus.de/

www.auslandsjob.de/auslandsjobs.php

www.ruf-jugendreisen.de/jobs

www.volunta.de

www.kulturweit.de

Text 4:
Early-Childhood Teachers Wanted in New Zealand [B2]

Duration: 12 months – permanent fulltime

Tasks and Duties:
Early childhood teachers will do some or all of the following:

- plan the centre's daily programmes, learning experiences and routines
- observe children individually and in groups to identify their abilities, strengths and interests
- constantly assess and record the individual learning and development of each child
- educate and care for children
- discuss children's progress with their parents or caregivers and other education professionals
- make or adapt learning resources
- attend social gatherings with children and their parents and caregivers
- support children to make the transition to school

Prospects: Demand for places in preschool education is growing and the employment prospects for early-childhood teachers are good. There is an ongoing shortage of suitably trained professionals.

Skills and Knowledge:
Early-childhood teachers need to have:

- teaching skills and knowledge of different teaching methods and learning styles
- the ability to plan programmes to encourage children's learning and development
- knowledge of early literacy and numeracy strategies
- knowledge of children's learning development, as well as the ability to identify children with special needs or learning difficulties
- skills in observing behaviour and evaluating children's progress
- communication skills and the ability to relate well to children and other adults
- understanding of a range of cultures
- the ability to supervise children in large areas
- research skills and knowledge of how to access information and resources
- administration and report-writing skills
- organisational skills
- problem-solving and decision-making skills
- first-aid skills
- computer skills may also be useful.

Personal Qualities:
Early-childhood teachers need to be:

- understanding and patient
- creative, imaginative and resourceful
- able to make quick decisions
- firm and fair
- good at listening
- adaptable
- sympathetic towards children
- enthusiastic

Minimum Educational Qualifications:
Diploma/Certification, preferably qualified early-childhood teachers, however for the right applicants with a background in childcare there are good opportunities.

Languages: Candidates must be competent in spoken and written English, as English is the medium of the classroom.

Salary/Pay: Suitably trained early-childhood teachers usually earn between $25,000 and $35,000 per year, depending on their qualifications and experience. Heads and senior teachers can earn up to $55,000 per year.

This programme is open to: Candidates of all nationalities, provided that their English is of an acceptable standard.

The application process involves: an online application form plus a letter of application, the provision of a CV, a phone interview in English, letters of reference, an in-person interview, a physical examination and an inspection of health records.

Work with me ISBN 978-3-582-77856-7

★ 1. **Working with the Text**

a) According to this job advertisement, what tasks must the early-childhood teacher carry out?
b) What job opportunities can well-qualified teachers look forward to?
c) Which qualifications are required?
d) What personal qualities must one have?
e) What steps does the application process involve?

★★★ 2. **Skills**

Write your own résumé (CV) and then reply to this advertisement with a letter of application for this job. (→ p. 232 ff.)

★★★ 3. **Role Play**

Get together with a partner and work out a series of likely questions and answers for a phone interview. Practise and make notes, then present your interview to the group.

Text 5:
Early-Childhood Teachers Needed Worldwide [B2]

Italy, Spain, Germany and More

Over the past 10 years there has been a tremendous surge in the number of private international schools abroad. This is not only because of the number of expatriates abroad who want a private education for their children, but also because more and more affluent local parents want their children to have a western-style education in English with an eye to attending university abroad. These are all very motivated parents who are willing to pay for their children to have the best start in life.

The number of preschools and primary schools abroad has far outstripped the number of other types of schools, opening up a wealth of opportunities for experienced directors and early-childhood teachers abroad. These are very exclusive posts, offering candidates the opportunity to live and work in exciting parts of the world such as Abu Dhabi, Italy, Singapore, India and China.

Europe: We have schools in Italy, Spain and Germany looking for teachers to start now. These jobs require applicants to be nationals of a European Union country. It is not possible to sponsor work permits for nationals from the USA or Canada.

Qualifications: Candidates must have a bachelors degree in early-childhood education or an equivalent degree focusing on education up to the age of six years. English will be the teaching medium and therefore a high level of competence in spoken and written English is an absolute minimum requirement.

The Application Process: This consists of an initial letter of application and a CV, a phone interview, letters of reference and an in-person interview. Successful appointments are conditional on a medical examination and the inspection of personal health records.

★★ 1. **Working with the Text**

a) Briefly explain the increasing need for early-childhood teachers abroad.

b) What arguments does this advertisement use to motivate potential candidates to apply?

★★★ 2. **Working with Words**

Find expressions in the text which are explained by the following:

a) a great increase

b) people who have left to live abroad

c) mums and dads who are very enthusiastic

d) jobs offering a rare opportunity

e) hoping to study in a foreign institution

★★★ 3. **Role Play**

Work with a partner and practise the in-person interview that is mentioned as a requirement in the advertisement above. Change your role, so that each one of you is employer as well as candidate.

★★★ 4. **Skills**

Write a letter of application in reply to this specific advert, applying for a job in Italy or Spain.

★★★★ 5. **Project**

Create your own application for employment portfolio. Include your CV and letters of application, references from former employers and practical work experiences, as well as all other materials which might make you seem attractive to future employers.

Text 6: A Gap Year in Australia [B1]

Work with me ISBN 978-3-582-77856-7

Claudia and Ben are both nineteen and have decided to go abroad after graduation. In the following text, they talk about their intentions, plans and experiences in Australia.

BEN: "I really wanted to go abroad after graduating from Secondary School. I needed a break before deciding what to do with the rest of my life. I also wanted to brush up on my English. My two older brothers, Tim and Ferdinand, had both gone to Australia and done "Work and Travel" for twelve months. They didn't organize their gap years in advance, and that was a bit too risky and adventurous for me. I wanted to know exactly what I'd be doing and where I'd be staying. My girlfriend Claudia suggested that we work as au-pairs. She'd done a lot of babysitting and I have two younger sisters, so taking care of children seemed like a good idea. Also, I'd have a place to stay. "

Claudia: "Ben and I graduated in June. We wanted to leave for our gap year in September. There were so many things we had to organize before leaving for Australia. We needed to apply for a "work and travel" visa. Luckily, Ben's Mum, who is American, helped us with the online forms. We also needed to find nice families to work for, and we needed to book flights to Melbourne. I didn't want to be too far away from Ben. Travelling together seemed much safer to me than going abroad on my own. I was really glad that Ben also wanted to be an au-pair.

Ben: "I found my au-pair family on Facebook. There is a group called "Au-Pair Australia". I joined this group and answered a post sent out by a family with two children. The boy was eleven and the girl was nine. Before I got to Melbourne, the mother sent me a list of things she expected me to do every day. Among my chores were getting the children ready for school, packing their lunches, walking the dog, cleaning, folding laundry, picking the children up after school and preparing dinner. I was paid 250 Australian Dollars per week and was allowed to use the family's car. I once got a speeding ticket, and it was very expensive. You have to drive very carefully in Australia!

Claudia: "My first au-pair family was absolutely horrible! They made me clean the whole house, and I wasn't allowed to eat any of the more expensive food, including fruit, or to leave the house without permission. They also didn't pay the salary we had agreed upon. Luckily, I'd made friends with other au-pairs and quickly found a new family with two baby boys. They were twins. Their mum was Australian, and their father was Asian. I was there when they started crawling and said their first words. I changed a lot of nappies and enjoyed my second family a lot.

Ben: "After working for eleven months, Claudia and I went on a road trip through Australia. We bought an old car, a tent and sleeping bags, and drove from Melbourne to Cairns. We stopped in Sydney, Byron Bay, Springbrook National Park, Noosa, Hervey Bay, Rockhampton and Airlie Beach. We drove a total of 3,622 km and had an exhilarating adventure. It was a perfect ending to our year abroad.

(554 words)

★★ 1. **Working with the Text**

a) What motivates Ben to plan a gap year in Australia?

b) According to Claudia, what must be arranged before the trip?

c) Which chores did Ben have to manage?

d) Why did Claudia leave her first family?

★ 2. **Working with Words**

a) Find synonyms for the following words:

careful, salary, chores, risky, exhilarating

b) Explain the following words using a complete sentence:

to organize, Work and Travel, speeding ticket, nappies

3. **Mediation & Creative Tasks**

★ a) Ben schreibt eine Liste der Aufgaben, die er als Au-Pair machen muss.

Folgende Dinge sind zu erledigen:
1.
2.
3.
4. …

★★ b) Claudia is talking to her Mum. She complains about her first au-pair family.
Write a dialogue between Claudia and her mum.

★★ c) Role Play: Claudia and Ben are spending a weekend together in Melbourne. They discuss the pros and cons of being au-pairs in Australia.

★★★ d) Now You

Would you consider spending a year abroad? Why or why not? Think of things such as finances, relationships, language, etc. …

★★★ 4. **Internet Search**

a) Research what it might have cost Claudia and Ben to get to Australia. Consider flights, a Work and Travel Visa, etc. …

b) Which other gap year situations can you find online? Present them to your fellow students.

Work with me ISBN 978-3-582-77856-7

VOCABULARY MODULE 7 Working Abroad

Info1: Early-Childhood Education		
early-childhood education	[ˈɜːliˈtʃaɪldhʊd ˌedjʊˈkeɪʃən]	frühkindliche Erziehung
(to) span	[spæn]	umfassen
Text 1: A Chat with Lydia and Doug		
(to) supervise	[ˈsuːpəvaɪz]	beaufsichtigen
preschool	[ˈpriːskuːl]	Vorschule
statutory	[ˈstætjʊtəri]	gesetzlich
(to) boil down to sth. [coll]	[bɔɪl daʊn]	auf etw. hinauslaufen
compulsory	[kəmˈpʌlsəri]	obligatorisch, gesetzlich
nursery school	[ˈnɜːsəri]	Kindergarten
reception class (UK)	[rɪˈsepʃən klaːs]	vergleichbar mit Kindergarten und Vorschule
Text 2: School Exchange Programmes		
mobility programme	[məʊˈbɪlɪti ˈprəʊgræm]	Austauschprogramm
induction course	[ɪnˈdʌkʃən kɔːs]	Einführungskurs
Text 3: Goodbye Germany! The Trend of Working Abroad		
tax burden	[tæks ˈbɜːdən]	Steuerlast
bureaucracy	[bjʊeˈrɒkrəsi]	Bürokratie
Text 4: Early-Childhood Teachers Wanted in New Zealand		
learning resources	[ˈlɜːnɪŋ rɪˈzcːsɪz]	Hilfsmittel zur Bildung
shortage	[ˈʃɔːrtɪʤ]	Mangel
resourceful	[rɪˈzɔːsfəl]	einfallsreich, findig
Text 5: Early-Childhood Teachers Needed Worldwide		
surge	[sɜːʤ]	Flut
expatriates	[ekˈspætrietz]	Nicht-Einheimische, Auswanderer
outstripped	[ˌaʊtˈstrɪpt]	überstiegen
affluent	[ˈæfluənt]	wohlhabend
Text 6: A Gap Year in Australia		
graduation	[ˌgrædjʊˈeɪʃən]	Schulabschluss
risky	[rɪski]	gewagt, riskant
adventurous	[ədˈvɛntʃərəs]	abenteuerlich
chores	[tʃɔːz]	Pflichten, Routinearbeiten
permission	[pəˈmɪʃən]	Erlaubnis
salary	[ˈsæləri]	Lohn, Gehalt
exhilarating	[ɪgˈzɪləreɪtɪŋ]	berauschend

Module 8

The Media

Part A The Traditional Media

In this part A you will have the opportunity to learn about

- the history of the media and its diverse forms
- television for young children
- advertising and its influence on young minds
- the regulation of advertising
- magazines aimed at an adolescent audience

Introduction

Match the time to the invention. You can discuss this with classmates using the phrases down below.

1900 BC
104 AD
1452
late 15th century
1672
1837
1837
1876
1877
1888
1895
1895
1925
1930
1970ies
1973
1977
1979
1996

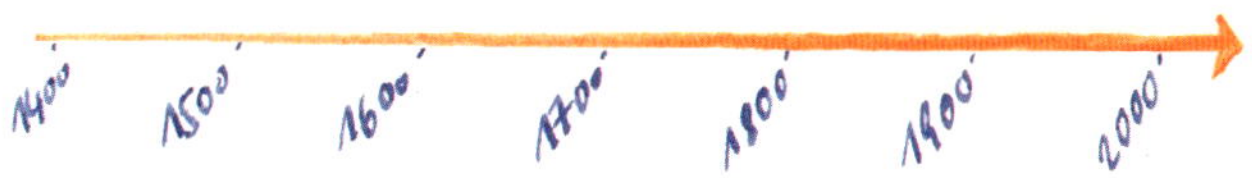

tape recorder
mobile phone
mechanical computer
newspaper
first movie shown in public
first alphabet
Internet
CD
magazine
paper
telegraph
video cassette
DVD
camera
telephone
phonograph/record player
radio
printing
television

(see solution page 97)

I think that was invented in …
What about …?
No, it was much earlier/later!
Surely not!
I can't believe it was that early/late
Do you agree?
It's between the (camera) and the (phone).

So early/late?
I think you're wrong/right.
What do you think?
(19…?) That's miles out!
18?? No way!!
You must be joking!

Work with me ISBN 978-3-582-77856-7

Text 1: A Revolution [B1]

Marconi's radio 1895
Early printing press by Gutenberg

The word "revolution" marks key dates in history: the Industrial Revolution in the 1700s in Great Britain; the French Revolution in 1789; the Russian revolution in 1917. "Revolution" describes a great change in human affairs which affects the lives of everyone. When did the great Media Revolution begin? Was it in 1452 when Gutenberg invented the printing press? Or later, perhaps in 1895, when Marconi's radio waves began the age of the mass-media?

The citizen of today has an immense wealth of information at his fingertips and gadgets which give access to it. Before Gutenberg invented printing, the only book most people saw was the bible. Nowadays the book is an everyday item and the Internet – possibly the most important invention in history – is an infinite library of information which grows daily bigger. Enter a keyword into a search engine and almost instantly hundreds and thousands of references appear. The Internet has revolutionised the way we live, entertain and inform ourselves and how we communicate and do business. We can contact friends thousands of miles away, watch films and tv, stram music, buy a car, a holiday, a house and even find out about the illness we are suffering from, without moving from our desks. And yet before 1970 the Internet did not exist.

A world without the Internet is now as unimaginable as a world without books.

(260 words)

Working with Words

★ 1. Which words in the text are defined by the following statements?
   a) electronic equipment which gives access to information
   b) It was the earliest book to be written out by hand and also to be printed.
   c) It is an ever-growing library of information.
   d) It describes a massive historical change.
   e) Put it into a search engine and lots of references are produced.
   f) Sources of information and entertainment for large audiences, such as newspapers, radio and television

★★ 2. Decide which words in the text these words could replace. Use a dictionary if necessary.
   a) inconceivable
   b) currently
   c) limitless
   d) a commonplace
   e) huge
   f) (to) permit
   g) devices
   h) links

★★★ 3. **Written Discussion**
   In no more than 100 words summarise the main points of the text, using your own words where you can.

Text 2: CBeebies [B2]

The first contact today's child will have with the media will be through simple story books and television programmes. Running from 6:00 until 19:00, CBeebies is a BBC channel on television entirely devoted to providing entertainment and educational programmes for very young children. It has a commercial counterpart, CITV, on which there is advertising. Some parents prefer their children not to be exposed to advertising pressure so they switch to CBeebies.

It is essential that programmes for small children stimulate their curiosity, imagination, language development and sense of humour. Programmes should also deliver simple messages about such issues as healthy eating, exercise, caring for the environment and respect for others.

For proper emotional development it is vital that children learn to empathise by identifying with the emotions of the characters they see. After watching TV, they can re-enact scenes they have watched and perhaps even take them further. Many programmes are linked to an activity – such as making a simple toy – thus encouraging children to be creative. Below is part of a day's schedule of programmes.

15:00	TWEENIES	Educational play with Bella, Fizz, Jake and Doodles the dog
15:20	POSTMAN PAT	The adventures of the loveable postie and his black and white cat Jess
15:35	BRUM	Motoring mayhem with the tiny car from Birmingham
15:45	CLIFFORD	The exploits of the gigantic dog and his owner Emily Elizabeth
16:00	BOB THE BUILDER	Bob and his dad build an observatory so that everyone can watch a comet pass over the valley
16:15	THE LARGE FAMILY	The adventures of a large family of elephants
16:30	LUNAR JIM	Adventures with the little astronaut
16:40	NINA AND THE NEURONS	Luke, the sight-neuron, helps Nina explain why things look small when they are far away
17:00	JAKERS	Animation in which a wise old pig tells stories of his childhood escapades
17:30	SPACE PIRATES	Musical fun with Captain DJ and the Pirate Posse
18:00	BEDTIME HOUR MAMA MIRABELLE	Fun for kids with the wise elephant and her friends
18:15	CHARLIE AND LOLA	Animation showing a boy's efforts to get his stubborn sister to try new things
18:25	RUBBADUBBERS	The exploits of a group of bath toys whose imaginations take them on incredible journeys
18:35	64 ZOO LANE	Animated animal tales followed by the CBeebies bedtime story

High-quality television for tiny tots is very important. Research is showing that a child deprived of stimulation and play in the early years is more likely to suffer from ADHD and other emotional, behavioural and learning problems, as well as being more likely to show delinquent tendencies.

(449 words)

Work with me ISBN 978-3-582-77856-7

★★ 1. **Discussion**
With your classmates study the CBeebies list of programmes and discuss some or all of the following themes:
- the duration of the programmes
- the number of cartoons
- the concept of outer space
- respect and liking for animals
- understanding simple science
- encouraging children to have a bath
- music
- stimulating the imagination
- the world of work
- story-telling
- adventures
- family relationships

★★★ 2. **Written Discussion**
"High-quality television for tiny tots is very important." In 150 words comment on this statement and the ideas in the text in your own words.

★★★ 3. **Group Work**
Situation: some young parents of children in your nursery group are confused about when, who with, how much and what kind of television their children should watch. In your group discuss Info 1 (and refer also to Text 2) and prepare a guidance brochure in English for parents.

INFO 1: Background TV Harms Toddlers, Even When They are not Watching

A study in the journal Child Development claims that parents who leave the television on all day are stunting the development of their children. Even when they seem not to be watching, it interferes with their concentration and hinders play with toys and other children. Children between one and three years are at particular risk. In an experiment 50 toddlers were invited to play for an hour. With the television set switched on, children played for shorter periods and spent less time focused on their toys.

Psychologists report that excessive TV watching can stunt language skills and reading development and lead to hyperactivity and poor behaviour. A study at John Hopkins University in the USA found that under-fives who watched TV for more than two hours a day were more likely to have behaviour problems. The American Academy of Paediatrics advises that children under two years watch no television at all.

(151 words)
(Adapted from the Daily Mail.

Work with me ISBN 978-3-582-77856-7

Text 3: The Media And Young Minds [B2]

From an early age, children are bombarded with messages by the media. The information they receive influences the way they think, speak and act. When asked which TV programmes they watch regularly, most older children mention the daily soap-operas. However, research shows that teenagers watch less TV these days. This is unfortunate because soaps often discuss important social problems like harassment, racism, street violence, domestic abuse, drug addiction, and alcoholism. Parents could help children understand these topics by watching with them.

Instead of TV, teenagers now mostly use smartphones to access the internet, where they can watch videos on platforms like YouTube, TikTok, Instagram, and Snapchat. Snapchat, however, can be risky for young users. Dangerous adults (catfish) may pretend to be children on these apps. Unlike TV, which is regulated to prevent harmful content, social media is less controlled. So, unsuitable content may be available. Online influencers can gain huge followings and earn money through advertising. Kids often admire footballers, pop stars, and lifestyle influencers, which is usually fine unless it causes them to have negative feelings about themselves or unrealistic dreams. Girls, in particular, may compare themselves negatively with the images that influencers post about makeup, beauty, and fashion.

However, some influencers can be harmful, spreading messages of misogyny, racism, or lies. Software can even make politicians or celebrities appear to say things they didn't actually say. Children have sometimes been tricked into sharing explicit photos of themselves or even been influenced toward self-harm. In this risky new environment, parents, teachers, and youth workers must actively work to protect children from these dangers.

(264 words)

★ 1. **Find the word in the text which best fits these gaps**
   a) Teenagers ... soap operas as their favourite viewing.
   b) Some online ... can cause harm to children.
   c) ... to drugs is a regular theme in soap operas.
   d) Children ... famous people in sport and music.
   e) Adults must ... children from risks online.
   f) Television and the internet contain all kinds of ... which children see and hear.
   g) Dangerous adults have ... children into sending photos of their bodies.

★★ 2. **Here are the answers. What might be the questions?**
   a) soap operas (What kind of programmes ...)
   b) daily (How often ...)
   c) through advertising (How do influencers ...)
   d) smartphones (How do children ...)
   e) explicit (What kind of photos ...)
   f) teachers and youth workers (Who should actively work)
   g) unrealistic (What kind of dreams ...)

Work with me ISBN 978-3-582-77856-7

★★★ 3. **Discussion**

In your group select programmes which you enjoyed when you were younger and programmes which are popular with younger Germans now. Discuss their good and bad points. Use the table for inspiration.

Some Structures to Use	General Points to Discuss
I used to watch … I thought it was funny/interesting/ educative … I particularly liked … I hated … because … My younger (brother/…) watches … I don't think … is very suitable for younger children I agree/disagree. It's too silly/violent…	There are (not) enough good programmes for children. Children watch too much TV. They should not watch TV after … p.m. Parents should check what they watch. Children should not watch TV in their rooms. … is very popular with children.

★★ 4. **Internet Research**

Go on the Internet to find out about the regulation of advertising in Germany. Find sentences similar to the ones in Info 2.

★★★ 5. **Translation**

KMK Translate the ASA Code from Info 2 into German and display it as a poster in your classroom.

Info 2: Children and Advertising in the UK

The Advertising Standards Agency in the UK applies strict rules governing advertisments aimed at under-sixteens (ASA Code). It decides which commercials on TV can only appear after 9:00 p.m. According to the ASA Code, children's advertising should not:

- *include material likely to cause children physical, mental or moral harm*
- *exploit a child's naivety, loyalty or inexperience*
- *encourage children to pester parents for (e.g.) sweets and toys*
- *exaggerate what a product, such as a toy, can do*
- *present children in a sexualised manner*
- *make a child feel inferior for not having a product*
- *promote unhealthy eating and lifestyle habits*
- *use verbal/visual ambiguity, confusion or irony in adverts aimed at the very young*
- *blur fantasy and reality*
- *use celebrities and characters well-known to children to promote products*

(For more details visit www.asa.org.uk)

Solution to page 92

1900 BC: first alphabet – 104 AD: paper – 1452: printing - late 15th century: newspaper – 1672: magazine – 1837: mechanical computer – 1837: telegraph – 1876: telephone – 1877: phonograph/record player – 1888: camera – 1895: first movie shown in public – 1895: radio – 1925: television – 1930: tape recorder – 1970ies: Internet – 1973: mobile phone – 1977: video cassette –1979: CD – 1996: DVD

Text 4: Teenage Magazines [B2]

General interest magazines are published for teenage girls in many countries, for instance, **Seventeen** and **Teen** in the USA, **More**! and **Shout** in Great Britain, **Jeune et Jolie** in France and **Yes** in the Netherlands. Publications for boys in this age group are about computer games, football, model-making and science fiction).

A newborn begins immediately to explore what its body feels like and what it can do. The body-image is constantly influenced by how others react to its appearance. A pre-adolescent girl, in particular, is already aware of what society's standards are for the "ideal body". In recent years an ever thinner body has been promoted by the fashion industry as the ideal for the young woman to aspire to.
No wonder then, that a survey of American girls aged nine and ten years showed that 40 % have tried to lose weight. Another survey of thirteen-year-olds showed that 53 % are dissatisfied with their bodies. By age 17 this figure increased to a very disturbing 78 %. Girls who watch lots of soap-operas and music videos are more likely to be unhappy with the way they look. And those who read teenage magazines are the most likely to suffer from "body dissatisfaction".

It is not difficult to see why. Years ago, characters in magazines used to be girls in school uniform having adventures and conflicts in and around the classroom. Today's teenage icon is radically different: She is typically a pretty, white, slim, blonde girl seeking a boyfriend – or more ways to gratify her boyfriend – and she enjoys shopping, fashion, make-up, skin treatments, manicures and popular culture.

The advertisements in the magazine are for clothes, cosmetics, hair products and fashion accessories. In fact, magazines frequently include a free gift of make-up to entice girls to buy them. The smell and feel of their glossy paper evoke luxury, femininity and the pleasures of self-adornment. The articles in them deal almost exclusively with dating and relationships. There is little space for politics, the environment, school or careers.

It seems that the teenage girl is being heavily stereotyped by the magazine industry. She is expected, one might conclude, to be interested solely in boys, sex, her appearance and celebrity. Many British parents are already very worried about the premature sexualisation of their young daughters. Professionals who work with young people are concerned that very young teenage girls are purchasing magazines, such as **Shout**, in order to appear as mature and as sexually experienced as girls five or six years older.

Apart from being brainwashed into having low educational and career aspirations – not to mention having very shallow personal values – are they not also more likely to experiment sexually at 13 or 14 years (with older boys), with the result that many develop genital diseases or become pregnant?

(465 words)

Work with me ISBN 978-3-582-77856-7

Working with Words

★ 1. In this summary of Text 4 the words in the box are missing. Put them in where they belong.

There are ___ general interest magazines for boys. Magazines ___ at teenage girls are causing ___ because they focus on consumerist ___ and ___ their readers to take ___ much interest in their personal ___ and their sex appeal. A high ___ of readers have told ___ that they are ___ with the size and shape of their own ___. Many younger girls are reading ___ which are meant (apparently) for older ___ and are perhaps, as a result, becoming sexually ___ at too early an ___.

encourage – percentage – teenagers – targeted – values – bodies – active – age – few – concern – appearance – dissatisfied – magazines – too – researchers

★★★ 2. Explain these terms in your own words.

a) body dissatisfaction
b) pre-adolescent
c) the ideal body
d) teenage icon
e) fashion accessories
f) the pleasures of self-adornment
g) premature sexualisation
h) brainwashed
i) low aspirations
j) shallow personal values

★★★ 3. **Discussion**
Bring in a German magazine for girls and discuss what messages, secret and obvious, it is transmitting. Consider
- photographs,
- cover,
- slogans and messages,
- advertisements,
- articles and
- feel of the paper.

★★★★ 4. **Written Discussion**
Write 150 words on this topic:
"Media-literacy should be part of the school curriculum."

★★★★ 5. Prepare a presentation to a female youth group on the themes and concerns in the text.

★★ 6. Prepare a questionnaire to a group of girls about these issues.
E.g. *Do you read teenage magazines?*
What interests you in them?

Work with me ISBN 978-3-582-77856-7

Part B The New Media

In this part B you will have the opportunity to learn about

- new problems which mobile phones have created in British schools
- the uses and misuses of the Internet

Text 5: A Dilemma [B1]

Mrs Stokes, headmistress of a school in Leicester has banned not only the use but also the possession of mobile phones by her pupils in school. Many parents are furious and a delegation of three, Mr Jones, Mrs Schofield and Ms Taylor, have arranged to see her.

Mrs Stokes: We have had so many problems with mobiles. They were taking up too much staff time – and even teaching time – that in the end I was forced to ban them. Reluctantly.

Mr Jones: But they keep our children safe! They can phone us to say where they are and we can phone them. If a child is approached by a stranger – or is abducted even – they can dial 999[1].

Mrs Schofield: Mobiles are part of modern life! What right have you to ban them?

Mrs Stokes: It was not an easy decision. Let me tell you what has been going on. Children were sending texts to each other in classrooms. Some left their phone on deliberately so that when it rang it disrupted the lesson. Others are sending other children nasty and threatening messages – which is bullying. Some parents even ring their children during lessons and think they have a right to.

Ms Taylor: But if my child is being bullied – and she has been – I want her to phone me straight away and take pictures of the bullies and record what they say with her phone!

Mrs Schofield: And what if there's an urgent matter, like a family illness?

Mrs Stokes: Every parent has the number of the school office. As far as bullying is concerned, our security cameras have almost eliminated it. But let me tell you what other impacts they are having on learning. First, so many pupils were arriving late for lessons because they were texting and calling friends. Teachers need to make prompt, clean starts to lessons, not spend the first ten minutes having arguments with pupils – who are frequently rude – about why they are late. I have a tray full of complaints from teachers and many other parents who want mobiles banned because of the loss of valuable time.

Mr Jones: Well, late-comers should be punished.

Mrs Stokes: Exactly! But that takes up so much time with form-filling and detentions, it's just getting out of hand. Mobiles also get lost or stolen. More time wasted!

Ms Taylor: But with a modern phone kids can get onto the Internet and do research for their projects.

Mrs Stokes: Or go to pornographic websites, like an eleven-year-old boy did recently! We have an ICT[2] room and computers in the library if a child wants to do research! There is so much competition now between kids to own the latest gadget, it's not healthy. I want

[1] 999: the emergency number for police, ambulance and fire service in Great Britain

[2] ICT: **I**nformation and **C**omputer **T**echnology

Work with me ISBN 978-3-582-77856-7

learning to be the focus in this school, not mobiles. And my staff – not just the English staff – worry about pupils' use of "textese"[3]. We are supposed to teach them correct spelling and punctuation, you know.

Mrs Schofield: Oh, what an exaggeration! Children know the difference between slang and proper English! They wouldn't use textese in an exam.

Mrs Stokes: Are you aware that many children are not sleeping well due to looking too long at screens? They arrive too tired to learn. I have been forced to make a very, very hard decision. Last week a vulnerable child was attacked on the way to school and lots of others filmed it fpr fun. What do I say to his mother? But what made my mind up was Monday's drama: a child had downloaded photos of his mother and her partner – naked together – from her digital camera. He showed them to his friend. He stole his mobile from his bag and sent the images to his contacts. Within an hour almost the whole school – rather than doing their school work – was looking at a couple having sex on a sofa! What do I say to those parents?

(691 words)

[3] textese: mobile phone language which uses special symbols and abbreviations

★★ 1. **Discussion**

In groups discuss the following issues arising from the dialogue.

- Is Mrs Stokes right to ban phones?
- What impact do mobile phones have on learning?
- Can Mrs Stokes please everybody?
- Can text language (textese) have a bad effect on proper written standards?
- Can it be right to film violence?

★★ 2. **Creative Task**

Mrs Stokes might give the school one last chance to use mobile phones responsibly. Draw up a code of conduct as a poster for school notice boards (alternative: a PowerPoint presentation). You could begin with:

PUPILS MUST NOT
- …

★★★ 3. **Written Discussion**

Write two summaries:

a) A letter to parents from Mrs Stokes explaining the reasons for the ban.

b) A letter from angry parents to the governors of the school explaining why children must be allowed to have their mobiles in school.

★★★★ 4. **Desktop Publishing**

Individually (or in pairs?) produce an article, with photos you might find online about the negative effects of social media on youngsters' mental health – for instance, *self-harming – using information from blogs, articles and examples from hearsay and personal experience.

* for example, cutting oneself

Text 6: The Dark Side of Cyberspace [B2]

Parents and teachers are calling for more control and censorship of the Internet, after the abduction and rape of a fourteen-year-old London girl by a man posing as a teenage boy in a chat room. The 47-year-old groomed the girl for weeks before arranging to meet her at a remote subway station after dark.

"Youngsters must be taught Internet safety at school," said Police Inspector Rose. "The Internet is like the Wild West. Naive teenagers can get hurt there. Girls are being put under pressure to send images of their bodies, so-called "sexting." The internet is an invaluable tool for educational purposes but like a lawless town it is also inhabited by dangerous paedophiles and contains pornographic and violent sites, wholly unsuitable for children."

Filtering

All schools have filtering systems in place but how many parents know as much about Internet technology as their children? In Australia every family receives a tax-credit to spend on filtering. Philip Norton, head teacher of an East Anglian primary school, phoned to tell our reporter that e-safety was an integral part of his ICT and PSHE[1] programme.

"Chat rooms can be great fun and they provide an ideal environment for our young pupils to exercise literary skills. As part of our 'Stranger Danger' initiative we teach even our six-year-olds about the threat of online paedophiles. We use two excellent websites – www.esafety.gov.au and www.thinkuknow.co.uk .

We hold open evenings for parents to learn about simple ways to protect their kids at home, such as parent controls, filter software, how to check web traffic and locking down applications."

"Another key area we deal with is cyber-bullying," he continues. "We have used an excellent U.S. government website (stopbullying.gov) which contains advice and resources, including downloadable fact sheets and film clips from YouTube."

Less Bullying

Mr Norton's LEA[2] is planning to introduce his programme into every primary school as there are far fewer incidents of cyber-bullying in the local secondary school which his pupils later attend. Linda Marston of the teachers union ATL[3] commented that 64 % of pupils in one Norfolk school reported being the victims of cyber-bullying. Two had even attempted suicide. Teachers too had been secretly photographed or even filmed and video-clips of them uploaded to YouTube.

"Most parents could not care less about what their kids log on to in their rooms," she said.

Empowered

A government spokesman told us: "Communication technology has empowered children and given them a degree of freedom and independence unprecedented in history. A remarkable number – the majority – use the Internet wisely. It is the minority we need to target – not only to prevent the harm they do others – but also, as we have seen so tragically, the harm they might do themselves."

He was referring no doubt to the Bridgend incident where in one year, in one small Welsh town, seven young people killed themselves. Where had they met and discussed suicide? In an Internet chat room.

(485 words)

[1] PSHE: Personal, Social and Health Education

[2] LEA: Local Education Authority

[3] ATL: Assistant Teachers and Lecturers

Work with me ISBN 978-3-582-77856-7

★ 1. **Working with the Text**
Read the text and decide if the following ideas are mentioned or not.
a) the kidnap of a teenage girl
b) the speed of Internet connection
c) helping junior pupils to grasp the perils of the Internet
d) bullying online
e) how Australian schools teach pupils to stay away from violent sites
f) how Mr Norton punishes cyber-bullies
g) how teachers become victims
h) new laws the government will pass to control the Internet

★★ 2. **Discussion**
Discuss how you use (or used to use) the Internet with your partner(s).

Some useful phrases:
These days …
When I was younger …
I visit … (website). I used to visit …
I enjoy chatting/playing/surfing …
I used to enjoy … writing/researching …

★★ 3. **Translation**
Translate into German all the comments in quotation marks from Text 6.

★★★ 4. **Working with Words**
In your own words explain these expressions.
a) censorship of the Internet
b) filtering systems
c) an invaluable tool for educational purposes
d) to exercise literary skills
e) Web traffic
f) cyber-bullying
g) social networking sites
h) to upload a film-clip

★★★ 5. **Creative Task/Role Play**
Write a dialogue where parents and youth workers discuss the following themes:
- The new media are causing many parents to lose control of their children.
- Children should play out more and log on less.
- Parents need to understand the Internet better.
- How much should parents control and check what their children log onto?
- How should they deal with cyber-bullying?
- Should children have Internet phones?
- Should their mobiles have special codes to activate Internet filters and controls?
- What more should Internet providers do to protect youngsters?

Practise it and perform the dialogue to your class.

★★★★ 6. **Written Discussion**
Inspector Rose compares the Internet to the Wild West. Explain the comparison in about 100 words.

7. **What is Artificial Intelligence?**
AI is the ability that computers have gained through design and programming. At first, computers were just calculating machines, able to do math tasks faster and more accurately than most humans. Today, the skills of the smartest machines go far beyond simple calculations. AI has led to robots that can communicate, understand, and even learn from experience. AI is also essential in smartphones and their apps, for example, in creating texts and images. It is used in medicine, transportation, at home, in industry, and in security.

★★★ **Discussion in small Groups**
Discuss how AI is used in your gadgets and the benefits it brings, but also think about the risks (search online for "the dangers of AI"). Write down any new words you find, and take turns looking them up in a dictionary. Share what you learn with other groups.

Work with me ISBN 978-3-582-77856-7

Vocabulary Module 8 The Media

Text 1: A Revolution		
printing press	['prɪntɪŋ pres]	Druckerpresse
gadgets	['gædʒɪts]	(technische) Geräte
infinite	['ɪnfɪnət]	unendlich
unimaginable	[ˌʌnɪ'mædʒɪnəbl]	unvorstellbar
(to) stunt	[stʌnt]	hemmen
Text 2: CBeebies		
devoted	[dɪ'vəʊtɪd]	gewidmet
counterpart	['kaʊntəpaːt]	Gegenstück
vital	['vaɪtəl]	unbedingt notwendig, unerlässlich
(to) empathise	['empəθaɪz]	sich einfühlen
deprived	[dɪ'praɪvd]	benachteiligt
ADHD	[ˌeɪ diː eɪtʃ'diː]	ADS
delinquent	[dɪ'lɪŋkwənt]	kriminell
excerpts	['eksɜːpts]	Auszüge
Text 3: The Media And Young Minds		
harassment	[hə'ræsmənt]	Belästigung, Mobbing
domestic abuse	[də'mɛstɪk ə'bjuːs]	häusliche Gewalt
drug addiction	[drʌg ə'dɪkʃən]	Drogenabhängigkeit
catfish	['kætfɪʃ]	Person, die in einem sozialen Netzwerk aus unlauterer Absicht ein Profil mit falscher Identität anlegt
unsuitable	[ʌn'suːtəbəl]	unangemessen, ungeeignet
misogyny	[maɪ'sɒdʒɪni]	Frauenfeindlichkeit
explicit	[ɪk'splɪsɪt]	hier: intim, freizügig
self-harm	[sɛlf-hɑːm]	selbstschädigend, selbstverletzend
youth worker	[juːθ 'wɜːkə]	Jugendbetreuer, Jugendarbeiter
Info 2: Children and Advertising in the UK		
(to) exploit	[ɪk'splɔɪt]	ausbeuten
(to) pester	['pestər]	belästigen, nerven
sexualised	[ˌseksju'ælaɪzt]	hier: zu früh geschlechtlich bewusst
inferior	[ɪn'fɪəriər]	minderwertig
(to) blur	[blɜːr]	verwischen
Text 4: Teenage Magazines		
(to) aspire to	[ə'spaɪər]	streben nach
(to) gratify	['grætɪfaɪ]	befriedigen, jem. gefällig sein
(to) entice	[ɪn'taɪs]	locken
(to) evoke	[ɪ'vəʊk]	hervorrufen
self-adornment	['self-ə'dɔːnmənt]	Selbstverschönerung
Text 5: A Dilemma		
reluctantly	[rɪ'lʌktəntli]	nur ungern
(to) abduct	[æb'dʌkt]	entführen
(to) disrupt	[dɪs'rʌpt]	stören
vulnerable	['vʌlnərəbl]	schutzlos, angreifbar
(to) eliminate	[ɪ'lɪmɪneɪt]	beseitigen
violence	[]	Gewalttätigkeit
Text 6: The Dark Side of Cyberspace		
invaluable	[ɪn'væljʊbl]	außerordentlich wichtig
lawless	['lɔːləs]	gesetzlos
(to) groom	[gruːm]	hier: präparieren, vorbereiten
(to) empower	[ɪm'paʊər]	bemächtigen
unprecedented	[ʌn'presɪdentɪd]	beispiellos
perils	['perəlz]	Gefahren

Work with me ISBN 978-3-582-77856-7

MODULE 9
People with Special Needs

In this module you will have the opportunity to learn about

- various disabilities
- caring for people with special needs
- getting support to cope with a disability
- working in a residential home for people with special needs

Introduction

⋆ 1. **Working with Words**
Write down five thoughts that come to mind when looking at the picture.

⋆⋆ 2. **Group Work**
Find a partner and discuss the stereotypes given in the box below about people with special needs. Write down whether you agree with them or not, giving reasons for your answers.

Stereotypes about people with special needs

They have a sad life.
They understand nothing of what is going on.
Working with them is so depressing.
One cannot teach them anything.

⋆⋆⋆ 3. **Role Play**
Situation: you are going for an interview at a residential home for young people with special needs. Prepare your reasons for wishing to work with them, and also think up questions to ask other candidates. Work with three or four classmates, taking turns to be interviewees and members of the interview panel.
Award points for good answers, self-confidence, etc. At the end decide who should get the job.

Text 1: Hearing Loss [B2]

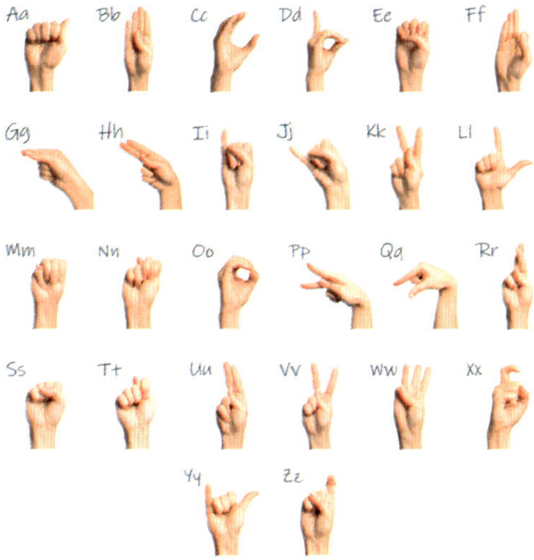

American Sign Language

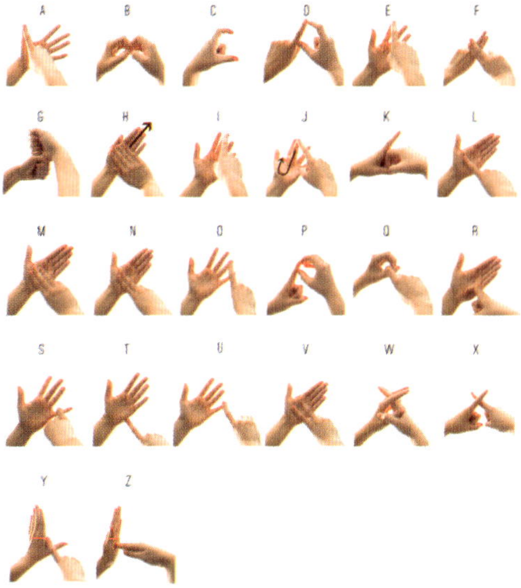

British Sign Language

Hearing loss describes an impairment which can occur in frequency or intensity, or both. The severity of hearing loss is defined by the range of frequencies or intensities which can be perceived. These are mostly connected with speech. The degrees of hearing loss are described as mild, moderate, severe or profound.

The word deaf describes a hearing loss so severe that even sounds of 90 dB (decibel) or higher are not heard. The sufferer is unable to hear or process speech and language information – even if given a hearing aid. People with a less severe impairment are called hard of hearing.

Impairment in hearing does not always affect both ears: Unilateral loss describes damage to one ear, bilateral loss damage to both.

Communication

People with a hearing loss use different means to communicate:

- speech is used for oral communication.
- sign language is used for manual communication,
- hearing aids are used for listening,
- lip-reading is used instead of listening for information (only a minority of affected people are able to use all of these means of communication).

Four Main Types

a) *Conductive:* Loss is caused by a problem in the outer ear or the middle ear. Usually all frequencies are affected to the same degree, but the hearing deficit is not severe in most cases.

b) *Sensorineural:* This problem can be found in the inner ear or the auditory nerve. Often a person's ability to hear some frequencies better than others is affected. Thus, sounds may seem distorted – even when a hearing aid is used. The range of this hearing loss is from mild to profound.

c) *Mixed:* This describes a combination of conductive and sensorineural losses.

d) *Central:* This problem occurs somewhere along the pathway between the inner ear and the auditory region of the brain, or even in the brain itself.

(306 words)

Work with me ISBN 978-3-582-77856-7

INFO 1: Hearing Aids

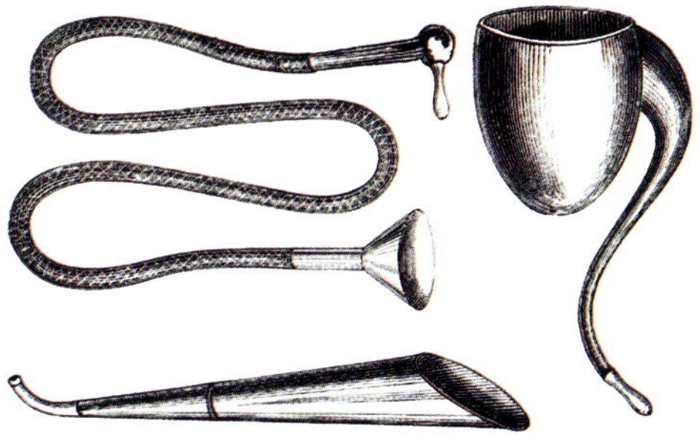

HEARING TRUMPETS.

Ear trumpets *were probably early man's first attempt at coping with hearing problems. In pre-historic times, hearing trumpets were simply hollowed-out horns of cows, rams or other animals. Later versions in wood and metal copied the same general shapes of natural horns.*

INFO 2: What Is a "Decibel"?

A ***decibel*** *(abbreviated* ***dB****) is the unit used to measure the intensity of a sound.*
Here are some common sounds and their decibel ratings:

- *Near total silence – 0 dB*
- *A whisper – 15 dB*
- *Normal conversation – 60 dB*
- *A lawnmower – 90 dB*
- *A car horn – 110 dB*
- *A rock concert or a jet engine – 120 dB*
- *A gunshot or firecracker – 140 dB*

Distance affects the intensity of sound and all of the above measurements were taken near the source.
Hearing loss can be caused by any sound above 85 dB. The degree of loss depends on the strength of the sound, as well as the length of exposure. Eight hours of 90 dB can cause damage to your ears. Any exposure to 140 dB causes immediate damage (and physical pain).

INFO 3: Disabilities Associated with Hearing Loss

About 30 % of children suffering from deafness or a hearing deficit also have one or more other developmental disabilities, such as mental retardation, cerebral palsy, vision impairment or epilepsy.
A child born with a hearing impairment, or whose hearing is impaired before the age of two, is likely to have problems in speaking and understanding spoken language.

★ 1. **Group Work**
Find out the decibel ratings of five different noises, tape them, play them to your classmates and let them guess what noise it is, as well as how high it is on the decibel scale.

★★ 2. **Internet Research**
Find out which hearing aids people use nowadays. Write down the pros and cons of each of them and list the different hearing aids in an order of recommendation.

★★★★ 3. **Project**
Imagine you are in a team of early-childhood teachers/social workers, and there is a child with hearing loss in your group. Plan a project in your nursery school or residential home to let your group know about hearing loss and how to live with it.

★★★ 4. **Discussion**
There are many different sign languages for people with hearing loss. Are you in favour of an international sign language or not? Give reasons.

★★★ 5. **Mediation**
KMK
Situation: you work in a school for children with hearing loss in Manchester. A German group comes on a visit and you have to tell them about the different types of hearing impairment. Give a presentation to a small group.

★★ 6. **Working with Words**
Make up a sentence in sign language, present it to your classmates and let them work out what it means in spoken language.

Text 2:

Intellectual Disability [B1]

Eileen and Emily, non-identical twins aged five, attend the same nursery school. Eileen shows average development but Emily has a cognitive disability. Jane has just begun working as a trainee at the nursery and asks Anne, her supervisor, about them.

Jane: Anne. May I ask you something about Emily's disability?

Anne: Yes, of course you can. What would you like to know?

Jane: Well, what exactly is her problem? All I know is that she's in the special needs programme. Yet her twin sister Eileen seems quite normal.

Anne: Emily has an intellectual or cognitive disability; sometimes called mental retardation. Children like her have below-average scores in intelligence tests and have a limited ability to manage in everyday life, for example in communication and in self-care. Coping with different social situations can be difficult for them.

Jane: Does it mean that Emily can't learn anything?

Anne: No, she *is* able to learn new skills, it's just that she needs more time to acquire them than a child of average intelligence and with good adaptive skills, such as her sister Eileen.

Jane: Is it the same for all children who have got her problem?

Anne: No, there are different degrees of intellectual disability which range from mild to profound. The degree of the condition is shown by scores in IQ – *Intelligence Quotient* – tests. Different children need different levels of support.

Jane: And what is Emily's main problem?

Anne: It's not always easy for her to let others know what she wants and needs. Taking care of herself is also not easy for her. Learning different skills and abilities, such as speaking, walking, dressing or eating without help, take her much longer and she has to make much more effort than other children. Later on, classroom learning will probably cause her problems. So I'm pretty sure she will have to be in a programme to focus on her special needs when she starts school.

Jane: Yes, that sounds quite probable to me. I would like to know how you found out about her cognitive disability in the first place.

Anne: Well, there are different signs to look out for. The most common ones – which were seen in Emily too – are:

- sitting up, crawling, and walking later than other children,
- learning to talk later, and having trouble speaking,
- finding it hard to remember things,
- having trouble understanding social rules,
- having trouble seeing the results of one's own actions and
- having trouble solving problems.

These signs were noticed early in Emily because the degree of her intellectual disability is quite severe. But nobody can tell how she will go on later, that is to say, how the disability will develop in detail. We only know that development depends to a great extent on the help a child gets. The earlier and more intensive the help, the more likely it is that Emily will reach her full potential.

Jane: How come Emily has an intellectual disability at all?

Anne: Oh, I wish I knew. There are so many possible causes. Symptoms can be found at different ages and can be traced back to structural dysfunctions in the brain, to injury or a disease. Intellectual disability is often triggered off by a problem before the baby is even born – possibly fragile-X syndrome, where the X-chromosome is abnormal. There are other genetic disorders or infections, and there is even a foetal alcohol syndrome which in Emily's case can be excluded, as I know the mother. But it can also

Work with me ISBN 978-3-582-77856-7

be caused during birth or soon after birth. My own daughter caught meningitis at the age of six months and now has learning difficulties. In some cases the cause of an intellectual disability cannot be found at all, and I think that Emily's case is like that.

Jane: Thank you for telling me so much about intellectual disability. That will be very useful in my career. I would love to help out with Emily to gain more experience.
Anne: Thank you Jane. It's good to know that you are so willing to help.
Jane: You're welcome!

(668 words)

★ 1. **Working with the Text**
Answer the following questions in your own words.
a) How is intellectual disability defined?
b) Are all forms of intellectual disability the same? Explain your answer.
c) Why do children with intellectual disability have problems in letting others know about their needs?
d) Are the reasons for intellectual disability post-natal only? Why (not)?
e) How can you find out whether a child is suffering from intellectual disability?
f) How can you stimulate the intellectually disabled child to reach their full potential?

★★ 2. **Internet Research**
Find out what help there is in your region for children with intellectual disability and their families. Create a brochure or booklet with addresses and short descriptions of the institutions.

★★★ 3. **Role Play**
KMK Situation: you work in a nursery school and suspect that a child has got an intellectual disability. Prepare a dialogue to tell the parents about your observations – the parents will be played by your partners. Practise it and perform it to the class.

★★★ 4. **Group Work**
Situation: you work as a team in a social institution of your choice. Your employer tells you that a child or a young adult with Down's syndrome is joining your group. List the kinds of support you can offer the child/young adult.

★★★★ 5. **Project**
Search the Internet and find different forms of intellectual disability; choose one and describe it in its cause, its appearance and its treatment to your classmates. Make sure you give an interesting presentation.

TEXT 3: Cerebral Palsy [B2]

The students at the department of education are working on the topic of cerebral palsy. Today Sam, who is a social worker in a school for children with special needs, has come to their class to do a presentation on the condition.

Hi, I'm Sam. I work in the special-needs school down the road. Your teacher has invited me to tell you something about cerebral palsy. Well, I'll try not to make it too theoretical, but there is quite a lot of information you need to know if you are going to work with people who have got cerebral palsy. Before going into detail, I'll write down a definition of it.

Definition Cerebral palsy
- Non-progressive brain abnormality
- Affects ability to move, to maintain balance/posture
- Cause: damage to part of brain which controls muscle tone
- Symptoms can change over lifetime

In practical terms, this means that an affected person is not able to keep their body or parts of it in a certain position, they are not able to sit up straight and keep their head up. Controlled changes by the muscles are just not possible.
I will explain the symptoms of cerebral palsy to you in more detail here.
The signs of cerebral palsy usually do not appear right after a baby is born. They often become clear during the first months or years of life. Some common symptoms include:
- Slow development – for example, not being able to sit by 8 months or not walking by 18 months.
- Muscles that feel either too stiff or too loose.
- Weakness in the arms or legs.
- Movements that are fidgety, jerky, or awkward.
- Sudden or uncontrolled body movements.
- Walking on tiptoes.
- Other possible difficulties – such as trouble swallowing, speaking, seeing, or learning.

The symptoms can be very different from person to person. Some people might only have mild issues, while others can be seriously affected.
I'll outline the four main types.

a) Spasticity

About 70 % to 80 % of affected people are spastic. The muscles are stiff because muscle tone is increased. Spastic cerebral palsy is generally differentiated by which part of the body is affected:

- Spastic diplegia describes spasticity mainly in both legs.
- Spastic hemiplegia means that one side of the person's body is affected.
- Spastic quadriplegia affects the person's whole body.

b) Athetoid or dyskinetic

- About 10 % to 20 % have the athetoid form.
- They show slow, writhing movements which they cannot control.
- Normally the extremities (arms and legs) are affected.
- Sometimes the face and the tongue are affected as well as speech.
- The tone of the muscle can change, even within a single day.

c) Ataxic

- About 5 % to 10 % have the ataxic form.
- Balance and depth perception are problems causing unsteadiness when walking.
- Quick or controlled movements (e.g. writing), cause trouble.
- Reaching for things is difficult □ poor hand/arm control.
- Tone of muscle increased or decreased.

d) Mixed

- Spasticity and athetoid movements combined
- Only affects a small percentage of people with cerebral palsy.

I hope I have shown you that the symptoms of cerebral palsy differ widely from one person to another. One person with a severe form of it might not be able to walk, while someone else, with a mild form, might just walk a little awkwardly. This is why the special help we give depends on the individual child and cannot be generalized.

Maybe you're wondering how cerebral palsy can develop. Cerebral palsy can happen

Work with me ISBN 978-3-582-77856-7

when a baby's brain does not grow in the usual way before birth, or if the brain is harmed during birth or shortly after.

Some possible causes of cerebral palsy are:

- Bleeding in the baby's brain or not enough blood and oxygen going to the brain.
- An infection the mother gets during pregnancy.
- Not enough oxygen to the brain for a short time during a difficult birth.
- Meningitis.
- A serious injury to the head.

However, in many cases, doctors do not know the exact cause.

Well, my presentation is over. If you are interested in getting to know more about cerebral palsy and how to work with affected children, you should let me know. Then I'll make arrangements for you to come and have a look around for a day.

(690 words)

★ 1. **Internet Research**

Find out what tasks your body has to do in order to move your right thumb.

★★ 2. **Group Work**

Make a list of places in your region where you can learn more about cerebral palsy. Concentrate on information for people with the condition and their families.

★★ 3. **Creative Task**

KMK

Imagine you work in a nursery school/ residential home for young people. A new group member with spastic hemiplegia cerebral palsy is arriving. Inform your group about her and her special needs. Plan a welcome party for her.

★★★★ 4. **Project**

For students doing a work experience in an institution for people with special needs

Choose a person who has a form of cerebral palsy. Describe their case to your classmates. In your description you should make sure you outline the cause of their cerebral palsy, their symptoms and special needs, as well as their daily routine.

★★ 5. **Working with Words**

Write down definitions for these words.

brain	posture	symptom
awkward	tongue	

★ 6. **Working with the Text**

Find questions to the following answers.

a) A person's ability to move and to maintain balance and posture is affected.

b) The affected person is, for example, not able to sit up straight and keep their head up.

c) Their muscles are stiff because the muscle tone is increased.

d) Cerebral palsy cannot be generalized because the symptoms are very different from one person to the other.

e) Yes, people with cerebral palsy can also be affected by other disabilities.

★★★ 7. **Discussion**

Have a look at the illustration showing the concept „inclusion" in practice.

a) Make a list of positive and negative aspects of this concept.

b) Describe how this concept should be realized.

c) Give reasons for a possible failure of this concept.

Work with me ISBN 978-3-582-77856-7

Text 4: Visual Impairment [B2]

The weekly youth magazine „Me and My World" includes a feature called "Things Which Make Me Angry".
It publishes readers' letters on that subject.
This week there is a letter from Catherine.

Dear Sir,

I'm a 16 year-old teenager who has been labelled "blind" since birth. It makes me angry that people think I cannot see a thing, just because my condition is described as severe. I am not blind! I am visually impaired!

The severity of visual loss can be described in different ways but low vision or blindness are the most common terms used to describe the problems affecting me and people like me. It is often assumed that our "blindness" means we cannot see at all, when it often only means that we have difficulty in doing tasks based on vision only, for example reading or filling in forms. This means we need special help and consideration from other people so that we can manage tasks like those. Other everyday activities, such as moving around the environment, can mostly be managed with the vision we still have.

The consequences of vision loss vary from one person to another, even when the degree of loss they have is equally severe. Some people just know better than others how to get the most out what vision they have. And attitude plays such an important part! While one person might say, "Okay, I'll make the best of it," someone else might just give up. And I definitely have not given up! I really want to get the most out of my remaining eyesight

Visual impairment, the public needs to understand, only means that a sufferer's eyesight is at a level below "normal", and that aids like glasses and contact lenses can do very little to help. The reasons for impairment are quite numerous. Often there is a loss of visual acuity which means that objects cannot be seen as clearly as usual. This is what I have got as well. Another common impairment is tunnel vision, where one is unable to see a wide area without moving the eyes or head.

My teacher gives me the level of support I need – not too much and not to little. He also helps me to evaluate my own visual function by observing me in different situations, where he focuses on the following aspects:

- Can I find someone or something by scanning the room?
- How much light do I need for doing different tasks?
- How do I use my remaining vision for moving around?

My visual impairment also affected my childhood development because I was unable to perceive information or have the experiences a child without vision impairment has. But I think myself lucky not to have had a developmental disability like mental retardation, cerebral palsy, hearing loss or epilepsy. These are found among almost two-thirds of children with my condition.

I hope readers will now see "blind" people in another light, and help them where they need help, but let them do as many things on their own as possible.

Yours sincerely, *Catherine*

(482 words)

Work with me ISBN 978-3-582-77856-7

INFO 4: The Braille Alphabet

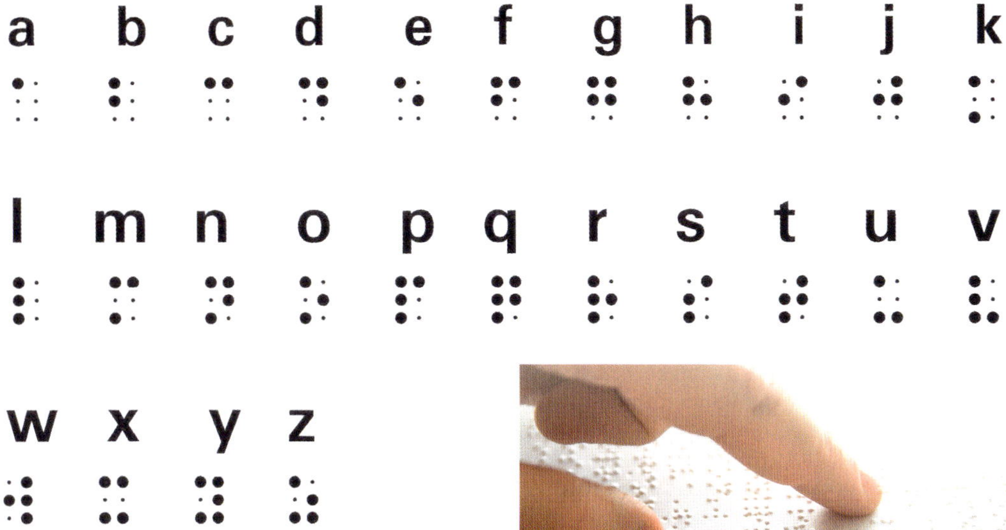

★ 1. **Working with Words**
Write down three English sentences in Braille using the Braille alphabet. Let your classmates work out what you wrote.

★★ 2. **Working with the Text**
Answer the following questions in your own words.
a) What does visual impairment describe?
b) Why is Catherine angry?
c) How do most blind people manage to move around in their own environment without help?
d) Explain why the consequences can be so different for two people with a medically equal loss of vision.
e) Why is it important to observe the individual in different situations?
f) What other problems do many visually impaired children suffer?

★★★ 3. **Internet Research**
Find as many types of visual impairment as you can and describe them briefly in your own words in a report – or present them to your group orally.

★★★ 4. **Role Play/Internet Research**
Imagine you work in a school for visually impaired children. Henry, aged 8, is one of your pupils. He can see very little. His parents want to know what can help to improve his eyesight. Tell the parents about existing aids and methods, list the pros and cons of each and then decide between you what further steps to take. Practise the role play and perform it to your class.

★★★★ 5. **Group Work**
Plan an activity for a group of children or young people with a visual impairment. Blindfold your classmates and do the activity with them. Afterwards you should reflect on what happened and ask your classmates for feedback.

★★ 6. **Creative Task**
Make a "Touch & Feel Braille alphabet" and put it with a self-designed little "Touch & Feel Braille book". It should contain pictures of things with their names underneath.

Work with me ISBN 978-3-582-77856-7

Text 5:

Working in a Residential Home for People with Special Needs [B1]

Hi, my name is Emma. I want to become an educational therapist. At the moment I'm doing a work experience in a residential home for people with special needs. There are five males and two females in the group I'm taking care of. They've got different needs, mostly linked to mental retardation.

Jake has got a condition called Trisomy 21 which I didn't know a lot about at the beginning of my practical training. So I had to do research on the Internet and read several books about it. Jake is a very nice young man and I enjoy working with him. But you have to keep your distance otherwise his emotions start running wild and he won't stop hugging and kissing you. On my first day in the residential home he asked me to marry him! I had a real problem explaining why I couldn't, without hurting his feelings. After talking to the rest of the staff about it, I found out that Jake falls in love very often and very easily. When I knew that, it was a lot easier for me to work with him.

My daily activities in the residential home include a lot of housework, like cleaning, doing the laundry and cooking. But I also have time to play games with the residents, accompany them on trips or go out for a walk with them. I think there's a lot for the residents to do here and they get plenty of exercise, according to their individual needs. And as for me, it's a job with so much to do that I never get bored.

Every day I am more and more fascinated by the way people with special needs live and experience things. Their way of life is so different to mine. They seem to live in an ideal world of their own, seeing everything through rose-coloured glasses, without making a fuss about little problems which would drive me mad. In a way I've been learning more from them than they have from me. To be honest, the experience has changed my own behaviour and attitude quite a lot. I've become more open-minded and tolerant in different situations now. It dawned on me that everybody experiences the world differently, in his or her own unique way. Things I would have considered as abnormal are very normal for the people I'm taking care of. And, anyway, who am I to judge what's normal and what isn't?

(410 words)

Work with me ISBN 978-3-582-77856-7

★ 1. **Working with Words**
Find a German equivalent to the following idioms.

a) Emotions start running wild
b) Living in an ideal world
c) Seeing everything through rose-coloured glasses
d) Stop making such a fuss!
e) Things drive me mad

★★ 2. **Working with the Text**
Answer the following questions in your own words.
a) Why do you have to keep your distance, working with Jake?
b) What did the staff tell Emma about Jake's marriage proposal?
c) What does Emma do so that the residents are not bored?
d) Why is Emma fascinated by the way people with special needs live their life?
e) How did Emma change her own behaviour and attitude?
f) Emma mentions things she would have considered abnormal. What things might she have meant?

★★★ 3. **Internet Research**
Find out the causes and symptoms of Trisomy 21. List aspects of good practice for working with children and adults who have the condition.

★★★ 4. **Mediation**
Translate the following German text into English. You may use a dictionary.

Heute können viele Menschen mit Trisomie 21 über 60 Jahre alt werden. Neue Forschungsansätze untersuchen, wie man geistige Fähigkeiten besser fördern und Menschen mit Trisomie 21 besser in die Arbeitswelt inkludieren kann. Dieser Bestandteil gesellschaftlicher Inklusion spielt eine wichtige Rolle hinsichtlich eines selbstständigen Lebens und der aktiven Teilnahme am sozialen Leben insgesamt, was entscheidend zu einem hohen Selbstwert beiträgt.

★★ 5. **Role Play**
Find a partner and make up a dialogue between Emma and Jake. She is telling him that she does not want to marry him after he has proposed marriage to her. Practise the dialogue and perform it to your class. Let your classmates give you feedback, especially about Jake's emotions.

★★★★ KMK 6. **Discussion**
Should people with Trisomy 21 have children or not? Give reasons for your opinion.

★★★ 7. **Project**
Find out what kinds of special needs people living in a nearby residential home have. Characterize them in terms of cause, symptoms and support needed. Communicate your findings to your classmates, using different methods of presentation.

VOCABULARY MODULE 9 People with Special Needs

Text 1: Hearing Loss		
loss	[lɒs]	Verlust
impairment	[ɪm'peamənt]	Beeinträchtigung
(to) perceive	[pə'siːv]	wahrnehmen
profound	[prə'faʊnd]	schwer, tiefgehend
deaf	[def]	taub
hearing aid	['hɪərɪŋ 'eɪd]	Hörgerät
sign language	[saɪn 'læŋgwɪdʒ]	Zeichensprache, Gebärdensprache
manual	['mænjuəl]	manuell
lip-reading	['lɪp-'riːdɪŋ]	Lippenlesen
auditory nerve	['ɔːdɪtri nɜːv]	Gehörnerv
distorted	[dɪ'stɔːtɪd]	verzerrt; entstellt
cerebral palsy	[ˌserəbrəl 'pɔːlzi]	Zerebralparese, zerebrale Kinderlähmung
Text 2: Intellectual Disability		
(to) lip-read	['lɪp'riːd]	von den Lippen lesen
(to) score	[skɔːr]	erzielen
(to) cope	[kəʊp]	bewältigen
skill	[skɪl]	Fertigkeit, Geschick, Können
(to) acquire	[ə'kwaɪər]	erwerben, annehmen
profound	[prə'faʊnd]	tiefgreifend, heftig
effort	['efat]	Anstrengung
(to) crawl	[krɔːl]	krabbeln, kriechen
(to) trigger off	['trɪgər ɒf]	auslösen
Text 3: Cerebral Palsy		
non-progressive	['nɒn-prə'gresɪv]	nicht fortschreitend
brain	[breɪn]	Gehirn
posture	['pɒstʃər]	Körperhaltung
muscle tone	['mʌsl təʊn]	Muskeltonus
athetoid		athetoid
athetosis		Athetose, Hammond'sches Syndrom (unwillkürliche umständliche Bewegungen bei Hirnläsion)
dyskinetic	[dɪskɪ'netɪk]	dyskinetisch, bewegungs(ablauf)gestört
spastic	['spæstɪk]	spastisch
spasticity	[spæs'tɪsəti]	Spastik
increased	[ɪn'kriːst]	erhöht; gesteigert
(to) differentiate	[ˌdɪfə'rentʃieɪt]	unterscheiden; differenzieren
diplegia	[daɪ'plɪːdʒiə]	Diplegie, doppelseitige Lähmung
hemiplegia	[hemə'plɪːdʒiə]	Hemiplegie, komplette Halbseitenlähmung
quadriplegia	[kwadrɪ'plɪːdʒiə]	Quadriplegie, Tetraplegie, Lähmung der vier Extremitäten
(to) writhe	[raɪð]	sich winden
extremity	[ɪk'stremɪti]	Extremitäten
ataxic		ataktisch, unsicher; ungeordnet, regellos
decreased	[dɪ'kriːsd]	reduziert, abgenommen, geschmälert
severe	[sɪ'vɪər]	schwer, heftig, hart
perception	[pa'sepʃən]	Wahrnehmung
Text 4: Visual Impairment		
visual acuity	['vɪʒuəl ə'kjuːəti]	Sehschärfe
perceive	[pə'siːv]	wahrnehmen
Braille	[breɪl]	Blindenschrift
Text 5: Working in a Residential Home		
educational therapist	[ˌedjʊ'keɪʃənəl 'θerəpɪst]	Heilerziehungspfleger/-in

Work with me ISBN 978-3-582-77856-7

Module 10
So Much Family Drama – Working with a Short Play

In this unit you will have the opportunity to learn

- about families with problems
- what might happen with children when families do not function as they should
- how to read, discuss, work with and analyse dramatic fiction

Introduction: A Family Portrait

⋆ 1. Describe the picture above. For which occasion and why might it have been taken?

⋆⋆ 2. Listen to the song "Family Portrait" by Pink without looking at the lyrics and try to write down words and sentences which you understand. After listening to the song, compare your notes as a class and try to find out what the song might be about. You may look at the lyrics (page 114) after you have finished.

Text 1: "Family Portrait" by Pink [B1]

Momma please stop crying, I can't stand the sound
Your pain is painful and its tearing me down
I hear glasses breaking as I sit up in my bed
I told dad you didn't mean those nasty things you said.
You fight about money, about me and my brother
and this I come home to, this is my shelter
It isn't easy growing up in World War III,
never knowing what love could be, you'll see.
I don't want love to destroy me like it has done my family.

Chorus:
Can we work it out? Can we be a family?
I promise I'll be better, Mommy I'll do anything.
Can we work it out? Can we be a family?
I promise I'll be better, Daddy please don't leave!

Daddy please stop yelling, I can't stand the sound.
Make mama stop crying, because I need you around.
My mama she loves you, no matter what she says
it's true. I know that she hurts you, but remember I love you, too.

I ran away today, ran from the noise, ran away
Don't want to go back to that place, but don't have no choice, no way[1]
It isn't easy growing up in World War III
Never knowing what love could be, well I've seen
I don't want love to destroy me like it did my family.

In our family portrait, we look pretty happy.
Let's play pretend, let's act like it comes naturally.
I don't want to have to split the holidays
I don't want two addresses
I don't want a step-brother anyways
and I don't want my mom to have to change her last name.

In our family portrait we look pretty happy
We look pretty normal, let's go back to that
In our family portrait we look pretty happy
Let's play pretend, act like it goes naturally

Daddy don't leave
Turn around please
Remember that the night you left you took my shining star?
Daddy don't leave
Don't leave us here alone.

Mom will be nicer
I'll be so much better, I'll tell my brother
Oh, I won't spill the milk at dinner
I'll be so much better, I'll do everything right I'll be your little girl forever
I'll go to sleep at night.

[1] Correct: I don't have a choice, there isn't any way

Work with me ISBN 978-3-582-77856-7

Working with Words

★ 1. Translate the following sentences into German.
   a) your pain is painful
   b) I don't want love to destroy me
   c) can we work it out?
   d) let's go back to that
   e) I'll be so much better

★★ 2. Explain these words and sentences in English.

a) she hurts you	b) family portrait	c) last name
d) don't leave	e) star	

Working with the Text

★ 3. What is the song about? What story does it tell?

★★ 4. Who is addressed in this song? How do you know this? Give examples from the text.

★★ 5. Why do you think the song was given the title "Family Portrait"? What does the title mean?

★★ 6. What does the singer Pink mean with "it isn't easy growing up in Word War III"? Explain this in your own words.

★ 7. How does this song make you feel? Think about the sound of the song, its beat and rhythm.

Creative Tasks

★★★ 8. „Draw" your own family portrait with words. Do this in the form of a text message (SMS).

★★★ 9. Watch Pink's video of "Family Portrait" on the Internet. Which methods does she use to portray her family life?

★★ 10. **Task Before Continuing: Discussion**
Find a definition of the word "family" either on the Internet or in a dictionary. Then compare your results in class and discuss the different definitions.
Here are some questions which might help you:
- How do more modern definitions differ from older ones?
- In which way do these definitions consider more open arrangements, such as blended families and gay couples with children?

When Families Do Not Function

Info 1: "Dysfunctional" Families

A dysfunctional family is one in which conflicts, misbehaviour and abuse are part of the family's daily routine. Dysfunctional families are most often characterized by problems which the parents experience – such as alcohol or substance abuse – as well as other addictions. One or both parents may also suffer from an untreated mental illness or a personality disorder. It is often the case that the characteristics of dysfunctional families are passed down from one generation to the next. Children who grow up in such an environment often start to believe that what they are experiencing at home is "normal" and may develop a certain behaviour in order to cope with the situation.
The following texts show different reactions which children may have and roles they may take on when living in a dysfunctional family.

Work with me ISBN 978-3-582-77856-7

Text 2: Roles in Dysfunctional Families [B2]

How do children from dysfunctional families behave? This depends, of course, on the character of the child and the nature of the dysfunction, making it impossible to argue that one set of circumstances will produce one particular outcome. However, the American psychologist Robert Burney has identified and described the following roles which children from troubled backgrounds may adopt.

The Responsible Child – a Family Hero

This child takes over the parental role at a very young age. He or she becomes very responsible and self-sufficient. These children give the family a feeling of self-worth because they look good on the outside. They are the good students, the sports stars, the "prom queens". The parents need this child to prove that they are good parents and good people. As an adult the Family Hero may become rigid, controlling and extremely judgmental of others and secretly of themselves. They achieve success on the outside and get lots of positive attention but are cut off from their inner emotional life. Because of their ability to adjust to such a dysfunctional situation, this child is often the child in the family who as an adult has the hardest time even admitting that there is anything within themselves that needs to be healed.

The Acting-Out Child – a Scapegoat

This is the child which everyone feels ashamed of, yet who often turns out to be the most emotionally honest member of the family. He or she acts out the tension and anger the parents ignore and provides distractions from what is really wrong. Scapegoats usually have trouble at school because they get attention the only way they know how – by behaving negatively. They often become addicted as teenagers and daughters may get pregnant. At the same time these children are usually the most sensitive and caring – which is why they feel such tremendous hurt. They may become very cynical and distrustful. They typically have a lot of self-hatred and can be very self-destructive. This often results in this child becoming the first person in the family to go into some kind of recovery programme.

The Mascot and Caretaker

This child takes responsibility for the emotional well-being of the family. They become the family's "social director" and/or clown, diverting the family's attention from the pain and anger. This child becomes an adult who is valued for his or her kind heart, generosity and ability to listen to others. His or her whole self-definition is centred on others and they do not know how to get their own needs met. They become adults who cannot receive love, only give it. They often have case loads rather than friendships – and get involved in abusive relationships in an attempt to save the other person. They often go into the helping professions and become nurses, social workers and therapists. They usually have very low self-worth and feel a lot of guilt which they work very hard to overcome by being really nice people.

The Adjuster or the Lost Child

This child escapes by trying to be invisible. He or she daydreams, fantasizes, reads a lot of books or watches a lot of TV. They deal with reality by withdrawing from it. They deny that they have any feelings and do not bother getting upset. These children grow up to be adults who find themselves unable to feel and they suffer very low self-esteem. They are terrified of intimacy and often have relationship phobia. They are very withdrawn and shy and become socially isolated because that is the only way they know to be safe from being hurt. A lot of actors and writers are "lost children" who have found a way to express emotions while hiding behind their characters.

(565 words)
(Sources: Burney; Wegscheider-Cruse)

Work with me ISBN 978-3-582-77856-7

★★ **Working with the Text**

1. In your own words sum up the different roles which children from dysfunctional families might take on.
2. According to the text, which problems might children who have grown up in a dysfunctional family have in adult life?

★★ **Discussion**

3. What do you think about the theories presented in the text? Do you agree that one specific role must always lead to the same behavioural patterns later in life?
4. Do you have any personal or professional experiences with children from dysfunctional families who have developed as described in the text? If so, in which category or categories might they fit?

So Much Drama – Working with a Short Play

"The Pressure Cooker" by Steve Skidmore and Steve Barlow

INFO 2: Short Play

A play is a dramatic work intended for performance by actors on a stage. The play you will be reading shortly is called "The Pressure Cooker". It was partly created by pupils attending a comprehensive school in Great Britain and later written in the form of a drama by two teachers and rather well known playwrights named Steve Skidmore and Steve Barlow.

INFO 3: Playing the Role

You will have a lot of fun by reading and acting this dramatic text out loud in class. Be sure to take this opportunity of improving your oral English skills! Remember that you are no longer yourself but playing a role. Feel free to improvise, exaggerate and "play" with your character and role.

For scene 1, get together in groups of three and decide who gets to read which character. Practice reading the play dramatically and with emphasis and then present it in front of your class. Then decide which group performed best and why.

★★ 1. **Pre-Reading Task**
Look up the following words in an English/English dictionary and translate them into German.

pressure – valve – lid – steam

★★ 2. **Discussion**
What might a play bearing this title be about?

Work with me ISBN 978-3-582-77856-7

Text 3: "The Pressure Cooker" by Steve Skidmore and Steve Barlow [B2]

Scene 1

[Outside school. Enter GRAHAM and ANDREA]

Andrea: She'll kill me.

Graham: Who will?

Andrea: My mum.

Graham: Why?

Andrea: Don't you listen to me?

Graham: Not usually.

Andrea: Graham!

Graham: Only joking. Look, so you get bad results. It doesn't mean that your mum's going to turn into Jack the Ripper and kill you.

Andrea: You don't know my mum.

Graham: [judge's voice] Andrea Payne. You have been found guilty of getting low marks in your mock exams. I sentence you to be hanged at dawn to set an example to other pupils who may…

Andrea: You're just not funny.

Graham: Sorry! Sorry I spoke. Sorry I breathe. Sorry I live.

Andrea: Shut up! I can't believe I did so badly.

Graham: Well, I'm rather pleased with my results.

Andrea: How did you get on?

Graham: Bottom in all of them! First time it's ever been done. A unique achievement, Mr Jones said.

Andrea: You're stupid. I don't know why I spend time with you.

Graham: Probably because of my stunning good looks, charm, wit, intelligence and above all, my great modesty.

Andrea: Grow up, Graham.

Graham: You're in a right mood.

Andrea: Didn't think I'd do so badly.

Graham: What does it matter?

Andrea: A lot. What am I going to tell mum?

Graham: Don't tell her.

Andrea: She knows I get the results today. What's she going to say?

Graham: I dunno. Mine won't say anything.

Andrea: Your mum's different from mine.

Graham: They're just mocks!

Andrea: I did badly in them. How am I going to do in the real ones?

Graham: Exams don't mean anything.

Andrea: Yes, they do! I want to go to drama college. What will I do if I fail them?

Graham: Do what I'm going to do – go on the dole.

Andrea: Oh yes, you can have a really great time on the dole.

Graham: There's no jobs anyway, even if you've got exams.

Andrea: I don't believe how stupid you are sometimes.

[Enter DAWN]

Dawn: What's wrong with you two?

Graham: It's her. Worried about her results.

Dawn: Well, they're only mocks.

Andrea: Don't you start. I suppose you did brilliantly.

Dawn: I did OK. Anyway, I didn't revise for them.

Graham: Neither did I.

Dawn: How did you do?

Graham: Came bottom in all of them!

Andrea: I did revise and I still did badly. Mum's going to murder me…

Graham: Here we go again.

Dawn: You could do retakes in the sixth form.

Andrea: I can't. Mum says she can't afford to keep me if I fail.

Graham: I thought your mum wanted you to go to university.

Andrea: She'll pay for me to do A levels. Not retakes. She thinks it's only fair because my brother did A levels and went to university.

Dawn: Mum and dad want me to go to university.

Andrea: Well, you're clever enough to get there.

Graham: I've not quite decided whether it's Oxford or Cambridge for me.

Dawn: University?

Graham: No. Dole Office!

Dawn: Very funny.

Andrea: You really are stupid.

Work with me ISBN 978-3-582-77856-7

Graham: That's what Jonesey said. Bottom in every subject, Dawn. A unique achievement, he reckoned.
Dawn: Well done! Anyway, I thought I'd remind you about my party on Saturday.
Graham: Great! I'm really looking forward to it.
Andrea: Who's going?
Dawn: Everybody. Starts at eight o'clock. Mum and dad are going out, so it should be good. Bring a bottle.
Graham: Will milk do?
Dawn: Ha ha! You ought to be on TV. Then we could switch you off. Are you coming, Andrea?
Graham: Of course she is.
Andrea: Yes, Mum says I can go.
Dawn: What are you two doing now?
Graham: Nothing.
Dawn: D'you want to come round to my house and watch a video? Mum and Dad are out.
Andrea: I can't. I've got to cook tea tonight. Mum's going to a meeting.
Graham: Stop worrying about your mum all the time. It's your life, not hers. Do what you want to do for a change.
Dawn: Put off telling her about the results.
Andrea: That's true.
Graham: Go on, live dangerously.
Andrea: Oh, all right.
Dawn: Good.
Graham: About time too. Stop worrying about everything. Enjoy life.
Andrea: Ok. Sorry. What's the video?
Graham: Zombie Zapping Vampire Flesh-Eaters? Or the Hacksaw Massacre?
Dawn: Actually, it's Bambi. I thought you'd like it, Graham.
Graham: Ha ha, very funny. Come on, lets go.

Working with Scene 1

★ 1. Which characters are introduced in this scene? What are their names? How do they behave?

★ 2. Which character can you relate to most? Why?

★★ 3. Which conflicts are introduced in scene 1? Give examples from the text in order to justify your statements.

★ 4. Having read scene 1, what do you now think the play is (will be) about?

★★ 5. **Written Skills**
Write a short summary of scene 1. Remember to watch your tenses! (see also appendix/Working with Me)

★ 6. **Working with Words**
Translate the following passages into German.
a) You have been found guilty of getting low marks in your mock exams.
b) There's no jobs anyway, even if you've got exams.
c) I did revise and I still did badly. Mum's going to murder me.
d) You could do retakes in the sixth form.
e) Stop worrying about your Mum all the time. It's your life, not hers. Do what you want to do for a change.

★★★ 7. **Creative Task**
Write your version of scene 2. It should take place at Dawn's house.

★★★ 8. **Internet Research**
Find information (in books, on the Internet) about the structure of the British school system. Compare it to the German system and find out where the characters of scene 1 stand academically.

Scene 2

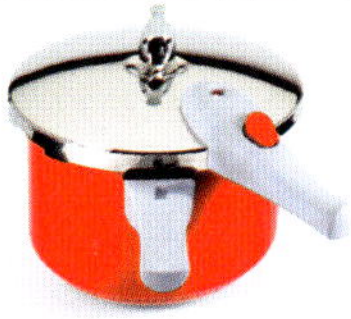

[MOTHER is getting ready to go out. ANDREA enters: She is surprised at seeing her MOTHER still in.]

Andrea: Oh!

Mother: So you've come home. What time do you call this?

Andrea: Sorry, mum, I was at Dawn's watching a video.

Mother: [Sarcastically] Watching a video! Never mind about getting tea ready; never mind your mother's got a meeting to go to. Andrea's at Dawn's watching a video. Very nice indeed. Well, thank you, Andrea.

Andrea: I said I was sorry.

Mother: Honestly, Andrea, it's not fair. I work all day so that you can have a decent home. I get no help from you. You do nothing in the home. Not a thing.

Andrea: That's not true.

Mother: When was the last time you hoovered or dusted? God knows it's hard enough without your father: I thought you might help out a bit.

Andrea: I do. You know I do.

Mother: Well, maybe you could do a bit more. For instance, you could cook the meal when you know I've got a meeting to go to.

Andrea: All right, mum. Don't go on.

Mother: 'Don't go on'! That's a fine thing to say: 'Don't go on'. Thank you, Andrea. Anyway, because you weren't here, I had to cook the meal. There's some meat in the oven and potatoes and carrots in the pressure cooker.

Andrea: You know I don't like spuds out of the pressure cooker. They go all soft.

Mother: Perhaps you should have thought of that when you were watching the video. I had to use the pressure cooker because I'm in a rush. So you'll have to like it. And don't try to take the lid off before it stops hissing. You're lucky to get anything at all.

Andrea: Sorry.

Mother: I should think so ... Pass my lipstick, will you, it's on the side.

Andrea: Here.

Mother: Thank you – oh yes, another thing; you were getting your results today. How did you get on?

Andrea: [Quietly] OK.

Mother: Oh, Andrea, you've not let me down, have you?

Andrea: Did my best.

Mother: What do you mean, you did your best? How bad were they?

Andrea: Bad.

Mother: How bad is 'bad'?

Andrea: Very bad.

Mother: I give up with you. How much revision did you do?

Andrea: No end. You know I stayed in and worked.

Mother: You obviously didn't work hard enough. How did the others do? How did Dawn do? I bet she did well, didn't she? I bet she did a lot of revision.

Andrea: Didn't do any.

Mother: But I'm sure she got good marks, didn't she? Andrea, you've got to work harder. If you don't, you'll never get to university.

Andrea: I don't want to go to university. I want to go to drama college.

Mother: Don't be stupid, Andrea. We've talked about this. Just because you're in the school play you think you're going to be a great actress.

Andrea: I want to go to drama college!

Mother: I'm not discussing this any more. We've decided you're going to university.

Andrea: You've decided.

Mother: I want you to do well for yourself. Like Ian.

Andrea: It's always Ian, isn't it? Ian this, Ian that. Isn't Ian wonderful?

Mother: Don't be so cheeky.

Andrea: You want me to be Ian.

Mother: No, I don't. Don't be so silly.

Andrea: I'm not Ian. I'm me. I want to do what I want to do, not what everyone else wants me to do. It's my life.

Mother: That's right. And I want what's best for you. I want you to go to university and get a decent job and do well. I want what's best for you.

Andrea: What's best for me is what I want to do.

Mother: Getting bad results?

Andrea: I didn't mean to get bad results.

Work with me ISBN 978-3-582-77856-7

Mother: You didn't mean to get good ones either. If you had, you'd have spent more time revising instead of seeing him.
Andrea: Who?
Mother: You know who I mean. You see far too much of that boy.
Andrea: He's got a name, mum. He's called Graham.
Mother: Yes, that's him. Graham. I don't know what you see in him. Honestly, I don't. How did he get on in the exams?
Andrea: What's it matter how he got on?
Mother: I see, as badly as you, I imagine. I've told you, Andrea, I'm not letting you stay on to do retakes.
Andrea: Mum, I worked as hard as I could, honestly.
Mother: You still went out though.
Andrea: I can't stay in all the time.
Mother: It wouldn't hurt. Perhaps if you had, you might have got better results. Ian never went out, and he got good results.
Andrea: Ian again. Ian. Little favourite Ian. Goody-goody Ian. [Mimics mother.] Oh, Ian's so clever. Andrea's so thick. My son, Ian, he's at university. I love Ian so much. He's a lovely boy. Is that why dad left? Because you loved Ian so much?
[MOTHER slaps ANDREA'S face. Andrea starts to cry.]
Mother: Don't you ever talk to me like that. It was because of you that he left – not Ian. You. Left me to bring up both of you. And I will. And you'll get good qualifications and a good job. I'll make sure you do. If you can't help yourself, then I'll have to do it for you. Understand? First of all, you're staying in. No more going out until the exams are over.
Andrea: You can't make me.
Mother: Can't I? Just you see. For a start, you're not going to that party tomorrow.
Andrea: You said I could!
Mother: Well, after tonight I've changed my mind.
Andrea: But I've told Graham I'm going.
Mother: That's another thing – no more seeing him. You've got work to do.
Andrea: That's not fair.
Mother: I don't care if it's fair, Andrea. You're staying in and that's that.
Andrea: I hate you.
Mother: You'll thank me in the long run.
Andrea: [running out and slamming the door.] No, I won't. I hate you.

Working with Scene 2

★★ 1. Re-read the text quietly to yourself and make a list of all the topics that Andrea and her mother fight about.

★ 2. Which of the conflicts suggested here have to do with Andrea's family life?

★ 3. Which of the conflicts are typical of a relationship between a mother and her teenage child?

★ 4. Describe the family structure which is presented here.

★★★ 5. This scene presents a huge fight between Andrea and her mother. Viewed metaphorically, we might even describe it as a "boxing match" in which both opponents "hit" one another with words as well as with hands. Which of Andrea's reproaches hit below the belt? Which of her mother's reproaches hit below the belt?

★★ 6. **Written Skills**
Characterise Andrea's mother. Give examples from the text in order to justify your statements. (see appendix/Working with Me)

★★ 7. **Analysis**
Analyse the symbol of the pressure cooker. What does it stand for in this scene? How does it reflect Andrea and her mother? (see appendix/Working with Me)

Work with me ISBN 978-3-582-77856-7

Discussion

★★★ 8. Do you think that a mother has the right to make her teenage daughter stay at home?

9. Comment on the following passage: *"And you'll get good qualifications and a good job. I'll make sure you do. If you can't help yourself, then I'll have to do it for you."* Can you understand Andrea's mother and the way in which she reacts? Why or why not?

10. How would you react if you were Andrea/Mother?

Creative Tasks

★★ 11. Imagine that Andrea calls her best friend right after leaving the room. What would she tell her about her fight with Mother? Work with a partner and write a scene in which one of you plays Andrea's role and the other plays her best friend.

★★★ 12. Re-write this scene into a harmonious one by turning Andrea's mother into an understanding and patient one.

Scene 3

[Outside school. GRAHAM is leaning against a wall. ANDREA enters looking embarrassed. He pretends not to notice her.]

Andrea: Hiya.

Graham: Oh, hello.

Andrea: Sorry.

Graham: Sorry? What for?

Andrea: The party.

Graham: What about it?

Andrea: Not going.

Graham: Oh, you were going to go, were you?

Andrea: Oh, come off it.

Graham: Off what?

Andrea: [With exaggerated patience] I'm sorry I couldn't go to the party with you.

Graham: Couldn't?

Andrea: That's right, couldn't. Mum wouldn't let me out.

Graham: Oh, well, that's ok. We had a great time.

Andrea: Yes?

Graham: Yeah, really great party. Pity you couldn't come.

Andrea: I couldn't!

Graham: You said.

Andrea: You don't understand.

Graham: Right.

Andrea: I really wanted to come.

Graham: So why didn't you?

Andrea: I told you. Mum wouldn't let me.

Graham: Oh, what did she do, then? Tie you to a chair? Lock you in your room and throw away the key? Make you take a bath and then wash all the towels?

Andrea: She says I'm seeing too much of you.

Graham: Oh, she does, does she?

Andrea: She says I've got to stop going out in the evenings. Got to stay in. Study.

Graham: And what do you say?

Andrea: I've got to get my exams …

Graham: So you're giving in. As usual. [Puts on a master of ceremonies voice] Ladeez an' Gennelmun, we proudly present – the world's leading ventriloquist, councillor Payne, with Andrea! "Now Andrea, I want you to stop seeing Graham." [As a doll] "Googye, Graham".

Andrea: Don't be like that.

Graham:

Andrea: We don't have to stop seeing each other. I mean, we can still walk to school together. And back.

Graham: Yeah, great relationship. Could talk a lot then, couldn't we?

Andrea: You're not talking to me now.

Graham: Of course I'm talking to you now – what d'you think this is?

Andrea: You know I'd 've come if I could.

Graham: No, it's not your mum at all. It's you. You don't want to see me any more – but that's all right, Andrea.

Andrea: It's not that!

Graham: Yes, it is. Getting dead snobby, you are. All this about going to drama college. What d'you want to go there for?

Work with me ISBN 978-3-582-77856-7

Doing stupid plays with a bunch of woofters. Won't be good enough for you then, will I? Just 'cos I'm not going to college you think I'm nothing.
Andrea: That's not what I think.
Graham: It's what your mum thinks, isn't it? So it's what you think.
Andrea: That's not true.
Graham: Isn't it? You could still go out with me, couldn't you? You wouldn't have to tell your mum.
Andrea: What if she found out, though?
Graham: What if she did?
Andrea: She said if I didn't stop seeing you, she'd stop me going to drama college.
Graham: [Sarcastically] Oh, well, that's all right, then.
Andrea: Look, I really love you – I've told you before.
Graham: You really show it, don't you?
Andrea: I do!
Graham: Just not enough. Why don't you fight her for once?
Andrea: I can't I'm not that strong. She overpowers me all the time.
Graham: You let her.
Andrea: Graham ...
Graham: What?
Andrea: Nothing.
[Pause]
Andrea: Good, was it? This party?
Graham: Yeah, we had a great time.
Andrea: We?
Graham: Yeah, well, everybody.
Andrea: Dance with anybody?
Graham: A few.
Andrea: Who?
Graham: Just girls.
Andrea:
Graham: Well, if you'd been there, you'd know, wouldn't you?
Andrea: Why don't you want to tell me?
Graham: Isn't that the bell?
Andrea: Graham?
Graham: [Sharply] Look – I went there on my own, right? You know I hate going to places like that on my own.
Andrea: She wouldn't let me out!
Graham: You didn't even phone to say you weren't coming.
Andrea: You knew when I wasn't there, I wasn't coming. You knew my mum'd kill me for my exam results.
[Dawn comes by]
Dawn: Hi Graham. Hello, Andrea. Come on, you'll be late for registration.
Graham: Coming.
Dawn: See you tonight then, Graham.
[DAWN goes. GRAHAM looks and sounds sheepish.]
Andrea: What's going on?
Graham: How d'you mean?
Andrea: Dawn. You. With – Dawn. At the party. My best mate.
Graham: So what if I was? Can't blame me, can you?
Andrea: Yes, I can. You just don't care, do you?
Graham: In a way, yeah.
Andrea: In a way?
Graham: I thought about you a bit.
Andrea: A bit? Oh, thanks, Graham.
Graham: Yeah, a bit. On the way there, I thought "I wonder how Andrea's doing".
Andrea: I thought about you all night. All the time. Couldn't do my work. Couldn't do anything. Thinking about you. And there you were. You and Dawn. Brilliant mates I've got.
Graham: So whose fault's that? Always somebody else's fault, isn't it? Me, your mum, Dawn. Not you. Never you.
Andrea: Don't.
Graham: Try thinking about someone else for a change. [ANDREA walks away.] Miss "I am". Me, me, me. I love me, who do you love? [Shouting after her] Who do you love, Andrea? Who loves ya, baby?
Andrea: [From a distance] Nobody.

Work with me ISBN 978-3-582-77856-7

Working with Words

★ 1. Match the words which have the same meaning.

sheepish – brilliant – stuck up – overpower – woofters – snobby – homosexuals – dominate – embarrassed – good

★★ 2. Translate these sentences into German.
a) So you're giving in. As usual.
b) You know I hate going to places like that on my own.
c) You could still go out with me, couldn't you? You wouldn't have to tell your mum.
d) So whose fault's that? Always somebody else's fault, isn't it? Me, your mum, Dawn. Not you. Never you.

Working with Scene 3

★ 3. Name five things that Graham criticizes about Andrea.
★ 4. How does Andrea defend herself in front of Graham?
★ 5. How does Graham defend himself in return?
★ 6. With which threat does Andrea's mum keep her from seeing Graham?
★★ 7. How does Dawn's role change in this scene?

Written Skills

★★ 8. Characterise Andrea and remember to give examples from the text. (see appendix)
★★ 9. Shortly summarize scene 3.

Discussion

★ 10. What do you think about the way in which Graham behaves toward Andrea?
★★ 11. What would you have done if you had been in Andrea's shoes?
★★ 12. How might the play continue?

Creative Tasks

★★ 13. Work in a group and write the scene of the party which Andrea has missed.
★★★ 14. Write an e-mail from Graham's point of view. Imagine he is writing to his best friend, explaining his relationship and ongoing conflicts with Andrea.

Scene 4

[School: The sixth form room. Several pupils are chatting. ANDREA is reading a magazine. DAWN and GRAHAM come in.]

Graham: [Snatching magazine] Studying again?

Andrea: Hey! That magazine's mine! Give it back!

Graham: Ought to be ashamed of yourself. What would Mummy say? What's this? Teentalk . Very intellectual.

Dawn: Ooh, don't you know some big words.

Graham: Watch it. Here, look, she's only reading the problem page, isn't she?

Dawn: Oh, Andrea.

Andrea: What's it got to do with you? It's my magazine – I can read any page I want. Give it here.

Dawn: Oh, sorry I spoke.

Andrea: Give it back, Graham, please.

Graham: Hang on a minute. Good for a laugh, these letters are. Here's one – listen to this: "Dear Emily ..."

Dawn: Emily?

Graham: That's her name: "Teentalk helpline – having problems with boys, your work, your parents, your body? Write to me, Emily ..."

Dawn: Emily!

Graham: Shut up and listen. "Dear Emily, I've got a boyfriend and I really like him,

Work with me ISBN 978-3-582-77856-7

but he keeps asking me to go to bed with him. I don't want to because I want to be a virgin when I get married and, anyway, it gives me a headache ..."

Dawn: Stupid! You made that up.

Graham: They're all made up, aren't they? No one'd really write a letter like that to go in a magazine where everyone'd see it.

Dawn: Nobody did write a letter like that.

Graham: All right, I'll read one out of here – oh, here's a good'un.

Andrea: No!

Graham: "Dear Emily, I'm only thirteen, but I have very big breasts for my age. [All the others in the room react: oooh!] My mum's very strict and she says I can't have a bra because I'm too young, but they keep moving under my pullover. [Dirty laughter] The boys in our class keep looking at me, and the girls think I'm showing off. What can I do?"

Dawn: I bet you made that up as well.

Graham: I never – it's here, look. You're not telling me somebody'd really write that to a magazine, are you?

Dawn: People do.

Graham: Come off it.

Dawn: Some of the advice they give is really helpful.

Graham: Could do better myself.

Dawn: Oh yes? Give it here, then. Let's try you out.

Andrea: Stop it. I want my magazine back.

Dawn: Just a minute. Right. "Dear Aunt Emily ..."

Graham: [Auntie voice] Yes?

Dawn: "When I was at junior school, I got worms. [Listeners' reaction: Uuurgh!] When I started secondary school, I got them again and my mum was furious and said if I got them again, I'd have to go into hospital and have an operation. Now I have got them again and I daren't tell my mum. I always wash my hands when I've been to the toilet, so it's not my fault. Worried Teentalk reader."

Graham: [Auntie voice] "Dear Worried Teentalk reader, the answer to your problem is very simple. After you've been to the loo, you must wash your hands before you bite your fingernails." [Others laugh]

Dawn: Oh, very funny.

Graham: Come on, then, I'll do one for you. Here we are – the Star Letter. From "Desperate reader". "Dear Auntie Emily ..."

Andrea: Graham! Stop it ! Give it back! Give it back!

[ANDREA fights to get the magazine. DAWN holds her back.]

Graham: Hey, hang on to her. She's going mad. Here we go: "Dear Auntie Emily, I'm writing to you because I don't know what else to do ..."

Andrea: No! Give it to me! It's mine!

Graham: Oh, don't be so mardy. "I haven't got a dad, only a mum and I can't talk to her, she's always out at meetings." Real tear jerker this, isn't it?

Andrea: Stop it. Please. Please stop it, Graham.

Graham: "Anyway, she doesn't listen. She wants me to go to university. We keep having rows about it. I want to go to drama college, but I've mucked up all my exams..." Hey, this could be you, Andrea. "On top of that, she's told me to stop seeing my boyfriend."

Dawn: Graham, pack it in.

Graham: Just a minute. Nearly finished. I really love him, but he's started going out with my best mate ..." [At last he becomes aware of the silence. Uncertainly] Hey, what's up?

Andrea: You pig. You filthy dirty pig.

[ANDREA takes the magazine from GRAHAM and leaves the room.]

Graham: What's got into her?

Dawn: You can be really thick sometimes, can't you?

Graham: You what?

Dawn: You even said it yourself.

Graham: You mean – she did write that letter? Andrea?

Dawn: Congratulations!

Graham: I never thought ...

Dawn: You never do. You've really upset her now.

Graham: Me? What about you? Best mate.

Dawn: You asked me out.

Graham: You didn't exactly fight me off, did you?

Dawn: You shouldn't have read that letter out.

Graham: How was I supposed to know?

Dawn: You shouldn't have teased her.

Graham: Oh, I might've known it was all my fault.
Dawn: I wonder if she's all right.
Graham: She's all right.
Dawn: I should go round and see her tonight ...
Graham: What about the film?
Dawn: We can go another time.
Graham: Finishes tonight.
Dawn: I suppose I could go tomorrow. Or the day after. Don't know why I should feel guilty, anyway – I didn't make her fail her rotten exams. Bet she wouldn't want to see me if I did go.
Graham: See you after school then.
Dawn: Yeah, see you. Poor Andrea. The look on her face. Bit of a laugh though, wasn't it.

Working with Words

★★ 1. Find the words in the text which match these definitions.
   a) to make fun of
   b) a sentimental story which makes people cry
   c) annoyed, fed up
   d) an argument
   e) to fail something
   f) to stop

★★★ 2. **Language Awareness.** This play is written in a way in which young people might speak aloud but not write in class tests or other more formal puposes. We call such utterances colloquial. Make a list of the colloquial and specifically oral phrases that have been uttered in the play so far and try to translate them into more formal English.

★★ 3. **False Friends.** It is sometimes hard to recognize a true friend! Which of these sentences contains a false friend? Identify and correct the wrong phrases.
   a) In my meaning Graham is a very mean boyfriend.
   b) Andrea will that everyone leaves her alone.
   c) When did Dawn become such an enemy?
   d) Andrea is very arm.
   e) Graham and Dawn's behaviour does not make any sin.

★ **Working with Scene 4**

4. How do Dawn and Graham behave towards Andrea in this scene? Describe their behaviour throughout the entire scene.
5. How does Graham react when he finally realizes that he has hurt Andrea?
6. How does Dawn rationalize whether or not to go see Andrea?

★★★ 7. **Skills**
   Characterize Graham using all four scenes of the play. (see appendix/Working with Me)

★★ 8. **Creative Task**
   Work in groups and create a talkshow in which:
   - Andrea and her mum fight
   - Graham and Andrea talk about their problems
   - Dawn and Andrea confront one another
   - Andrea's mum and brother Ian confront Andrea about their family situation

Work with me ISBN 978-3-582-77856-7

Scene 5

[Outside ANDREA'S house. DAWN rings the doorbell. IAN answers.]

Dawn: Oh, hello. Is Andrea in?
Ian: No.
Dawn: Oh, uhm – you're Ian, aren't you? Andrea's brother?
Ian: That's right. Are you a friend of Andrea's?
Dawn: Yes – at least – we had a bit of a row ... She hasn't been at school for a day or two. I wondered ...
Ian: Are you Dawn?
Dawn: Yes.
Ian: You'd better come in. Through here – in the kitchen. I'm just cooking supper. Don't want to leave it.
[The pressure cooker is whistling.]
Dawn: What's that noise?
Ian: Pressure cooker. I'm doing the spuds. The safety valve's letting off a bit of steam. I'll turn the heat down: it'll stop in a minute.
Dawn: Makes a racket, doesn't it?
Ian: You've got to have a safety valve on a pressure cooker. Could blow up if you didn't.
Dawn: Will Andrea be home soon?
Ian: No.
Dawn: Well, I could come back tomorrow.
Ian: How'd she been? These last few days?
Dawn: Well ...
Ian: Bit upset would you say?
Dawn: A bit, yeah.
Ian: Any idea what about?
Dawn: Well, exams. And she was worried her mum might not let her go to drama college.
Ian: And?
Dawn: We had a bit of a row, like. About a boy. I wanted to make it up.
Ian: That all?
Dawn: Well, there was this letter. In a magazine.
Ian: I found the magazine.
Dawn: We were laughing about it. At school. Didn't know it was her. She was upset. A bit.
Ian: A bit. Just a bit. Only a bit.
Dawn: Look, can I see Andrea?
Ian: Andrea's in hospital.
Dawn: What?
Ian: That's why I'm here. Mum called me at university.
Dawn: But – what? – I mean ... was it an accident?
Ian: Not an accident. She swallowed mum's sleeping pills. Nearly the whole bottle. Mum was out.
Dawn: Oh my God ... I never thought ... not Andrea. Why?
Ian: Don't you know?
Dawn: I can't believe it.
Ian: You can go and see her – she's all wired up like Frankenstein's monster – tubes going in, tubes coming out, in her arms, down her throat.
Dawn: I'll go and see her – or is your mum ...?
Ian: Mum's at a meeting.
Dawn: At a meeting? Not at the hospital?
Ian: There's no point. Andrea's in a coma. Know what that means?
Dawn: 'Course I know what it means. Don't the doctors know when she'll wake up?
Ian: The doctors don't know if she'll wake up.
Dawn: Oh, God, it's my fault. Poor Andrea.
Ian: Bit late to be sorry, isn't it?
Dawn: What d'you mean?
Ian: Pity you weren't sorrier a bit earlier – you and Graham.
Dawn: How d'you know about ... How did you know who I was?
Ian: She mentioned your names. In the note.
Dawn: Note?
Ian: They always leave a note. [Pause; the pressure cooker stops whistling] There, see, it's stopped.
Dawn: What?
Ian: The noise of the steam. That means the pressure's back to normal. Unless the safety valve's got blocked. I've heard of that happening. Then you could be in dead trouble. You can't always tell, can you? They said they'd ring if anything happened.
[In another part of the house, the telephone starts to ring.]

★ **Working with Scene 5**

1. How does Ian behave towards Dawn in this scene?
2. How does Dawn feel about herself?
3. Which role does Andrea's mother play in this scene?

★★ 4. **Analysis**
In which way does the pressure cooker reflect Andrea's situation in this scene?

★★ 5. **Discussion**
What do you think of Andrea's reaction? Can you understand her? How might she have reacted instead?

★★★ **Creative Tasks**

6. Write an alternate scene 5 which completes this drama in a different way.
7. Write scene 6 of this play. How might the open ending end?

★★ **Final Discussion**

8. How did you like reading the play aloud in class? How did this oral experience make you feel?
9. Which title would you give this play, now that you know what it is about?
10. Which was the scene that you enjoyed most/least? Why?
11. If you had to pick a favorite character, who would that be and why?

★★★★ 12. **Project**

Agree on a topic and write your own class play. Perhaps your teacher can help you to correct your play before you perform it in front of others.

Work with me ISBN 978-3-582-77856-7

VOCABULARY MODULE 10 So Much Family Drama

[coll] (colloquial): umgangssprachlich

Text 1: "Family Portrait" by Pink		
(to) tear s.o. down	[teər daʊn]	jem. herunterziehen
(to) split	[splɪt]	trennen, teilen
Info 1: "Dysfunctional Families"		
dysfunctional	[dɪs'fʌŋkʃənəl]	dysfunktional, funktionsunfähig
abuse	[ə'bju:z]	Missbrauch, Misshandlung
untreated	[ʌn'tri:tɪd]	unbehandelt
personality disorder	[ˌpɜ:sən'æləti dɪ'sɔ:dər]	Persönlichkeitsstörung
(to) cope	[kəʊp]	verkraften, bewältigen
Text 2: Roles in Dysfunctional Families		
self-sufficient	['self-sə'fɪʃənt]	unabhängig
prom queen	[prɒm kωi:n]	Gewinnerin eines Popularitätswettbewerbs beim Abschlussball der High School (USA)
rigid	['rɪʤɪd]	rigide, starr
judgmental	[ʤʌʤ'mentəl]	wertend, kritisch, selbstgerecht
cut off	[kʌt ɒf]	abgeschnitten, abgeschirmt
(to) act out	[ækt aʊt]	ausleben
tension	['tentʃən]	Anspannung
distraction	[dɪ'strækʃən]	Ablenkung
scapegoat	['skeɪpgəʊt]	Sündenbock
tremendous	[trɪ'mendəs]	riesig
distrustful	[dɪ'strʌstfəl]	misstrauisch
case load	['keɪs ləʊd]	etwa: starke Belastung
adjuster; (to) adjust	[ə'ʤʌstar]	jem. der angepasst ist; sich anpassen
(to) withdraw	[ωɪð'drɔ:]	sich zurückziehen
relationship phobia	[rɪ'leɪʃənʃɪp 'fəʊbiə]	Beziehungsangst
Text 3: The Pressure Cooker		
mock exams	[mɒk ɪg'zæmz]	Probeklausuren
unique achievement	[jʊ'ni:k ə'tʃi:vmənt]	einzigartige Leistung
modesty	['mɒdɪsti]	Bescheidenheit
dunno [coll]	[də'nəʊ]	I don't know
dole [coll] BrE	[dəʊl]	Arbeitslosengeld
(to) revise	[rɪ'vaɪz]	üben
retakes	[ri:'teɪks]	Wiederholungen
D'you	[du: ju:]	do you
(to) put off	[pʊt ɒf]	hinauszögern
(to) hiss	[hɪs]	Zischen
cheeky	['tʃi:ki]	frech
thick [coll]	[θɪk]	dumm, begriffsstutzig
come off it [coll]	[kʌm ɒf ɪt]	hör auf damit
master of ceremonies	['ma:stər 'ɒv 'serɪməni:z]	Zeremonienmeister
ventriloquist	[ven'trɪləkwɪst]	Bauchredner
woofters [coll]	['wʊftərs]	"Schwuchteln"
'cos [coll]	[kəs]	(because) weil
(to) overpower	[ˌəʊvə 'paʊər]	übermannen, überwältigen
sheepish	['ʃi:pɪʃ]	verlegen
(to) snatch	[snætʃ]	wegschnappen
(to) make sth. up	[meɪk ʌp]	sich etw. ausdenken, erfinden
good'un [coll]	[gʊd ωʌn]	a good one (in etwa: guter Witz)
mardy [coll]	['mɒ:di]	schlecht gelaunt, brummig
tear jerker [coll]	['tɪəˌʤɜ:kər]	Schnulze
(to) tease s.o.	[ti:z]	jem. ärgern, aufziehen

Work with me ISBN 978-3-582-77856-7

Module 11

Children on the Fringe

In this module you will have the opportunity to learn about

- problems with fitting in
- being different in our community
- children at risk
- peer-mentoring

Introduction

★ Look at these photos. Say what makes these children and teenagers different and why they might not fit in. Use these words:

race – clothes – posh – Islamic – old-fashioned – artistic – briefcase – obese – poor – religion – culture – appearance – studious – untidy – complexion – odd

Work with me ISBN 978-3-582-77856-7

TEXT 1:
The Misfit [B1]

Jeremy's family has recently moved from Aberdeen in Scotland to a small town in Eastern England. He has joined the local church youth club, St. Peter's. His youth worker, Jane Robinson, is disappointed that he is not making friends. She decides to talk to some of the other children.

JANE: Children, can I have a word? I need your help. It's about Jeremy. I saw that he was playing on his own again. I think he must be very lonely.

HAYLEY: We play with him sometimes but we don't like him. He's always in a bad mood.

JANE: I'm disappointed to hear that. I put him in your group because you are nice children and I felt sure that you would look after him and make him feel welcome.

TOM: Well, he's not very nice to us and we can't tell what he says.

JANE: He's from Scotland, so he's bound to sound different to you. He has a Scottish accent.

HAYLEY: You can understand him sometimes. He swore at Chloe and stole her chocolate biscuit.

CHLOE: And he spat at me on the lawn.

JANE: That is horrible. Why do you think he did that? Did you do anything to provoke him?

CHLOE: No. I only told him off because he pushed Damian off the climbing frame.

TOM: He said his dad's a pilot but Damian said he couldn't be, because he doesn't live in a posh enough house. He tells lies.

JANE: When people make things up they usually have a reason.

STEPHEN: We've tried to make friends with him but he always bosses us about. Can he sit on another table, Jane? He keeps annoying us – and he smells!

TOM: He does. He smells like my granddad. He smokes.

HAYLEY: He's scruffy as well. My brother says we should call him Mucky Mac.

JANE: Well, you mustn't. We can sort all these problems out. Children, I am worried that Jeremy looks so unhappy. We need to try and help him.

(333 words)

★ 1. **Working with the Text**
Decide whether these statements are true or false. Correct the false statements.
a) Jeremy has recently joined a school.
b) The children find his speech easy to understand.
c) Jeremy has problems at home.
d) Jeremy has some unpleasant habits.
e) He is a truthful and honest boy.
f) He can be violent.
g) He has complained to the youth worker.
h) Jeremy looks untidy.
i) He annoys the children at his table.
j) The other children never involve Jeremy in their games.

★★ 2. **Role Play**
In groups of three, list the reasons for the children's dislike of Jeremy. Select one of these reasons and write a short role play involving Jeremy and two other children. Practise it and perform it to your class.

★★ 3. **Working with Words**
You are the youth worker. Before you decide what action to take, you need to speak to Jeremy. Ask him if he did what the children claim.
Example:
Did you write on the table?
Did you spit at Chloe?

★★ 4. **Role Play**
Study Jeremy's behaviour and give him some good advice.
Jeremy, you should(n't) …

★★★ 5. **Role Play**

What advice would you give to the other children to help them cope with Jeremy's behaviour? Use the words and phrases in the boxes below to make sentences.

If he annoys you ...	you must / mustn't
(Use the examples found in the dialogue)	you should / shouldn't
	you could
	you might

Be friendly – Retaliate – Tell him to come to me – Ask if he needs help – Invite him to play with you – Tell him how you pronounce it – Swear back at him – Smile at him – Offer to share your biscuits with him – Tell a youth worker – Invite him to sit next to you – Tell him he smells – Ask him to repeat it – Ask him why he's angry – Show him what to do – Get angry with him – Be patient – Gang up on him – Call him names – Call him a liar – Laugh at his accent

★★★ 6. **Written Discussion**

Invite Jeremy's parents to come to see you to discuss your concerns for his wellbeing. Complete the letter and try to use the expressions given. Write 80–100 words of your own.

Dear Mr and Mrs Duncan,

As we reach the end of Jeremy's first month at St. Peter's Youth Club it has become apparent that he is experiencing certain difficulties in settling in. I would welcome the opportunity to speak to you about the following issues.
I am concerned that ...

(Choose from ...)

Nouns	**Adjectives**	**Verbs**
complaints	unhappy	to assault
theft	short-tempered	to communicate
friends	isolated	to mix with
aggression	self-reliant	to insult
hygiene	uncertain	to swear
lies	domineering	to notice
relationships	unpleasant	
odour		
appearance		
cooperation		
(un)willingness		

Please contact me to arrange an appointment at your earliest convenience.

Yours sincerely,

Jane Robinson
Youth Worker, St. Peter's Youth Club

Work with me ISBN 978-3-582-77856-7

TEXT 2: Charter of Respect [B1]

St. Peter's Youth Club has a Charter of Respect which all members must follow.

CHARTER OF RESPECT

We think it is important for members of the club not to pick on or discriminate against others who are different. These differences include:

- nationality
- personality
- interests
- religion
- sex
- sexuality
- race
- appearance
- accent
- name
- popularity

- fitness
- state of cleanliness
- clothes
- abilities and disabilities
- intelligence
- age
- weight
- height
- friends
- family
- opinions

- taste in music
- reputation
- personal habits
- economic background
- where people live
- being new at the club
- suffering from an illness
- being popular with the youth workers
- being clumsy

Different individuals make up this club. Difference is not a crime.
Difference means variety. We are all different.
We can learn from each other.

★★ 1. **Group Work**

The Club Council, a mixture of youth workers and children, can consider members' misbehaviour and decide what action to take. In groups of four decide which aspects (sometimes more than one) of the Charter of Respect have been infringed in these cases:

a) Charlotte keeps calling Tom "a fat whale".
b) Simon keeps kicking Melanie under the table because the youth worker praised her.
c) Freddie calls Wayne a "thicko" because he has help with his reading at school.
d) Sean goes to ballet lessons and Martin say's he's gay.
e) Christopher throws paper aeroplanes at Davinder Singh and tries to hit the top-knot on his head.
f) Clare is always excluded when the children play games as she is not sporty.
g) Elliot always "forgets" his trainers as they are cheap and unfashionable.
h) Children avoid Connor as they say he stinks.
i) The boy who started last week is a from a travellers' camp.
j) Sophie plays the cello and a group of girls teases her.

★★ 2. **Group Work**
This is an activity which members of the club have really enjoyed. Can you do it? First, sort the comments into positive/respectful and negative/disrespectful. Then put them into pairs according to the subject being discussed.

A She's really embarrassing. During the film she dropped her crisps, spilt her drink and then fell over in the toilet.

B I've not heard many of their songs. Perhaps we can swap some CDs or downloads and check out each other's music.

C If you were any skinnier, you'd be a stick insect! My mum reckons you've got an eating disorder.

D I don't want to sit with her! She's such a loner and has no friends. People will laugh at me.

E She seems very clever. We should talk to her and share ideas.

F I think your mum's really kind to invite us to stay over. I've never met an Asian family before. I'd love to try the food.

G You still listen that old band?! That's so out of date and uncool! Everybody laughs at your bad taste.

H Let's all play together as a team. If we all try hard we might even win!

I We're worried you're losing too much weight. We think you look great as you are. There's no need to put your health at risk.

J Your dad's offered us a lift to the cinema? That's really kind. What time shall we go?

K She always answers the questions. She's such a know-all and a teacher's pet. I bet she does nothing else but homework in the evenings.

L Your mum's got a funny accent. I can't understand a word she says. It's about time she learnt to speak English properly.

M We saw a brilliant movie. We had to apologise to the staff, because we made a mess with our crisps and drinks, but we had a great laugh.

N We don't want her in our team. She's so slow and can't hit the ball. Everyone will laugh at us.

O I wouldn't be seen dead getting in your dad's car. It's so old and it's such a horrible colour.

P I'll sit with her as I don't know her very well and it'll be a good opportunity to make friends.

Work with me ISBN 978-3-582-77856-7

★★★ 3. **Creative Task**
In groups choose 5–10 other areas from the Charter of Respect and make cards with other positive and negative comments. Try to avoid using the word or phrase in the charter. Give your finished cards to another group for them to put into pairs.

★★★ 4. **Written Discussion**
Write 80–100 words about an incident you have either witnessed or experienced where an individual was excluded because of something which made them different from others.

Text 3: Perry's Plight – A Profile of Deprivation [B2]

Wigan Social Services have called a case conference for a 13-year-old boy, Perry Allen, who is on the At-Risk Register[1]. They need to review his case following notification from the police that Perry has been arrested for theft. Present at the meeting are a social worker, a police officer, Perry's mother and his pastoral teacher. Below are the reports of each agency and his mother's statement.

The Police
On 25th May Perry Allen was arrested for breaking into a car and stealing an iPad on the Braunstone estate. He was in breach of a court order to stop vandalism and the harassment of local residents. He is frequently picked up late at night and returned to his mother. He has often been drinking. He truants from school and associates with a gang of older, unemployed youths who carry knives.

Social Worker
Perry has been on the At-Risk Register for three years due to abuse of his mother by a

[1] **At-Risk Register:** a list of children who are at risk

former partner who has restricted parental access to Perry's younger siblings. The family is currently in emergency accommodation following a fire at their council house. Conditions are cramped; the only bedroom is occupied by Perry's mother, her new partner and two younger children. Perry and his older sister, who suffers from cerebral palsy, are forced to sleep in the living room. The partner has convictions for possession of drugs and is unemployed. There has been no wage-earner in the family since Perry started school. His mother has had to give up her cleaning jobs as she is six months pregnant. We must seriously consider taking Perry into care as he now beyond parental control.

Pastoral Teacher

Perry Allen is frequently absent and has had several short exclusions from school for disruptive and aggressive behaviour. The educational psychologist originally diagnosed ADHD[3], possibly caused by an unstable environment in early childhood and a lack of play opportunities, and now this has been exacerbated by overcrowding at home. He has no Internet access, study space or books. Our Behaviour Support Team offers to work alongside pupils in class but Perry has rejected this help. He is, however, following an anger-management programme in the hope that it will help him to avoid permanent exclusion from school. Perry is of above-average intelligence but underachieves. There is no family history of further education and Perry feels the loss of his natural father who has severed contact with them. Therefore, a young male mentor has been allocated in order to provide Perry with a positive role-model and address his depression, low aspirations and lack of self-esteem. In my opinion it would be disastrous to place Perry in care. We know that there is a shortage of skilled foster carers and that educational outcomes for children in care are very poor – only 12 % achieve five good GCSEs.

Mother

Perry is not a bad lad. He often looked after his sister and the twins when I was at work. He started getting into trouble when the twins' dad kept beating me up and my nerves were bad all the time. He won't take his Ritalin[4] and I can't make him. The GP has told me to keep him off junk food but I can't afford fruit and fresh vegetables and he won't eat them anyway. He'd rather go hungry and nick sweets from the shop. The older lads are a bad influence, but he's too big to keep in and I don't want them round home. There's no room anyway. There's nothing to do on the estate, he gets bored and then he gets into trouble. If he goes into care, I'm frightened I'd lose touch and never get him back.

(609 words)

[3] **ADHD** (Attention Deficit Hyperactivity Disorder): affects mainly boys; they cannot concentrate or stay on task for long

[4] **Ritalin:** a drug which helps ADHD sufferers to concentrate and to be calm

Working with the Text

★ 1. Say which pieces of the jigsaw puzzle are mentioned by the mother, the social worker, the pastoral teacher, the police officer or no-one.

★★ 2. Answer the following questions in full sentences, using the word in the brackets, if you can.
   a) Why has Perry been arrested? (steal)
   b) How is he a nuisance on the street? (neighbours)
   c) What does Perry often do in the evening? (alcohol)
   d) Why does he get into trouble during the day? (absent)
   e) What are the family's sleeping arrangements? (overcrowded)
   f) Why is the mother unemployed? (expecting)
   g) What circumstances can lead to ADHD? (stimulation/toys)
   h) Explain why Perry is unlikely to go to university. (tradition)
   i) When did Perry's poor behaviour begin? (witness/violence)
   j) How would you describe Perry's diet? (unhealthy)

Work with me ISBN 978-3-582-77856-7

★★ 3. **Translation**
Choose a paragraph from the case conference and translate it into German.

★★★ 4. **Group Work**
Form groups of those who have translated the same paragraph. Take it in turns to read out German sentences slowly. The others – without seeing the text – have to translate it back into English. Help each other!

★★★★ 5. **Creative Task**
Get into groups of four and make a set of 35 cards with one of the words from the box on each card. Take it in turns to pick up a card from the pack, look at the word(s) and then decide who you should be. Say "I am the teacher/social worker/police officer/parent."
Make a comment about Perry's case using the word on the card. You may invent other details if you wish. Other members of the group may ask you questions which you must answer.

OVERCROWDING

BOOKS – FATHER – ALCOHOL – ROLE-MODEL – SELF-ESTEEM – UNEMPLOYMENT – CONCENTRATION – OVERCROWDING – HOMEWORK – EXCLUSION – CRIME – HEALTH – FURTHER EDUCATION – INSTABILITY – RECREATION – HOUSING – DRUGS – FIRE – ATTENDANCE – NEGLECT – YOUNG CARER – POVERTY – DEPRESSION – BEHAVIOUR – PARENTAL CONTROL – ABUSE – GANG – PREGNANT – ADHD – GP – MENTOR – DIET – BOREDOM – NEIGHBOURHOOD – INTERNET

★★★★ 6. **Creative Task**
Perry has been mentored and encouraged to express his feelings about his life in writing. He has produced this rap:

Sometimes when I'm dreaming, I dream I am free
Of this dark, scary prison built specially for me.
You ask why I'm angry? You would be as well
If you knew what it's like to be trapped in this cell.
From my window I just see a part of the sky
A square in old concrete where birds never fly.
I can't breathe. I can't think. There's bad air. There's no space.
Why should I have to live in this terrible place?
Who cares if I go, if I do well in school?
That's why I behave bad and act like a fool.
The teachers advise me but glance at the time
They know I'm a loser whose future is crime.
I swear to be good for my mum when she cries
But she lies with a man who I fear and despise.
I'd really try harder if it was just her and me
And sister together, all happy, we three.

In groups you could practise this rap, record it and play it to the class. Could you add ideas to it – or produce a similar rap of your own on themes in Perry's life which he has not included?

Text 4:
Mentoring the Child on the Fringe [B1]

For many years, mentoring by adults has been successful in helping to shape the development of the child in the school environment. More and more schools are now discovering the contribution that peer-mentoring can make in supporting youngsters who need help.

Piravinth (13) and Lewis (15) are being interviewed by a BBC reporter at an event to promote peer-mentoring, which took place at Westminster, London.

INTERVIEWER: Piravinth, you're from a Sri-Lankan family but you were actually born and brought up in Germany. So you arrived here a couple of years ago speaking very little English. Tell us about your feelings at the time, having to start at a new school in a strange country.

PIRAVINTH: I couldn't talk proper English, I didn't know how to speak to people, so that was a problem. I worried that people wouldn't talk to me.

INTERVIEWER: Your English is very good!

PIRAVINTH: Because I talked a lot to Lewis, my mentor.

INTERVIEWER: At the beginning, what were the thoughts going through your mind?

PIRAVINTH: I was scared. If you go to a different country you should know how to communicate. But after I got to know the language, I made more friends.

INTERVIEWER: So you met with Lewis on a regular basis?

PIRAVINTH: Yeah. And he helped me with my learning, talking, language … all sorts of stuff.

INTERVIEWER: Lewis, do you want to tell us what happened? How were you able to help Piravinth?

LEWIS: I helped Piravinth with the basics. Being in an English environment, he did pick up words and if he didn't know what the words meant, I explained them to him and set him spelling tests.

INTERVIEWER: Piravinth, how quickly were you able to develop your English and make progress with your school work?

PIRAVINTH: After one or two months! My parents said that I learnt English really quickly.

INTERVIEWER: I'm sure they were impressed. Lewis, can I just ask you finally, what has peer mentoring meant to you? After all, it isn't the sort of thing many young men would want to do, is it?

LEWIS: I don't know. It just appealed to me. I wanted to help other people and it sort of gives you a sense of personal satisfaction. And when you're in the school environment, you sometimes see things like bullying and it's nice to know that you can help to prevent that from happening. The older generation doesn't always see what's going on.

INTERVIEWER I'm sure that there are many things that you could teach us. Congratulations, boys, on forming a successful mentoring relationship. Thank you. We wish you both all the best.

(440 words)

(Adapted from an online-audio interview at www.mandbf.org.uk)

Work with me ISBN 978-3-582-77856-7

Info 1: Mentoring

Here are some of the areas where mentoring is currently being used to help children and young people:

- *transition from one school to another*
- *transition from one culture to another*
- *English as an Additional Language (EAL)*
- *behaviour improvement*
- *anti-bullying*
- *self-harm*
- *looked-after children[1]/children leaving care[2]*
- *raising attainment*
- *Special Educational Needs (SEN)*
- *youth offending*
- *young people with disabilities*

[1] children in foster care
[2] children who have been in foster care

★★ 1. **Working with the Text**
List all the benefits of mentoring for Piravinth and Lewis.

★★★★ 2. **Internet Research**
Google mosaicyouth.org.uk which offers support to youngsters who are or who think they are LGBT (lesbian, gay, bisexual and transgender). Click on Young People and select aspects from the list which are of interest to you as a youth worker. Report your findings to the group.

★★★★ 3. **Role Play**
Invent a situation where you, a pupil, are affected by one of the above issues. Explain to your partner how you feel. Your partner will be your peer-mentor. Then mentor your partner about his/her problem.

Key Phrases to Use

I think you should …
Why not (speak) …?
Have you thought about …?
Might it be a good idea to …?
If I were you, I would … try to …
You should perhaps consider …
Have you spoken to …?

★★ 4. **Working with Words**
Put the following situations into the same order as the bullet points from Info 2 to which they are linked. Two of these match none of them.

a) Priti's father will not allow her to wear shorts for Physical Education.
b) Lech has just come from Poland and can speak no English.
c) The Religious Education teacher wishes to take a class on a visit to a mosque and a Sikh temple.
d) The local police wish to come in to speak about drugs.
e) Chinese pupils are unwilling to make eye-contact with staff and answer questions.
f) There is no wheelchair access to the school hall.
g) Black girls attain higher results than black boys.
h) Two thirds of the pupils are of Polish origin. There are no Polish teachers.
i) A Jamaican footballer from Leicester City FC is mentoring a group of disaffected West Indian boys.
j) Su Ying's uncle has agreed to give judo lessons in the gym after school on Fridays.

Info 2: Racial Equality and Schools

Schools have a legal duty to promote racial equality. They must:

- *monitor the progress of all pupils to narrow the achievement gap between ethnic groups*
- *improve race relations by celebrating diversity*
- *improve pupil behaviour so that no one group has more exclusions for poor behaviour than any other*
- *take account of religious or cultural traditions when setting rules for school uniform or appearance*
- *ensure staff are well-informed about cultural differences in behaviour*
- *encourage parental and cultural involvement*
- *recruit a diverse workforce at all levels*
- *support newly-arrived pupils to integrate*

Work with me ISBN 978-3-582-77856-7

Text 5: New Kids on the Block [B2]

Many children need language support. The proportion of children with English as an additional language (EAL) is rising (google EAL learner statistics in regional English Primary Schools to research data.)
At Challney High School nearly 95 % of pupils are drawn from minority ethnic groups and forty languages are spoken!

Roberta Martin, attendance and pastoral support manager at a catholic school in Leeds, Yorkshire, attended a course entitled *"Polish Pupils, British Schools"*. She reports.
"We have a dozen Polish pupils in the school and I wanted a better understanding of their background and culture. I was concerned about their low attendance. The course leader was Polish and she said that there was less emphasis on perfect attendance in Poland. She explained that it was quite normal for new children to go through a quiet phase and that staff should not be concerned or put pressure on them if they sit silent in lessons. It can be tempting to get older Polish pupils to help younger ones, but this must not detract from their own learning.
There was excellent advice on dealing with parents. It is normal for them to be overprotective when they are new to the country and unsure of its culture. The course provided me with materials including standard school letters translated into Polish. I became aware of cultural differences I had not considered. In Polish schools teachers are authoritarian. There is a danger that too much English politeness could be perceived as weakness. 'Perhaps it would be a good idea not to run in the corridor' should be expressed as 'Don't run!' "

Elizabeth Cope, a Religious Education teacher at a school in Kent, is keen to explore ethnic diversity in order to promote respect for other religions and cultures.
"Music, dance and cookery can give pupils an insight into religion. We suspended the timetable to have a Spirituality Day. I invited into school a gospel choir and an Indian dance group. We held a Jewish cookery workshop. The children made traditional dishes and learnt about the importance of food rituals. There was an ICT project where pupils designed places of worship as part of a housing development, thinking about the religious needs of the community and whether it's a good idea to have multi-faith centres."

Sue Seifert's school in north London has won a national award for involving its local community.
"We invited parents into school. A Somali group helped children with special educational needs, a Turkish group helped children with maths and a Bengali group ran an Arabic class to study the Koran. We persuaded many parents whose English was weak that it was fine to use their own language and that we can all teach and learn from each other. We have had Albanian parents who wished to improve their ICT skills learning alongside their children. I myself am from a family of Jewish refugees so I know that newcomers to a country are particularly keen on education, seeing it as a way out of poverty. Education liberates people."

(541 words)

Work with me ISBN 978-3-582-77856-7

★ 1. **Working with the Text**
Sort these words taken from the text into three columns.

parent – understanding – attendance – emphasis – pressure – tempt – detract – protective – translate – excellent – polite – perceive – suspend – invite – development – special – liberate – educational

Nouns	Verbs	Adjectives
…	…	…

★★ 2. With the help of a dictionary find the related nouns, verbs and adjective to complete a word family table in your exercise book.

Nouns	Verbs	Adjectives
persuasion	(to) persuade	persuasive
…		

★★★ 3. When you have completed your table write a sentence for each new word you have found.

★★★★ 4. **Discussion**
"Faith schools are divisive." In groups, discuss this idea, thinking of arguments for and against. Consider these key themes:

- building bridges in a multi-ethnic society
- preserving the cultures of minorities
- the parental right to choose
- religious fundamentalism
- religious tolerance

Structures You Might Use

- In my opinion/In my view/ In my experience …
- As far as I'm concerned …
- I think/fear/feel/believe/am certain (convinced)/I would argue that …
- I (dis)agree …
- You're right/wrong!
- That's a good point!/That's true!
- I hadn't thought of that!
- Is it not the case that …?
- I have heard/seen/read that …
- There is the danger/possibility/risk that …
- On the one hand … and on the other hand …
- One could say/argue/suggest that …
- (That) might encourage/discourage/prevent …/lead to …

★★★ 5. **Written Discussion (Creative Task)**
The Outsider: Have you ever been in a situation where you were the new kid on the block? How did it feel? Discuss the experience with a partner and/or write about it in around 100 words. Try to use the words and expressions in the box. Perhaps a group of you could write a short play about being on the fringe and perform it to the class.

a good impression – anxious – lonely – self-conscious – self-esteem – shy – stressful – vulnerable

★★★ 6. **Creative Task**
Plan a summer party in an educational institution of your choice. You should involve parents of different cultural backgrounds in your planning as you wish to promote cultural understanding. Furthermore, you want as many parents and children as possible to come into contact with each other so that integration can take place more easily than it did before.

Hint: Activities in teams and good food are brilliant helpers when it comes to getting into contact with each other.

Work with me ISBN 978-3-582-77856-7

TEXT 6: An Email to the Newspaper [B2]

From: collins@stpeter-church.co.uk

To: editor@yorkshire-weekly.co.uk

Subject: St Peter's Might Close!

Dear Editor,

We are writing to your newspaper in protest at the possible closure of our church youth club due to the ending of financial support given by our town council. We know that the town budget is tight but without the annual grant of six thousand pounds we receive for help with energy bills, repairs, materials, equipment and the part-time employment of our youth worker (five helpers are volunteers) we will be unable to continue.
Do our readers realise how valuable youth work is?
We have attached a file showing, in a "word-spider", all the benefits of our precious youth club to the whole community. We hope you will print it as a special feature,

Faithfully Yours,
On behalf of the Church Elders,

Reverend Janice Collins

INFO 3: Useful Phrases for Formal Emails

- ***Stating your purpose*** *The reason I am writing is... / I would like to draw your attention to... / The purpose of this email is to...*
- ***Making requests*** *I would be grateful if you could... / Could you please... / I would appreciate it if you would...*
- ***Giving information*** *I would like to inform you that... / Please note that... / I am pleased to tell you that...*
- ***Expressing opinions politely*** *In my opinion... / I believe that... / It seems to me that... / From my point of view...*
- ***Closing*** *Thank you for your time and consideration / I look forward to hearing from you / Please do not hesitate to contact me*
- ***Sign-offs*** *Yours sincerely (name known) / Yours faithfully (name unknown) / Kind regards*

Work with me ISBN 978-3-582-77856-7

★ 1. **Working with Words**

Find in the text words which match these definitions below.

a) The local administration
b) A job for a few hours
c) A report out of the ordinary
d) Money to be spent in a small community
e) People who work without payment
f) Items such as paper, pens, paints, brushes
g) Money donated every year

★★★ 2. **Creating a Mind Map: Committee Meeting**

Your group is the church committee, meeting to create a word-spider (mind map), attached to the email for the attention of the editor. In the centre of the spider write HAPPY COMMUNITY.

Brainstorm each other for useful phrases to write on the legs of your spider. Use the box of nouns for ideas. Post your completed spiders on the board. Compare and criticize (nicely!) (Mind map: see appendix p. 228)

Example for the first leg: "keeping children off the street"

CRIME NUISANCE FITNESS DISCUSSION ADVICE SAFETY
DRUGS ALCOHOL SKILLS CONFIDENCE

★★★★ **Projects**

3. Your group is responsible for organising a special day to celebrate cultural diversity at a youth club. Decide what each youth worker could contribute with the help of the children.

4. Your group is responsible for publicising a multicultural festival. Organise posters, emails to the local paper, invitations to local celebrities and messages on the club's website. Discuss also how to use any profits for charities and good causes.

★★★★ 5. **Internet Research / Discussion**

a) Work in pairs or small groups. Use the internet to research **youth crime in England and Wales.**
Focus on:
– What types of crimes are most common among young people (ages 10–17)?
– What does the data say about the ethnicity of young offenders?

b) Make a short presentation (2–3 minutes)
Present your findings to the class. You can use a poster, a slide show, or simply speak freely. Or:

c) Write a short reflection in English (80–100 words). Consider the questions below:
– What did you learn about youth crime?
– Did anything surprise you?
– What do you think could help reduce youth offending?

Vocabulary Module 11 Children on the Fringe

Introduction		
complexion	[kəm'pləkʃən]	Teint
Text 1: The Misfit		
mucky [coll]	['mʌkɩ]	schmutzig
(to) retaliate	[rɪ'tælieɪt]	sich rächen
Text 2: Charter of Respect		
infringed	[ɪn'frɪnʤd]	verletzt, verstoßen
thicko [coll]	['θɪkəʊ]	„Dummkopf"
travellers' camp	['trævələrz kæmp]	Travellers: Leute, die in Wohnwagen wohnen
Text 3: Perry's Plight – A Profile of Deprivation		
plight	[plaɪt]	Notlage
deprivation	[ˌdeprɪ'vaɪʃən]	benachteiligte Situation, Mangel
neglect	[nɪ'glekt]	Vernachlässigung
absentee	[ˌæbsən'tiː]	Abwesende/-r
absenteeism	[æbsən'tiːɪzəm]	Krankfeiern
(to) be in breach of	[biː ɪn briːtʃ ɒv]	gegen etwas verstoßen
harassment	['hærəsmənt]	Belästigung
(to) truant, (to) play truant	[(pleɪ) 'truːənt]	schwänzen
siblings	['sɪblɪŋs]	Geschwister
cramped	[kræmpt]	eng
convictions	[kən'vɪkʃənz]	Vorstrafen
disruptive	[dɪs'rʌptɪv]	störend
(to) exacerbate	[ɪg'zæsəbeɪt]	verschlechtern
overcrowding	[ˌəʊvə'kraʊdɪŋ]	Überfüllung
anger management	['æŋgər mænɪʤmənt]	Selbstbeherrschung
(to) underachieve	[ˌʌndərə'tʃiːv]	unter dem erreichbaren Leistungsniveau bleiben
(to) sever	['sevər]	abbrechen, trennen
(to) allocate	['æləkeɪt]	(Mittel) zuteilen
self-esteem	[ˌself-ɪ'stiːm]	Selbstachtung
outcome	['aʊtkʌm]	Ergebnis
lad [coll]	[læd]	Bursche
estate	[ɪ'steɪt]	Wohnsiedlung
Text 4: Mentoring the Child on the Fringe		
on the fringe	[ɒn ðə 'frɪnʤ]	am Rande, in der Randzone
mentoring (peer)	['mentɔːrɪŋ (pɪər)]	Beratung (von seinesgleichen)
all sorts of stuff [coll]	[ɔːl sɔːts ɒv stʌf]	allerlei Sachen
Info 1: Mentoring		
transition	[træn'zɪʃən]	Übergang
youth offending	[juːθ ə'fendɪŋ]	Jugendkriminalität
attainment; (to) attain	[ə'teɪnmənt, ə'teɪn]	Leistung; leisten
disaffected	[dɪsə'fektɪd]	unzufrieden, desillusioniert
Text 5: New Kids on the Block		
(to) exceed	[ɪk'siːd]	übertreffen
(to) detract from	[dɪ'trækt frɒm]	beeinträchtigen
multi-faith centre	[mʌlti-'feɪθ sentər]	Zentrum verschiedener Religionen
divisive	[dɪ'vaɪsɪv]	spalterisch
Text 6: A Letter to the Newspaper		
town council	[taʊn 'kaʊnsᵊl]	Stadtrat
tight	[taɪt]	angespannt
annual grant	['ænjuəl grɑːnt]	jährlicher Zuschuss
benefit	['bɛnɪfɪt]	Vorteil; Nutzen
precious	['prɛʃəs]	wertvoll
special feature	['spɛʃᵊl 'fiːʧə]	Sonderbeitrag
on behalf of	[ɒn bɪ'hɑːf ɒv]	im Namen (von)
church elders	[ʧɜːʧ 'ɛldəz]	Kirchenälteste, Ältestenkreis
Reverend	['rɛvᵊrᵊnd]	Pfarrer/Pfarrerin

Work with me ISBN 978-3-582-77856-7

Module 12
Outdoor Education

In this module you will have the opportunity to learn about

- the aims of outdoor education
- its history and development
- a range of outdoor activities
- the importance of reflection and the rules for feedback
- the development of ecological awareness through activities

Introduction

★ 1. **Working with Words**
Express any ideas which come to mind when you look at the photograph.

★★★ KMK 2. **Role Play**
Find a partner and prepare a dialogue between two of the people shown above. Present the dialogue in form of a role play to your classmates. You may use the words in the box.

mountain – sun – tired – heavy – blisters – campsite – hungry – team – lost – idea – bandages

★★ 3. **Group Work**
Work in a group and make a list of items the people shown in the picture may have in their rucksacks. Give reasons for your choices.

Text 1: Outdoor Education [B1]

Outdoor education can be defined as organized learning taking place outdoors. Programmes are often based on experiences around a base camp or ones encountered on a trip. Participants can be challenged by different activities, such as hiking, climbing, canoeing, abseiling and group games. Outdoor education can be connected theoretically with experiential and environmental education. Although adventure education is often linked with it as well, adventure trips rarely take learning about the environment into consideration.

Education outdoors takes place all over the world. Only the mix and importance of various activities differ from country to country, depending on their environments and the cultural context. So it is not surprising that outdoor education means the same as environmental education in some countries, whereas the concepts are different in others.

Outdoor training courses are mostly targeted at adults, especially corporate teams. Trainers offer programmes which are similar to the ones for children and teenagers, but they do not mention the word "education" because a lot of grown-ups are convinced that they do not need to be educated any more. Nevertheless, training courses are in fact based on learning through experience.

Info 1: Different Outdoor Programmes

Organizations offering outdoor programmes of different types are quite numerous. You can find experiential education programmes for children, teenagers, adults, families, school classes etc. People with special needs are of course welcome, as programmes can be designed to suit each individual and every group.

Aims

What are the aims of outdoor education? The answer comes as a surprise to a lot of people who think outdoor education is about *mastering skills* outdoors, for example, rock-climbing or canoeing. This is not accurate. Outdoor education is much more about the experience one gets when trying to fulfil different tasks. According to the theory of experiential learning, the main issue is not about mastering skills but about learning how to overcome difficulties in new situations, how to work in a team and how to develop a deeper relationship with nature.

There are three target areas:

1. the Self
2. Others
3. the Natural World

In an outdoor education programme these three aspects are the focus. Any of these can be emphasized, depending on the needs of the individual. For example, within the area of *Self*, outdoor education allows many young offenders to develop their personalities and change their attitudes. It provides an opportunity for them to escape the environments which have contributed to their criminal behaviour and can give them a chance to lead a non-criminal life.

Within those three main areas of outdoor education there are other objectives:

- enhancing teamwork
- teaching outdoor survival skills
- promoting spirituality
- understanding natural environments
- developing leadership skills
- improving problem-solving skills

(402 words)

Work with me ISBN 978-3-582-77856-7

Info 2: Re-Offending

Re-offending means repeating criminal or unwanted behaviour after the negative consequences of that behaviour have already been pointed out. The term is frequently used in conjunction with substance abuse, vandalism, assault and theft.
Outdoor education is a vital tool in helping disaffected youngsters to learn normal and accepted patterns of behaviour.

★ 1. **Working with Words**
Choose five of the aims mentioned in Text 1 and explain them in your own words.

★ 2. **Working with Words**
Find synonyms for these words.

a) programme
b) trip
c) participant
d) different
e) vital

★★★★ KMK 3. **Group Work**
Consider the areas of Self, Others and the Natural World. Choose a target group (of children, teenagers or adults – with or without special needs) and design a poster. Show what their different characteristics are and which activities in an outdoor training programme might be suitable for them.

★★★ KMK 4. **Creative Task**
Situation: you have to explain to a group in your workplace that it is not the outdoor activity itself but the way they work at it, which is the most important. Anticipate comments and questions from your "clients" in response.
The presentation to your classmates could be in form of a role play or a taped dialogue, if you wish to work in pairs.

★★ 5. **Internet Research**
Do an Internet search and find out what is meant by "experiential education" and "environmental education". Prepare a presentation to inform your classmates about it.

★★★ 6. **Project**
Work in a group. Search the Internet and list different outdoor activities. You could even try them out, if possible.
- Evaluate their suitability for different age-groups.
- Assess their practicability in the workplace.
- Finally, think about learning outcomes for participants.

Work with me ISBN 978-3-582-77856-7

Text 2: Outdoor Education and Its Roots [B2]

Outdoor education is not just a modern trend. The philosophy of getting the best out of the individual can be traced back to the Ancient Greeks. The philosopher Plato stated that the ideal community can be achieved by education focussing on the good qualities of people. In the 18th century **Jean-Jacques Rousseau** stressed the natural goodness of human beings and he developed a theory of education to encourage their best qualities. His book "Emile" shows in detail how this could be done.

About a hundred years later, philosopher **Henry David Thoreau** argued that the desire for unnecessary goods was ruining the individual and that it was vital to concentrate on the important things in life in order to be spiritually free. The longing for certain luxuries made individuals obsessed with obtaining and owning them. The pursuit of wealth made people forget to live as a consequence. Thoreau argued that they could reduce their need for goods to a minimum and still be free to lead a good life. He also stressed that it was important to live in accord with nature and not against it.

Info 3: Thoreau

Henry David Thoreau (1817–1862) practised his theory with his "Walden Project": for several years he lived in a hut near Walden pond, reducing his needs to the basics. You can find a detailed description of his life there in his book "Walden".

Kurt Hahn, a German educator, is recognised as the founder of modern outdoor training based on pedagogical theory. In 1941 he founded his "Outward-Bound Schools". The first outdoor training centre was opened in Aberdovey in Wales during the Second World War.

Info 4: Hahn

Kurt Hahn (1886–1974), observing the different problems which youngsters had, summarized them in four statements:

1. *a lack of empathy*
2. *a lack of carefulness*
3. *a lack of bodily fitness*
4. *a lack of initiative and spontaneity*

His solutions to these problems were the following:

- *helping each other*
- *project work*
- *bodily training*
- *trips and expeditions*

Nowadays you can find "Outward-Bound Centres" all over the world. Depending on region and climate, trainers stress different activities as the core of their programmes. But whatever the activities may be, the humanistic theory is the basis of all of these programmes. The philosophical works of Comenius, John Dewey, William James, Aldo Leopold, John Locke, John Muir, Rousseau, Thoreau and Pestalozzi, Hahn and Willi Unsoeld can be considered as the foundations of outdoor pedagogical activities.

(410 words)

Work with me ISBN 978-3-582-77856-7

★★ 1. **Internet Research**
Find out different countries in which there are training centres for outward-bound education. Outline what they focus on.

★★ 2. **Creative Task**
Create a diagram showing the historical roots of outdoor training.

★★★ 3. **Mediation**
KMK
Situation: your German boss knows nothing about outdoor education, so you have to tell him or her about the roots of it, as well as the theory behind it. Otherwise you will not get any money for visiting an outward-bound centre with your group!

★★★★ 4. **Project**
Work in a group to find out about the philosophical work of one of the above-mentioned historical figures. Find out how their ideas relate to modern outdoor education. Present your findings to your classmates.

★ 5. **Working with Words**
Here are the answers. Form questions asking for the underlined part of the sentences.

a) Outdoor education can be traced back to the Ancient Greeks.
b) Jean-Jacques Rousseau stressed the natural goodness of human beings.
c) The desire for unnecessary goods was spoiling the individual.
d) Kurt Hahn founded outward-bound schools.
e) John Locke's work is recognised as one of the bases for outdoor learning.

Text 3: Activities, Reflection and Feedback [B1]

Activities

The activities below are used to achieve a range of learning outcomes such as team-building skills, citizenship and emotional literacy.

- abseiling
- archery
- bushcraft
- canoeing
- indoor climbing wall
- environmental education
- forest school
- gorge-walking
- hill-walking
- Jacob's ladder
- John Muir Awards
- kayaking
- labyrinth
- orienteering
- raft-building
- rock climbing

Whatever the activity undertaken in an outdoor training course, it must be environmentally friendly. It is also vital that participants are able to get an insight, not only into their own motivation, but also into their behaviour towards others. Reflection and feedback are therefore crucial if learning from activities is to take place.

(114 words)

Reflection

Outdoor trainers are often asked why participants in a programme have to "reflect all the time". The answer to that is very interesting. Reflection is a diagnostic instrument to investigate reactions to an event, at a group or personal level. Without the diagnosis further steps cannot be taken. In addition, reflection makes it clear how behavioural patterns in an activity occur in everyday life as well. One can subsequently take different skills learnt on an outdoor training course and transfer the most successful ones to other situations in life. In a very practical sense reflection is the basis for change.

Work with me ISBN 978-3-582-77856-7

But how should reflection best be done? Simon Priest, a researcher in the area of outdoor education, has created a framework for reflection. By answering the questions listed below in order, it is possible to reflect successfully on any activity:

Questions for Reflection

1. What has happened?
2. What has been triggered off?
   How did you feel about the situation?
3. What did you learn?
4. Is there any possible transfer into everyday life?
5. Save the insight: How would you behave in similar situations in future?

By following this process of reflection, the experience may lead one to an awareness of those personal characteristics which one needs to change in order to gain more success, for example, in social and career terms. Sometimes the individual might wish to undertake this reflection process alone, as an introspective act. Other times it might help to discuss the answers to the questions with other participants. Requesting group feedback can help everyone to gain, by developing a better insight and understanding of one's own as well as others' experiences and emotions.

(279 words)

Feedback

For good feedback you should stick to a few rules.

Feedback

1. **Request and give feedback often**
   If you start working with a new group of people, you should start the feedback cycle by asking for feedback, so that people get used to the dynamics before you – the team leader – start giving feedback yourself.
2. **Provide feedback early**
   It makes it easier to understand something if the feedback is close to the event.
3. **Giving feedback is about sharing your feelings**
   Give feedback in "me" terms. Instead of saying "You are rude", you should say "Sneezing in my face make me feel belittled and angry". A good template is: "when you do that, it makes me feel like this".
4. **Don't evaluate or judge**
   Good feedback gives the recipient information on their behaviour and gives that person a chance to change.
5. **Receiving feedback is about listening to someone else's feelings**
   By keeping this idea in one's head, it is much easier not to take a defensive stand. It is important to realise that one is only listening to someone else's point of view.
6. **Feedback can refer to negative as well as positive sides of behaviour**
   Feedback telling other people what was negative about their behaviour is the best possible chance to bring about change. It is difficult and awkward to give and receive such feedback but it helps participants to see themselves from another point of view. Receiving positive feedback is also not easy for a lot of young people, but it helps to strengthen their self-esteem and increases confidence in themselves and in their actions.
7. **Talking about the feedback is called meta-feedback**
   Meta-feedback is a great way to become better at the art of giving and receiving feedback. It will also help everyone relax and really listen to what is being said, instead of just trying to defend opinions.

(316 words)

Work with me ISBN 978-3-582-77856-7

★ 1. **Working with Words**
Explain these expressions in your own words.

a) researcher
b) obvious
c) process
d) characteristics
e) rude

★★★★ 2. **Group Work**
Work in a group to discuss how the mentioned activities can be useful for the development of the individual. Concentrate on different age-groups as well as on people with and without special needs.

★★★★ 3. **Working with Words**
Reflection is an important part of experiential learning. Work with your partner and list questions which stimulate reflection about an activity. Sort your questions into different categories, for example:

Social	Emotional	Technical	Diagnosis	Transfer	Perspective	...
...						

★★ 4. **Group Work**
Work in a group to find different activities/methods of reflection. Try them out with your classmates and discuss their advantages as well as disadvantages. Set up a list of the ten best activities/methods of reflection.

★★ 5. **Creative Task**
Find symbols for the feedback rules (for example, an ear for "listening", a clock for "feedback time"). Prepare them in such a way that you could take them outdoors in all weather conditions. Explain the meaning of the symbols to your classmates and let them give you a feedback on your symbols.

★★★ 6. Give a short explanation of the meaning behind the five impulses of the STATE method.

The STATE method for effective feedback:

S → T → A → T → E

S	T	A	T	E
Share the facts	Tell your story	Ask for other´s path	Talk tentatively	Encourage testing

Read this offer regarding outdoor training for migrant children and teenagers:

Erlebnispädagogik mit Kindern und Jugendlichen mit Migrationshintergrund

Viele Fachkräfte in Erziehungs- und Bildungssituationen sehen sich täglich mit der Herausforderung konfrontiert, Kinder und Jugendliche mit Migrationshintergrund in das alltägliche Geschehen in der Institution vor Ort zu integrieren. Regeln für das Zusammenleben sowie bestehende Wertvorstellungen sind ebenso zu vermitteln, wie Arbeit in der individuellen Sprachförderung zu leisten ist. Oftmals wünschen sich sozialpädagogische Fachkräfte und Lehrer mehr Zeit, um den individuellen Bedürfnissen der Kinder und Jugendlichen nachkommen zu können.

Eine Lösung für die Problematik stellen erlebnispädagogische Programme dar. Sie unterstützen den Einzelnen dabei, seinen individuellen Platz in der Gesellschaft zu finden. Beispielsweise werden Stärken in einzelnen Übungen und Aufgaben herausgefunden und in ihrer möglichen Übertragung auf die Alltagswelt reflektiert. So erfährt der Einzelne, dass er Fähigkeiten und Fertigkeiten hat, die wertvoll sind und er bereits einbringen kann, obwohl er noch viel in anderen Bereichen lernen muss, bevor er das gesellschaftliche System vor Ort komplett versteht. Er erkennt den Wert seiner Person, der sich in vielen Fällen durch traumatisierende Erlebnisse in der Vergangenheit nicht ausbilden konnte oder ihr abgesprochen worden ist. Das Erkennen des Selbstwerts ist aber entscheidend für den Aufbau des Selbstbewusstseins, das der Einzelne benötigt, um die Anforderungen des Alltags gesund zu bestehen und realistische Ziele für sein Leben zu finden, vor anderen zu vertreten und schließlich dauerhaft zu verfolgen.

Weiterhin zeigen erlebnispädagogische Programme Wege der Umsetzung von Vorhaben im Alltag auf. Fragen, wie bestimmte Ziele erreicht werden können, finden ihre Beantwortung beispielhaft in Vertrauen- und Teamübungen, die den Wert von Unterstützersystemen untermalen. Reflexionsrunden gehen auf den individuellen Transfer im Alltag ein. Dabei wird die gegenseitige Unterstützung in ihrer Relevanz für das gemeinschaftliche Leben deutlich. Die soziale Komponente des Gebens und Nehmens erhält eine herausragende Bedeutung, die durch die eigene Erfahrung in entsprechenden Übungen und Aufgaben erlebt wird.

Ebenso wird die Notwendigkeit von Ausdauer, Sorgfalt, Flexibilität und Spontaneität für das erfolgreiche Abschließen von Vorhaben in der Erlebnispädagogik durch angepasste Projekte herausgestellt und praktisch geübt. Dies ist gerade für Jugendliche mit Migrationshintergrund von besonderer Relevanz, da sie meist zeitnah in das Berufsleben wechseln wollen, in welchem diese Charakteristiken zu den Schlüsselqualifikationen gezählt werden können, um beruflich erfolgreich zu sein.

Da erlebnispädagogische Programme meist in der Natur durchgeführt werden, bietet sich den Kindern und Jugendlichen mit Mi-

Work with me ISBN 978-3-582-77856-7

grationshintergrund außerdem ein Lebens- und Erfahrungsfeld in der neuen Umgebung, das ihnen häufig in dieser Form unbekannt war. Die Nähe zur Natur und der Wert der natürlichen Umwelt wird direkt als schützenswert erfahren. Ein positives Umweltbewusstsein wird thematisiert und in seiner aktiven Umsetzung im Alltag beispielhaft trainiert.

Gesamt gesehen bietet Erlebnispädagogik Kindern und Jugendlichen mit Migrationshintergrund die Chance, das zu erfahren, was für ihr Leben und ihre Integration in die Gesellschaft notwendig ist. Zudem wird die individuelle Erziehungs- und Bildungsarbeit durch erlebnispädagogische Programme unterstützt. Warum sollte man sie also nicht durchführen?

★★ 1. **Mediation**
Write a mediation of this text for your English speaking colleague who is responsible for migrant children and teenagers who have only just come to Germany.

★★ 2. **Discussion**
Discuss the pros and cons of accepting this offer for an international group of children and teenagers who live in the residential home you work in, and draw a conclusion.

★★★ 3. **Role play**
Your English speaking colleague has got some questions he'd like to ask the manager of the programme offered. As the manager speaks English fluently you prepare a telephone conversation with him. Act out the conversation and make an audio recording that you play to some classmates. Don't forget to ask them for feedback on it.

★★★ 4. **Creative Task**
You are planning to book a one-week outdoor programme. Create an information sheet about educational outdoor training for the international group of children and teenagers at the residential home where you work. Present your information sheet to your classmates and ask them for feedback.

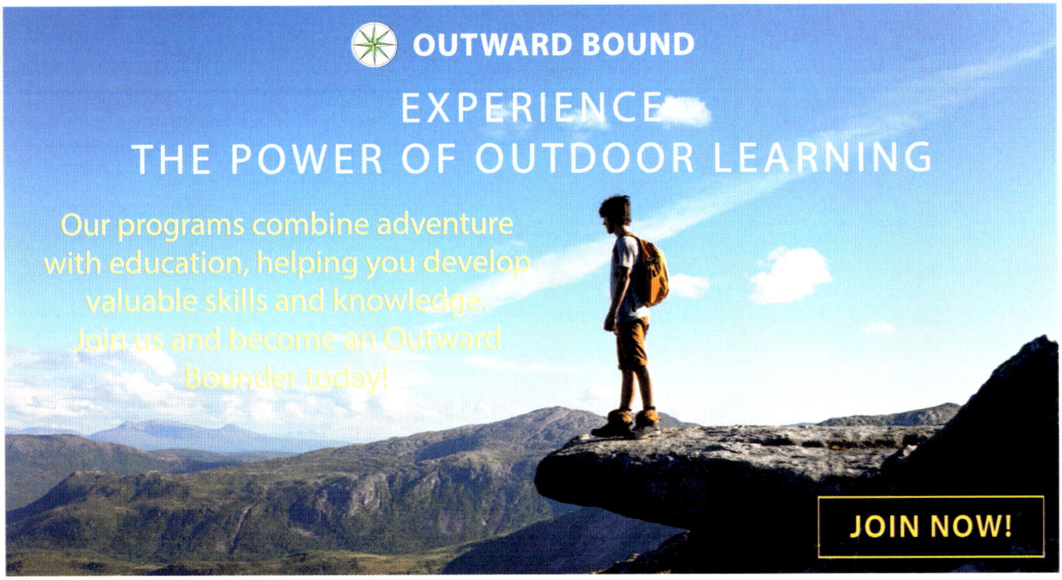

Text 4: Eco Schola in Romania [B1]

"Eco Schola" is a programme implemented by "Outward-Bound Romania" and the local Romanian Scouts. The programme is intended to help high-school students learn ecology "hands-on" in their natural surroundings. They are empowered to work together to identify local environmental issues and solutions they can implement themselves.

This programme is part of the Agenda 21 programme, one goal of which is to train local people and involve them in the planning and implementation of sustainable development projects.

Info 5: Agenda 21

This programme is a comprehensive plan of action to be taken globally, nationally and locally by organisations of the United Nations, governments and groups in every area in which humans have an influence on the environment.

More than 178 countries committed themselves to follow the principles of Agenda 21 at the United Nations Conference on Environment and Development (UNCED) held in Rio de Janeiro, Brazil in 1992. Every five years there is a review of the progress being made by each of the participating countries.

Countries not taking part in Agenda 21 are regularly asked to sign the treaty and take adequate action.

Earth Summit

In 2003, biology students from three Romanian high schools were selected with their teachers to participate in "Eco Schola", which includes a mix of classroom discussion and preparation, local observations as well as team-building and problem-solving activities at the Outward-Bound Centre in Sovata, Romania.
Students spend time in class learning about ecological issues and the impacts of human behaviour on their environment. Then they participate in a weekend programme at the Centre where they examine local flora and fauna as well as take part in normal outward-bound activities such as abseiling, hiking and activities with environmental themes.

It is hoped that by taking the classroom lessons out into the field and using hands-on activities, students will begin to incorporate those environmental lessons into their everyday life. For many, this is a first step in thinking practically about their environment – the first real step in following the "Patagonia Philosophy":

The Patagonia Philosophy

The Natural Steps:

1. Do not take anything from the Earth's crust which you cannot put back.
2. Maintain the integrity of natural ecosystems.
3. Do not spread long-lasting human-made materials around the environment.
4. Leave enough for others.

(275 words)
(Source: www.outward-bound.org)

Work with me ISBN 978-3-582-77856-7

★ 1. **Working with the Text**
The Patagonia Philosophy tells you in short how to respect nature. Explain in detail what is meant by each of the four statements.

★ 2. **Working with Words**
Find a partner and create a crossword puzzle, using words from the text "Eco Schola in Romania".

★★ 3. **Creative Task**
Draw up a plan of how you would get your group to follow the Patagonia Philosophy when outdoors.

★★★★ 4. **Group Work**
"Outward-Bound Romania" is a shining example of how to combine experiential and environmental learning. Create a programme to show how this sort of learning might look in detail. Stick to the age-group you want to work with and the given surroundings.

★★★ 5. **Project**
Find out what opportunities for experiential learning there are in your region. Prepare an interview (for example, by inventing a questionnaire) with one of the organisations and get to know what it is doing to protect the environment.
After carrying out the interview, you should present the result to your classmates. Decide which organisation best addresses environmental matters.

Text 5:

Jill and Her Outdoor Training Experience [B1]

Hi, my name is Jill and I'm 15 years old. I live in a residential home for children in Liverpool. Life in the residential home is kind of okay, though the social workers want us to do crazy things sometimes. Like, not long ago – they went and booked a one-week outdoor training programme for some of us: me and Jane, who is 13, Sid, who turns 17 next week, ten-year old Ella and Henry, who is my age. The guys are all okay and we get along with each other, I suppose, though we do have rows and quarrels sometimes. Anyway, the social workers wanted us to go on this training course so we would get along even better with each other and grow up a bit.

To be honest, none of us wanted to do any kind of psycho-thing. We all were against the idea of training and decided not to let ourselves get brainwashed by some psycho-blokes. Even Ella said she would kick them if they made her do things she didn't want to. But the social workers insisted on us going to this outward-bound centre. And so we went.

On arrival we got to know our trainers for the week. Well, they weren't what we'd expected them to be. Steven and Cleo weren't psycho-kind of people at all, but really cool. They welcomed us just how you'd welcome friends, so we felt fine - and important. During the week my attitude to the programme changed completely. The activities we did weren't babyish or anything to do with stupid brainwashing methods and the trainers took what we said seriously. They didn't force any of us to do things we didn't like. But they got us thinking about ourselves and the people around us. If you look at the programme of our outdoor education week, you can see that we did real grown-up things:

Work with me ISBN 978-3-582-77856-7

The Outreach Centre (Cheshire, UK) Outdoor Education Programme				
Monday	**Tuesday**	**Wednesday**	**Thursday**	**Friday**
– Welcoming the group – Problem-solving activities – Reflection – Lunch – Participants organize a trip – Dinner – Reflection	– Breakfast – Start of the trekking trip (– Lunch boxes) – Reflection – Putting up tents – Solo – Dinner – Reflection – Relaxing at the campsite	– Breakfast – Taking down tents – Trekking – Lunch – Reflection – More difficult problem-solving activities – Reflection – Return to the Outreach Centre – Dinner	– Breakfast – Canoeing (– Lunch boxes) – Reflection – Dinner	– Breakfast – Reflections on the week – Feedback – Saying goodbye – Lunch
+ Reflection and feedback when necessary				

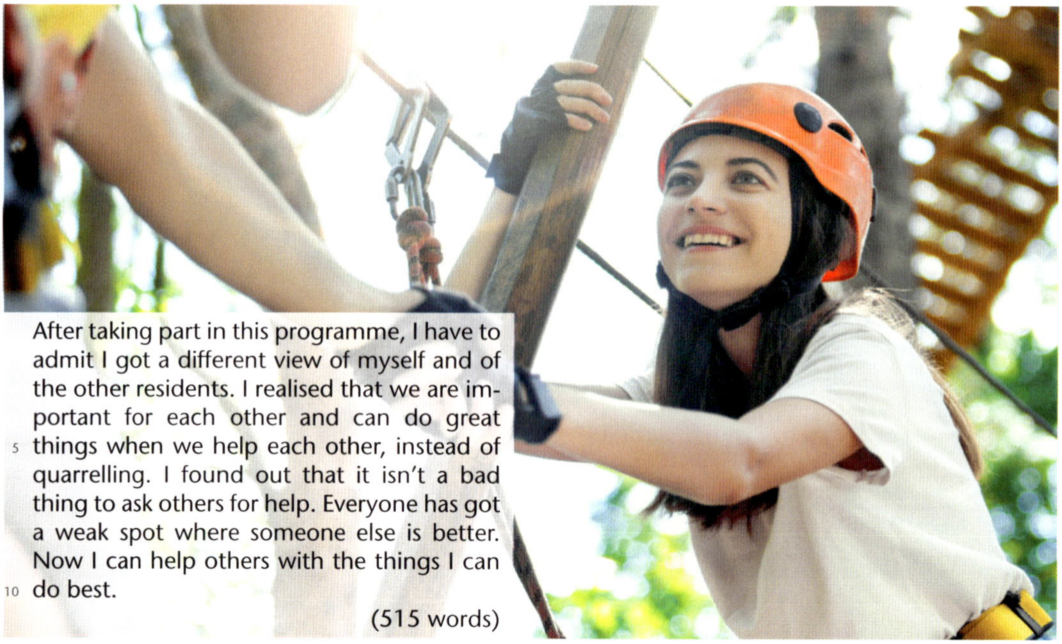

After taking part in this programme, I have to admit I got a different view of myself and of the other residents. I realised that we are important for each other and can do great things when we help each other, instead of quarrelling. I found out that it isn't a bad thing to ask others for help. Everyone has got a weak spot where someone else is better. Now I can help others with the things I can do best.

(515 words)

Info 6: The Structure of Outdoor Education

Outdoor education is based on the philosophy of humanism. The basics of outdoor education are:

- *problem-solving activities*
- *ropes courses (high and low)*
- *projects*
- *solo (being on your own for a certain period of time, in order to think about yourself and your life)*
- *expeditions and trips*
- *outdoor sports*
- *city-bound (outdoor education transferred to town)*

Work with me ISBN 978-3-582-77856-7

★ 1. **Working with Words**
Everyone in class writes their name on a piece of paper. Pass the papers round. Think of the strengths of each classmate and write them on their paper. Pass them back.

★★★ 2. **Creative Task**
Prepare dialogues between Jill and her social worker before and after the outward-bound course. Tape the dialogues and present them to your classmates.

★★ 3. **Internet Research**
Search the Internet for the pros and cons of outdoor training. State why you would or would not like to participate in an outdoor training programme.

★★★★ 4. **Role Play**
Situation: you are Jill's social worker and want children to go to the Outreach Centre the following year. Write a report about the experience to present at a team meeting where there are youth workers who are not in favour of outward-bound activities. Practise it and perform it to your class.

★★ 5. **Working with the Text**
Compare the activities in Jill's programme with Info 6. Decide which activities belong with which aspect.

★★★ 6. **Project**
Situation: you work in a youth club and are planning to take the children on a trip. Your supervisor wants you to create a two-day programme of activities to promote experiential learning. Justify the activities you choose. Present your programme to your classmates who will give you feedback on it.

★★★ 7. **Discussion**
Do you think you need a qualified trainer to organise experiential education programmes? Or can you set up programmes yourself by combining some activities?

Although the problem itself may change, one thing remains constant – the more prepared, calm, and empowered you and your team are, the better outcome you can expect.

Vocabulary Module 12 Outdoor Education

Text 1: Outdoor Education		
outdoor education	[ˈaʊtˌdɔːr ˌedjʊˈkeɪʃən]	(vergleichbar mit Erlebnispädagogik, kein deutsches Wort vorhanden)
(to) encounter	[ɪnˈkaʊntər]	begegnen
hiking	[ˈhaɪkɪŋ]	(Berg-)Wandern
experiential education	[ɪkˌspɪəriˈentʃəl ˌedjʊˈkeɪʃən]	Erlebnispädagogik
environmental education	[ɪnˌvaɪərənˈmentəl ˌedjʊˈkeɪʃən]	Umweltpädagogik
adventure education	[adˈventʃər ˌedjʊˈkeɪʃən]	Abenteuerpädagogik
rock climbing	[rɒk-ˈklaɪmɪŋ]	Felsenklettern
offender	[əˈfendər]	Straftäter/-in
survival skills	[səˈvaɪvəl skɪlz]	Überlebenstechniken
problem-solving skills	[ˈprɒbləm-sɒlvɪŋ skɪlz]	Problemlösefähigkeiten
Info 2: Re-Offending		
re-offending	[riː-əˈfendɪŋ]	Rückfälligkeit
substance abuse	[ˈsʌbstənts əˈbjuːz]	Drogenmissbrauch
assault	[əˈsɒlt]	Körperverletzung
theft	[θeft]	Diebstahl
disaffected	[ˌdɪsəˈfektɪd]	unzufrieden, desillusioniert
(to) anticipate	[ænˈtɪsɪpeɪt]	erwarten, vorausahnen
Text 2: Outdoor Education and Its Roots		
obsessed	[əbˈsest]	besessen
(to) obtain	[əbˈteɪn]	beschaffen, erlangen
pursuit	[pəˈsjuːt]	Streben
wealth	[welθ]	Reichtum
Info 3: Thoreau		
hut	[hʌt]	Hütte
Text 3: Activities, Reflection and Feedback		
archery	[ˈaːtʃəri]	Bogenschießen
bushcraft	[ˈbuʃkraːft]	extension of "survival skills" (using tools for building a shelter, making fire, hunting ...)
gorge-walking	[ˈgɔːdʒ-ˈwɔːkɪŋ]	Marschieren in einer Schlucht
Jacob's ladder	[ˈdʒækəʊbs ˈlædər]	Jakobsleiter, Himmelsleiter (Strickleiter)
John Muir Award	[ˈdʒɒn mjuːə əˈwɔːd]	Zertifikat für Teilnehmer von mehrtägigen Outdoor-Education-Veranstaltungen, mit den Bereichen Discover – Explore – Conserve – Share (vgl. www.jmt.org)
raft-building	[raːft-bɪldɪŋ]	Floßbauen
reflection	[rɪˈflekʃən]	Reflexion, Rückblick
subsequently	[ˈsʌbsɪkwəntli]	anschließend
feedback	[ˈfiːdbæk]	Rückmeldung
(to) trigger	[ˈtrɪgər]	auslösen
template	[ˈtempleɪt]	Vorlage
Text 4: Eco Schola in Romania		
scouts	[skaʊts]	Pfadfinder
hands-on	[ˈhændzɒn]	praktisch, spielerisch
(to) implement	[ˈɪmplɪmənt]	durchführen, anwenden
Info 5: Agenda 21		
treaty	[ˈtriːti]	Abkommen, Vertrag
ropes course	[rəʊps kɔːs]	Seilgarten

Work with me ISBN 978-3-582-77856-7

Literature Project

"The Curious Incident of the Dog in the Night-Time"

In this module you will have the opportunity to learn

- how to create a plot-outline and describe a character
- about the difficulties of non-verbal communication
- about Asperger's Syndrome
- about detective work
- about family problems

Introduction

★★ **Double Circle: Different Categories**
Get together in groups and discuss the following questions. Make sure everybody takes notes.

a) What might these books be about? Give reasons for your opinion.
b) Find categories for these books (e.g. adventure, crime, love story).
c) What other categories do you know?
d) What is your favourite category? Give reasons for your opinion.
e) What might the favourite category of the children or teenagers be who you work with? Give reasons for your decision.

After discussing the questions in your group, form a double circle (see appendix *Working with Me*). Make sure that your group members are either all in the inner or the outer circle so that you can find a partner from a different group. Tell your partner what you have found out about the different questions.

Info 1

The following texts and tasks are divided into three sections:

Pre-Reading Activities *raise expectations about the book and make it easier for the reader to access the story.*

While-Reading Activities *help readers to focus on the important aspects of the story and give them a chance to develop a creative contextual examination.*

Post-Reading Activities *encourage readers to reflect upon what they have read and to stimulate them to go beyond the reading and to work with their new knowledge.*

Pre-Reading Activities:

"The Curious Incident of the Dog in the Night-Time" by Mark Haddon

Group Work: Create a Story

★★ 1. Have a look at the title. What might this book be about?

★★ 2. Choose one category from page 163 and suggest a possible story.

★★ 3. To create a good story you have to think of different aspects. Read Text 1 "How to create a story". This will help you with your plot-outline. Also do some drawings to highlight the key elements of the plot. With that you can visualise your story and therefore help the other students to follow your presentation.

★★ 4. After finishing your outline, create a cover for your book and explain your choice.

★★ 5. Present your story to the class. Show the chosen cover and tell your story by using your drawings. Let your classmates guess which category you have chosen.

Text 1: How to Create a Story [B1]

Everyone, especially children, loves a great story but it is often difficult to write or tell one. Unfortunately, most people never take the time to learn basic writing techniques and when they try to tell their story after finishing it, they find themselves losing their audience. Others refuse to study story-writing techniques because they fear they will lose their creativity by using story structures.

However, it is important for an early-years teacher or a youth worker to know how to build an interesting story which hooks the audience. Therefore, like building a house, there are definite things you need to know in order to write or tell a story. Learning how to read blueprints, how to swing a hammer and how to install a roof are as essential to a roofer as learning how to set up a story is to the writer and storyteller - as well as how to write a basic plot-outline and how to write a scene. So here is a quick primer on how to create a story.

Stories consist of three parts: **The beginning, the middle** and **the end**. Traditionally, this is why stories are broken down into three acts. There are six parts of a story contained within these three segments.

Act I: The Beginning
(Introduction and Early Action)

The beginning (Act I) has three goals. The first goal is to "get the ball rolling" by introducing the main characters and the setting they are in. The second goal is to hook your audience with something that is exciting and interesting. The third goal at the start of a story is to introduce the villain and the main point of the story.

Act II: The Middle
(Complications and Crisis)

Complications in the story make things more interesting for the characters and the reader. Often a plot-twist is introduced here which will force the main character to change, to become fully committed and to strengthen or clarify his motivation. This will often be a point of no return. The crisis is the lowest point in the story where everything looks hopeless. This will force the characters to

Work with me ISBN 978-3-582-77856-7

make a decision, leading to the climax of the story.

Act III: The End (Climax and Resolution)
The final climax of the story is a scene that everything in the story has been pointing towards. It can be a surprise, but it should be a logical progression of the events in the past. Sometimes in a short story the climax will be the first (and perhaps the only) scene.
The resolution is a final scene which shows the outcome of the events of the story. This is where the storyteller shows the consequences of the actions taken in the story.

(452 words)

(adapted from: Mark O'Bannon, "How to Tell a Story")

Pre-Reading Activity:
Character Anticipation

This food box was found on a train. It belongs to the main character of the novel.

Group Work

- ★ 1. Describe the content of the food box. Who could it belong to?
- ★★ 2. Create a picture of the possible owner considering the following aspects: sex, age, appearance, character and hobbies.
- ★★ 3. What are your expectations about the book? Write down your thoughts about what might happen in this book.

While-Reading Activities (Chapter 29):
The Difficulties of Non-Verbal Communication

- ★ Describe your feelings today with one of the faces.

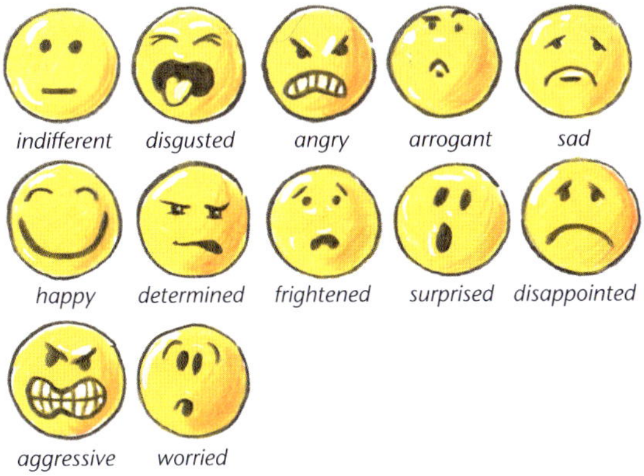

Emotions:

aggressive	= agressiv
angry	= wütend
arrogant	= arrogant
determined	= entschlossen
disappointed	= enttäuscht
disgusted	= angeekelt
frightened	= ängstlich
happy	= glücklich
indifferent	= gleichgültig
sad	= traurig
surprised	= überrascht
worried	= besorgt

Christopher's Feelings at the Beginning of the Book

1. **Silent Written Discussion**
   - ★ a) Have a look at Christopher's thoughts. How does Christopher feel? What makes him feel like that?
   - ★★ b) What do you think about Christopher's feelings? Do you agree?
   - ★★ c) Write your statements in a thought bubble like Christopher and put them on a table in the middle of the room. Walk around and read the other comments in silence.
   - ★★ d) Find a partner and talk about the different opinions on Christopher's comment.
2. **Group Work: Spot the Emotion**
   - ★★ a) Have a close look at the different pictures of this girl. How does she feel?
   - ★★★ b) Which face belongs to which (smiley) picture from page 165? Discuss it in your group.
   - ★★★★ c) Get back together in a circle of chairs with your classmates and explain to the others why you made that decision.

Useful Words

Augen = eyes

Ausdruck = expression

Mundwinkel = corner of the mouth

Falten = wrinkles

hochziehen = to lift

Lid = lid

Linien = lines

Lippen = lip

Lippen kräuseln = to purse one's lips

Nase = nose

Wangen = cheeks

weit = wide

verengen = to narrow

Work with me ISBN 978-3-582-77856-7

3. **Evaluation of the Group Work**
   ★ a) Was it easy/difficult to match the smiley pictures with the faces?
   ★★ b) What are the problems of non-verbal communication?
   ★★★★ c) Why is non-verbal communication so important, especially in your job as an early-childhood teacher or youth worker? What do you have to consider in your job regarding non-verbal communication?

While-Reading Activities (Chapter 2–59): Christopher – a Portrayal of the Main Character

Working with Words

★ 1. Have a look at the picture. Why does it appear as a puzzle?

★★ 2. What aspects do you have to consider when you want to describe a character? Create a mind map for character description.

KMK Group Work

★ 3. Find text evidence in the book which shows what Christopher likes and dislikes. Use the symbols ☺ and ☹ and make a list. Make sure you write down where you found the evidence in the book.

★★ 4. Find text evidence in the book of how Christopher relates to the people around him. The following questions may help you:
   a) How does he interact with these people?
   b) What do other people's emotions mean to Christopher?
   c) How does he behave in terms of social rules in his environment?

   Use the symbols ☺ and ☹ and make a list. Make sure that you write down where you found the evidence in the book.

★★★ 5. Find text evidence in the book which describes Christopher's use of language and his manner of communication. The following questions may help you:
   a) How large is his vocabulary in general and with regard to his favourite topics?
   b) Does he use a lot of repetition?
   c) Is he able to understand implied meanings?
   d) Is he able to understand non-verbal clues?

   Use the symbols ☺ and ☹ and make a list. Make sure you write down where you found the evidence in the book.

★★★★ 6. Find text evidence in the book which explains Christopher's way of thinking. The following questions may help you:
   a) What do you get to know about Christopher's imagination?
   b) How easily can Christopher handle changes?
   c) What does "routine" mean to him?
   d) How sensitive is he towards his environment?

   Use the symbols ☺ and ☹ and make a list. Make sure you write down where you found the evidence in the book.

★★ 7. **Creative Task**
   Use all your lists (3.–6.) to design a poster to show Christopher's character.

Work with me ISBN 978-3-582-77856-7

★★ 8. **Working with Words: The "Special" Me**

a) What is "special" about Christopher?

b) What is "special" about you? Write a list of things that other people may find unusual about you. Collect and mix up your classmates' descriptions. Pick one and let the others guess who it might be.

KMK 9. **Discussion**

★★ a) What does "being special" mean in our society?

★★★ b) What do you think about integrating children with special needs in a regular nursery school or school? Express your opinion and justify it.

★★★ c) Do you want to work with children who have special needs? Give reasons for your decision.

Info 2: Asperger's Syndrome

Asperger's Syndrome is one of several autism spectrum disorders. It is a milder variant of an autistic disorder. It is characterised by difficulties in social interaction and non-verbal communication. The sufferer's speech may have a repetitive pattern.

Sufferers usually show eccentric behaviour during their childhood. They usually have restricted, stereotyped interests which leave no space for more age-appropriate, normal interests.

(See also www.autisticaspergers.com)

Text 2:

Living with Asperger's Syndrome [B1]

Some Questions and Answers
By Wendy Lawson

Question: When did you first realise you were different?
Answer: I think that I always knew that I was not like others ... but I didn't know why or how.

Q. How did it affect your family relationships? For example, did your parents realise you were different?
A. My parents were so busy with having a large family and often running their own business that I was just 'Wendy being Wendy'! I was mostly left to my own devices. At times I felt as if there was a lot of anger directed towards me, but I never understood why. I didn't really receive the help and support that I could have benefited from as a child.

Q. As a child, did you find it hard to make friends with other children or were you not really interested in that?
A. This was very difficult and I had very little success! I was viewed as a "know-all" and the only way that I could relate to other children was if we had an interest in common, e.g. dogs or medicine (in my teens I read medical books because they fascinated me). I was interested, at a distance, in having a friend ... but I lacked the social 'know-how' of reciprocity and quite often would go overboard to 'buy' friends, influence others with my knowledge or become their 'helper' – just to gain a friend.

Q. Did you have rituals or obsessions at an early age? If so, how did they develop?
A. Yes, I always had rituals and obsessions! Yes, they changed over time. However, they

Work with me ISBN 978-3-582-77856-7

were always based around my interests: animals, insects and medicine. I like to wear clothes that are familiar (new ones hang around for ages), eat foods that are the same (I could live on baked beans on toast, mashed potato, carrots and gravy or McDonalds!). I hated it when routines changed and I would become quite miserable and almost lose motivation to do anything. I needed to be sure of what would happen; I need to know so that I can know what will happen, what to expect ... I am still like this today. However, I am more flexible than I was as a child!

Q. What was your experience of school like?
A. Yuck! At first I was interested in school, but after getting into trouble constantly and not understanding what was going on around me, school became a nightmare! I was bullied and teased mercilessly. I just wanted the world to stop so that I could get off and go back to being with my dog! This did change when I left school and moved on to college. However, I think it changed because I am academic more than social and at College and University I met others who were more like me - interested in study.

Q. What about sensitivities to sound/touch/light etc. – are these a problem?
A. Yes. My ears are very sensitive to particular sounds and certain noises really hurt me – even today. I wear tinted glasses to help me cope with the light that hurts my eyes and I only wear cotton next to my skin because of discomfort with how other materials feel. I don't know why this is so, but it always has been. I haven't noticed much improvement over time though.

Q. Are you able to empathise and understand other people's emotions? Can you tell someone's state of mind by looking at his or her face?
A. I'm not good at 'reading' another's body language ... I often 'feel' that if someone is unhappy, then it must be my fault. I make others angry ... I am learning that this isn't always the case but I still find this difficult. I don't 'feel' the emotions of others, unless it impacts upon me. However, I have learnt how to 'listen' to others and how to ask them how they are feeling and what this might mean for them. I am naturally inquisitive about human behaviour and driven to understand both myself and others. This means asking lots and lots of questions all of the time (this can be very demanding on people and is not always appreciated!).

Q. How did you learn to compensate for being different? Did you have to learn social skills by trial and error?
A. Yes. I did learn social skills by trial and error! Yes, they have become easier over time (lots and lots of time). I compensate, if you like, by specialising in one area and becoming good at that. Then I have something to offer, something that others are interested in.

Q. What situations do you find the most difficult to deal with?
A. Anything that I am not in control of! Public transport, pubs, clubs, parties and so on. I love to talk about things I am interested in and will generally steer a conversation that way.

Q. What's the most important advice you would give to a parent whose child has just been diagnosed with Asperger's Syndrome?
A. This is difficult ... A parent needs lots of support and they need to know that that's okay. Teachers, psychologists and other professionals will not always see things the same way that a parent does. This can be upsetting but as parents we need to fight for our children and not be put off by the ignorance of others. All of this means that for parents it is better to join with others and share the experience, rather than try to go it alone!

(928 words)
(Wendy Lawson, 1998)

Working with the Text

★ 1. Sum up the key facts of Wendy's behaviour and the resulting problems with her surroundings.

★★★ 2. Why is it difficult to live with somebody who has Asperger's Syndrome?

★★★ 3. **Creative Task/Internet Research**
Design a brochure for parents giving a definition and advice about living with a child who has Asperger's Syndrome. Include a list of what parents should and shouldn't expect of their child. You could use the following websites:

National Autistic Society: www.autism.org.uk
Autism Research Centre: www.autismresearchcentre.com
Autism Society of America: www.autism-society.org
Guide for people with the disorder: www.tonyattwood.com.au/

While-Reading Activities (Chapter 59–139):

Christopher's Investigation into the Murder of Wellington

1. **Working with Words: Detective Work**

★ a) Who is the person on the picture?
★ b) What does he do?
★ c) Write down as many words as you know linked to the word "detective".
★★ d) Put them into a Picture Lotto, a crossword puzzle or a maze and let the other students guess the words. With that you will have a lot of new vocabulary you may need for the next tasks.

Working with the Book: The Suspects
Situation: imagine you are Christopher. You want to find out which of your neighbours could have killed the dog. Therefore you decide to go and ask some of the people who live in your street.

★ 2. Complete the map from chapter 67 in the book with the names of the neighbours.

★★ 3. Develop a "WANTED" poster where you write down all the information you may get from the neighbours. You will ask
- Mr Thompson
- the black family
- Mr and Mrs Wise
- Mrs Alexander
- Mrs Shears

★★★ 4. Who is the prime suspect? Give reasons for your decision.

★★★★ KMK 5. **Role Play: The Trial**
Your prime suspect has been arrested. Today is the trial. The whole community of Swindon is interested in the trial because nobody can understand why the innocent dog had to die. Prepare yourself for the trial as:
- Judge (at least one student or the teacher): you control the action in court. You decide who can present the arguments and you make sure that the trial is fair.

Work with me ISBN 978-3-582-77856-7

- Jury: you listen to the details of the case presented in court and decide whether the suspect is guilty or not.
- Prosecutor and team (at least three students): you are the lawyer who brings the charges against the suspect. You co-operate with your team who prepare your arguments. You also have to produce witnesses who can testify against the suspect.
- Defender and team (at least three students): you try to prove that your client (the suspect) is not guilty by establishing an alibi. You co-operate with your team who prepare your arguments. The suspect has to testify in front of the court. You also have to produce witnesses to testify for the suspect.
- Journalists: you work for the local media. You sit in court and have to prepare a report for the television news after the trial. Take notes while you are listening to the arguments and then make your report.

While-Reading Activities (Chapter 149–179):

The Mysterious Letters

Working with the Book

* 1. Who might have written this letter to Christopher? Give reasons for your opinion.

** 2. What has happened to Christopher's mother since she left Swindon? Reconstruct it by analysing the letters.

** 3. What has happened to Christopher's father since his wife left Swindon? Reconstruct it by analysing his conversation with Christopher.

KMK 4. **Role Play: What happened before Christopher's mother left?**

** a) Group A: get together in your group and work out reasons why his mother might have left.
Group B: get together in your group and find out how his father might have behaved while the family was still living together.

*** b) Mix the groups and discuss your explanations of his parents' behaviour.

*** c) Create a role play of the situation where Christopher's mother decides to leave her family. Practice it and perform it to the class.

5. **Working with the Book: Christopher the Runaway**

* a) Explain why Christopher decides to run away from his father.

** b) Christopher takes his rat Toby, his coats and a scarf, a Milky Bar, two liquorice laces, three clementines, a pink wafer biscuit and his red food colouring with him. Do you think this a good choice? Give reasons for your opinion.

** c) What would you take with you if you ever wanted to run away from home? Design a picture with your choices and present it to the class.

*** 6. **Group Work**
KMK Find out about different institutions which provide help for young people who want to run away from home. What do they do? Create an "emergency folder" with the most important information for these children and teenagers.

**** 7. **Discussion**
Work out a job description for people who work in this field (e.g. street worker) and find arguments for and against this kind of work (dangers, rewards). Can you imagine working as a street worker?

While-Reading-Activities (Chapter 181–227):

Christopher's Trip to London

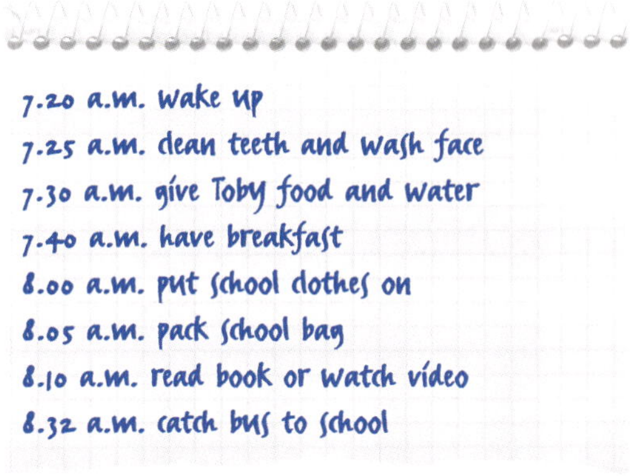

1. **Working with the Book: Christopher's Daily Routine**
   - ★ a) Describe Christopher's daily routine shown at the beginning of chapter 193.
   - ★★ b) How would you feel if it were your daily routine?
   - ★★★ c) Compare this daily routine to what he experiences on his trip to London. How does he cope with all the changes and experiences? What helps him to find his way?

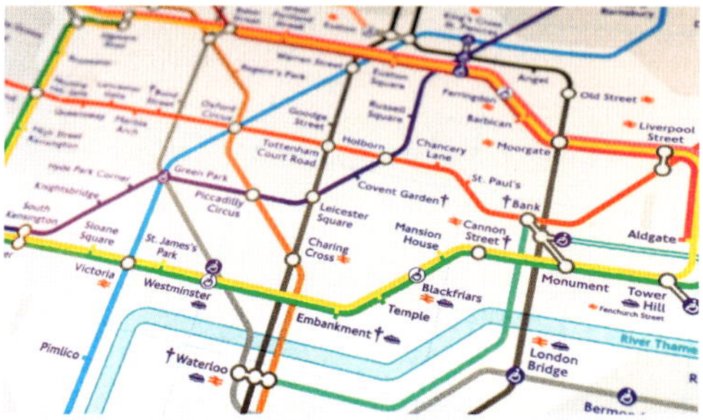

★★★ KMK 2. **Working with Words: Finding Tourist Attractions**
   - a) Get a map of London. Mark the train stations on it. Prepare some cards with important places to see in London (e.g. the Tower, London Eye, Madame Tussaud's). Divide the class into groups and give them some of the cards. The groups have to write down directions to find these places.
   - b) Imagine your class has arrived in London by train. Give the other students directions to a tourist attraction without mentioning it. If they "arrive" there safely (by following your directions on the map), you get one point. The group with the most points wins.

3. **Project on Advertising**
   - ★★ a) Describe Christopher's reaction to the advertisements he sees on his trip to London. What could be the reasons for his behaviour?
   - ★★ b) What is your reaction when you see a lot of advertising? When does it catch your eye?
   - ★★ c) Find out what the letters "AIDA" stand for.
   - ★★ d) Find good/bad advertisements for children on the Internet, in newspapers, magazines etc. How do they affect children?
   - ★★★ e) What can you do as an early-childhood teacher to deal with this issue in the nursery school?
   - ★★★ f) What can you do as a youth worker to deal with this issue in the youth centre?

Work with me ISBN 978-3-582-77856-7

While-Reading Activities (Chapter 229–End):
Going Back to Swindon

★★ 1. **Role Play: Breaking up**
KMK
The night before Christopher and his mother leave, Christopher's mother has a row with Mr Shears. Act out their arguments in a role play. Practice it and perform it to the class.

2. **Working with the Book: The Father-Son-Project**
- ★★ a) Why does Christopher not want to live with his father?
- ★★ b) Why does the father want to start this Father-Son-Project?
- ★★ c) What does he bring for Christopher at the start? Why is that a good idea?
- ★★★ d) Help Christopher's father in planning the Father-Son-Project. What can they do together?

★★ 3. **Working with the Book: Christopher the Mathematical Genius**
- a) Why can Christopher still do his maths A-Level?
- b) How does he feel about it?
- c) What does he want to do after he passes his maths A-Level?

★★ 4. **Internet Research**
Do you think a person with Asperger's Syndrome can become a scientist? Find out about people who are successful even though they have a handicap or a disorder.

Post-Reading Activities:
"The Curious Incident of the Dog in the Night-Time"

Group Work: Reflection

★ 1. Do you like the ending of the book? Use the smilies from the beginning to state your opinion.

★★ 2. Show Christopher's development during this story. Create a new poster of Christopher and compare it to the one you did at the beginning.

★★ 3. Does the ending match your expectations? Make a list of your expectations and compare it to the ending of the book.

★★★ 4. Write a review of this book.

★★★ 5. Write a letter to
- Christopher's mother,
- Christopher's father

… and tell them how you feel about their behaviour during the story.

★★★ 6. **Role Play**
Talk Show "My Neighbour Ran Away with My Husband"

Situation: imagine American talk show host Oprah Winfrey inviting the characters of this book to her show because she wants to discuss difficult relationships.

You are …
- Mrs Shears
- Mr Shears
- Christopher's father
- Christopher's mother

Prepare yourself for the show and explain your view of the situation.

★★★★ 7. **Group Work: What If …?**
KMK
Imagine what might have happened if the characters had behaved differently to how they did in the book. Rewrite the story:
- What if Mrs Shears had continued her affair with Christopher's father?
- What if Christopher had stayed at home?
- What if Christopher's mother had returned from London while Christopher was investigating the murder?
- What if Christopher had gotten lost during his trip to London?
- What if Christopher had never found the letters?
- (…)

Present your new story to the class.

VOCABULARY Literature Project

Introduction/Info 1		
(to) access sth.	['ækses]	Zugang zu etw. haben
curious	['kjʊərɪəs]	neugierig, hier: ungewöhnlich, merkwürdig
incident	['ɪntsɪdənt]	Vorfall
plot-outline	[plɒt 'aʊtlaɪn]	Handlungsumriss
key elements	[kɪː 'elɪməntz]	Schlüsselelemente
Text 1: How to Create a Story		
(to) hook	[hʊk]	hier: fesseln, auf sich ziehen
blueprints	['bluːprɪntz]	Blaupause; hier: Entwurf
primer	['praɪmər]	Grundierung; hier: Ausgangspunkt
early action	['ɜːli 'ækʃən]	Spannungsbogen
villain	['vɪlən]	Schurke, Ganove
point of the story	[pɔɪnt ɒf ðə 'stɔːri]	Ziel der Geschichte
plot-twist	[plɒt-twɪst]	Wendung in der Handlung
climax	['klaɪmæks]	Höhepunkt
resolution	[ˌrezə'luːʃən]	Lösung
progression	[prə'greʃən]	Fortschritt, Entwicklung
Character Anticipation		
anticipation	[ænˌtɪsɪ'peɪʃən]	Vorannahme, Erwartung
appearance	[ə'pɪərənts]	äußere Erscheinungsform
Christopher – a Portrayal of the Main Character		
in terms of	[ɪn tɜːms ɒf]	im Hinblick auf
implied meanings	[ɪm'plaɪd 'miːnɪŋs]	implizite Bedeutung
non-verbal clues	[ˌnɒn'vɜːbəl kluːz]	nonverbale Hinweise
Asperger's Syndrome		
autism spectrum disorders	['ɔːtɪzəm 'spektrəm dɪ'sɔːdərs]	Bandbreite der autistischen Störungen
variant	['veəriənt]	Variante, Form
repetitive pattern	[rɪ'petətɪv 'pætən]	sich wiederholendes Muster
stereotyped	['stəriətaɪpt]	klischeehaft
appropriate	[ə'prəʊpriət]	angemessen
left to my own devices [coll]	[dɪ'vaɪsəs]	auf mich allein gestellt
know-all	['nəʊɔːl]	Alleswisser
(to) lack	[læk]	fehlen an
reciprocity	[ˌresɪ'prɒsɪti]	Gegenseitigkeit, Austausch
(to) go overboard [coll]	['əʊvəbɔːd]	hier: überstrapazieren
obsession	[əb'seʃən]	Leidenschaft, Manie
(to) tease	[tiːz]	ärgern
(to) emphasise	['empfəsaɪz]	betonen, hervorheben
inquisitive	[ɪn'kwɪzɪtɪv]	wissbegierig
(to) steer	[stɪər]	lenken, steuern
Christopher's Investigation on the Murder of Wellington		
prime suspect	[praɪm sə'spekt]	Hauptverdächtige(r)
trial	[traɪəl]	(jur) Gerichtsverfahren
judge	[dʒʌdʒ]	(jur) Richter
court	[kɔːt]	(jur) Gericht
prosecutor	['prɒsɪkjuːtər]	(jur) Ankläger
lawyer	['lɔːɪər]	Anwalt
(to) charge	[tʃaːdʒ]	anklagen
(to) testify	['testɪfaɪ]	etwas bezeugen
defender	[dɪ'fəndər]	(jur) Verteidiger
The Mysterious Letters		
runaway	['rʌnəweɪ]	jmd. der von zuhause wegläuft
Going Back to Swindon		
row	[raʊ]	Streit

Work with me ISBN 978-3-582-77856-7

Tenses in English – a Quick Summary

Tense		**Watchwords**
Simple Present	describes events which take place day in, day out *We eat at seven.*	regularly, usually, mainly, always
Present Continuous	**1** describes events happening at that very instant *We are eating!* Can you phone back? **2** describes events happening soon *We are eating at seven.* Can you come?	now, at the moment, at present, as I speak today, tonight, tomorrow, on Sunday
Simple Past	describes events which began in the past and are now complete *We ate at seven.*	yesterday, last night, on Sunday
Past Continuous	**1** describes past events which were not complete at a certain time – What were you doing at seven? – At seven? *We were eating.* **2** describes events which were interrupted *We were eating* when the doorbell rang.	when, while, at three o'clock
Present Perfect	**1** describes events in the recent past *We have just eaten*, thank you. We're not hungry. **2** describes past events which have been repeated *We have eaten* at Luigi's many times. **3** describes events which have never happened (so far) *We have never eaten* curry (before, up to now, till now). **4** describes events which began in the past but which are still happening in the present *We have eaten in this restaurant* since 1997.	just, already (BUT NOT ago: We <u>ate</u> a few minutes ago.) often, regularly, frequently since 2008, for many years
Present Perfect Continuous	describes events of long duration which began in the past and which have continued <u>uninterrupted</u> into the present *We have been eating* for three hours. I feel sick.	for the past hour, for weeks, for the last few days, continuously
Past Perfect	describes events which took place BEFORE a <u>more recent event</u> It <u>was</u> eight o' clock. *We had already eaten at seven.*	already, just, never, once, not yet
Past Perfect Continuous	describes a past event of long duration, which took place before a more recent past event interrupted it *We had been eating *for **ten*** minutes when the chef ran out shouting "Don't touch the fish!" *This tense stresses the **length of time** of previous events	for, since
Will-Future	describes a future event about which the speaker makes a clear, emphatic* decision at that very moment Where shall we eat tonight? Mmm … I know! *We'll eat at Luigi's!* Oh no, we won't. *OH YES, *WE WILL!*	
Going-to-Future	describes an event in the future about which a decision has <u>already</u> been made *We are going to eat at Luigi's tonight.* NB: *We are eating at Luigi's tonight* (see above) is easier and more usual. The future distance of an event makes no difference. It is a very common mistake to think that the far-future* needs "will". *We're going to visit Paris *next October.* (Decision already taken) I know! *We'll go to Paris tomorrow!* (Decision made now)	next week, next year, tomorrow

NB = nota bene (lat.), take notice
Continuous = Progressive

Working with Grammar

If you are able to read and understand this, then your knowledge of *basic** English grammar, which you acquired in school, must in general be good. The authors assume that

- you have mastered (for example) rules of word order,
- that you can conjugate common verbs,
- can form adverbs and
- can understand the comparison of adjectives and adverbs etc.

* We define as "basic" any rule which is identical or very close to German grammar, such as the comparison of adjectives.

We feel it is unnecessary, therefore, to revise simple material and in this section you will only find explanations of the **more difficult and advanced grammar** required for good grades or for the test for the "Fachhochschulreife" (FHR). The exercises will provide you with an opportunity to practise these rules and improve your competence.

Exercises:
Exercises are colour-coded according to whether they are easier or harder. The most difficult questions will usually appear as numbers 6, 7, 8. You will find the solutions to the grammar exercises at the end of this book.

Abbreviations:
Ae1 = A Adverbs, exercise 1; De3 = D Gerunds, exercise 3
(A5) = see A Adverbs rule number 5 "The position of adverbs in English" for rule
NB = nota bene (lat.), take notice

Aspects of grammar are listed alphabetically:

Work with me ISBN 978-3-582-77856-7

A Adverbs

1 The following verbs (Zustandsverben) describe a condition and not an activity. Adjectives (NOT adverbs) are used with them.

become – feel – get – keep – look – remain – seem – smell – sound – stay – taste

She speaks quiet**ly**	BUT	She **seems** quiet.
In this garden beans grow **well**	BUT	The beans **taste** good.

2 A few adverbs have the same form as the adjective.

early – far – fast – hard – high – ill – late – long – near

A fast train	The train goes fast.
An early bus	The bus went early.

3 Words whose meaning is changed by the addition of -ly

English	**German**
fair/fairly	gerecht/ziemlich (auch: auf gerechte Weise)
hard/hardly	hart/kaum
high/highly	hoch/sehr
late/lately	spät/neulich
near/nearly	nah/fast

4 Irregular Adverbial Forms
badly – worse – worst
far – farther/further – farthest/furthest
(further im übertragenen Sinn) I have nothing further to say.
(farther nur in Strecken) London is farther (also: further) than Paris from Stuttgart.
much – more – most
well – better – best

5 The position of adverbs in English is less strict than in German, but here are some general rules.

a) Adverbs of time and place usually appear at the end of the sentence.
Time: The pupil arrived **late** …
Place: … and he went to sleep **in the corner**.

b) If there are adverbs of place and time in the same sentence, the adverb carrying the more relevant information is usually placed **at the end**.
(**When** does the Calais ferry sail?) The ferry sails from dock three **at midday**.
(**From which dock** does the Calais ferry sail?) The ferry sails at midday **from dock three**.

c) Adverbs of manner can come at the end of the sentence, at the beginning, after the verb or before the verb!
He came into the room **quietly**. **Quietly** he came into the room.
He came **quietly** into the room. He **quietly** came into the room.

d) But adverbs of manner NEVER appear between the verb and the direct object!
~~She ate slowly the spaghetti.~~ She ate the spaghetti **slowly**.

e) Most adverbs of time and place can also begin sentences.
Time: **Finally** she sat down. **At two o'clock** the film began.
Place: **Nearby** there was a park. **Over the road** there was a café.

But some adverbs NEVER do:	late	early	ever	always
(or only do in poetry:	never	rarely	seldom)	

f) You should put adverbs of frequency (Häufigkeit) after the subject (or after the *auxiliary verb/**the modal verb).

always – never – occasionally – often – seldom – usually

We **always** go to Majorca in the summer.
They *do **occasionally** go to Italy.
I **can **seldom** understand what he says.
We *have **never** been to Greece.
She **may **often** seem depressed.

▶ Exercises

Ae1 VERBS WHICH USE ADJECTIVES, NOT ADVERBS. Decide which adjective you should write in the gap. (A1)

Example: Please turn the light on! It's getting so ____ in here. (____ = dark)

1 She cooked the fish to perfection. It **tasted** ____.
2 I must go to the doctor. I **feel** ____.
3 He must have a problem. He **looks** un____.
4 You should wash the towels. They **smell** ____.
5 He has a bad temper. Be careful how you speak to him. He **gets** ____ very easily.
6 You **seem** ____. Perhaps you should go to bed earlier.
7 The winter weather is not improving. Tomorrow it will **remain** ____.
8 Have you got a sore throat? You **sound** ____.

Ae2 Put the adverbs from the brackets into the correct or best position. (A5)

Example: We are going to the park (today)
➔ Today we are going to the park. OR We are going to the park today.

1 Have you met my brother? (ever)
2 You should do your homework. (carefully)
3 Rapidly she ate her hamburger. (greedily)
4 From which platform does the Munich train leave Hamburg?
– It leaves (from platform 4/at six a.m.)
5 He came into the room, looked around, glanced at his watch and sat down. (finally)
6 I did like the book but the film was boring. (quite, rather)
7 The supervisor welcomed the parent who sat down and read the report she had been given. (silently, carefully)
8 The new boy can speak English but cannot understand if you speak with an accent. (fast, well)

Ae3 Translate these sentences into English with the correct form of the adverb. (A2, A3, A4)

1 Müssen wir sehr viel weiter laufen?
2 Er ist in letzter Zeit krank gewesen.
3 Sie hat kaum vier Stunden geschlafen.
4 Du sprichst zu schnell.
5 Ich war höchst entzückt.
6 Sie waren ziemlich hungrig.
7 Er hat schwer gearbeitet.
8 Sie war *schlecht geeignet, in einem Kindergarten zu arbeiten. (*do not use "badly")

Work with me ISBN 978-3-582-77856-7

B Auxiliaries and Modal Verbs

What do I need them for?
- to build proper sentences
- to express yourself in different tenses (see → **K Verbs in the Past Tenses** on page 204)
- to express more complex meaning and attitudes (Will you help me? vs. Can you help me?)

→ *NB: You will find a table of the most common irregular verbs and their main forms on page 207f.*

Auxiliaries (to be, to have, to do)

1 **To be + Present Participle**

The Present Progressive
I am eating You are going He is seeing

a) The present progressive describes an action which is taking place at that moment.

WATCHWORDS: now, at the moment, presently, as I speak …

I'm on the bus. **I'm going** to the doctor's. (Perhaps overheard on a mobile phone)

b) It also describes a future activity already planned.

WATCHWORDS: soon, tomorrow, next week, on Friday, in a moment …

I can't come and see you. Tomorrow I'm visiting my aunt.

→ *NB*: Other continuous tenses using the verb "to be" are discussed in:
- *future continuous/B12*
- *past continuous K2/K3/K5*

▶ Exercises

Be1 You are on a work-placement in a nursery school observing Peter, a child of three. Write your notes on his activities as they take place.

Example: 9:00 eat/biscuit → He is eating a biscuit.

1 9:15 play/swings
2 9:30 paint/clown
3 9:45 ride/tricycle
4 10:00 drink/milk
5 10:15 argue/Natasha
6 10:30 build/tower/bricks
7 10:45 try/jigsaw/friend
8 11:00 cry/(hurt finger)

Be2 Parents are on the phone, wishing to speak to the nursery school director, but she is very busy. Tomorrow she will also be unavailable. Play the part of the receptionist and explain to English callers why she cannot speak to them.

Example: Kantine/Mittagessen ➔ She is having her lunch in the canteen.

Im Moment …	1	Konferenz (teilnehmen an)
	2	Bein/Kind (verbinden)
	3	Büro/ Eltern (sprechen)
	4	Kind/Krankenhaus (fahren)
Morgen …	5	London (fliegen)
	6	Budget (diskutieren)
	7	Hochschule/über Umweltpädagogik (Vorlesung halten)
	8	kanadische Studenten (empfangen) (Deutschland besuchen)

2 To do + Infinitive

"**Do**" and "**does**" are sometimes used with the infinitive.

a) To stress that an action really takes place.
They are not keen swimmers but they **do** go to the pool sometimes.

b) "**To do**" is always used in questions.
Does she/**Do** they go swimming?

c) "**To do**" is always used in negative statements.
She **doesn't**/They **don't** go swimming very often.

3 The past form "**did**" is also sometimes used with the infinitive.

a) To stress that an activity really took place.
She was not a keen swimmer but she **did** go swimming sometimes.

b) "**Did**" is always used in questions and in negative statements.
Did she go swimming last week? No, she **did**n't go swimming.

➔ *NB:* Short forms can replace the main verb.

Do/did you go swimming?	
Confirmation	**Negation**
Yes, I do.	No, I don't.
Yes, I did.	No, I didn't.

▶ Exercises

Be3 Play the role of a supervisor asking a carer questions (*does/did he …?*) about a child's behaviour.

Example: books (look at, sometimes) ➔ Does he sometimes look at books?

1 play with Michael? (play, ever)
2 toilet? (go, very often)
3 food/other children? (occasionally, steal)
4 violent pictures? (draw, sometimes)
5 much/neighbours? (speak, usually)
6 any marks/bruises? (have, ever)
7 late? (yesterday, arrive)
8 temper? (last week, lose)

Work with me ISBN 978-3-582-77856-7

Be4 Translate this discussion into English. Use "do", "does" and "did" + infinitives.

1 Meinst du, das Kind in der Ecke ist krank?
2 In der Tat sieht das Mädchen sehr traurig aus.
3 Hat sie etwas in der Pause gegessen?
4 Sie hat eine Banane gegessen ...,
5 ... hat aber nichts getrunken.
6 Sie ist heute nicht rechtzeitig angekommen ...
7 ... und ihre Mutter sah wütend aus.
8 Sie macht den Eindruck, nicht sehr froh zu sein.

4 To have + Past Participle (Present Perfect)

a) It is used to describe actions which have just finished ...
I have just eaten.

WATCHWORDS: just, in the last (few) minutes ...

b) ... and actions which began in the past but are **not yet complete**.
You haven't eaten all of your ice-cream!

WATCHWORDS: yet, up to now, so far ...

c) It is used to describe actions which have not happened but which might happen in the future ...
I have never been to New York.
Have you ever been to Chicago? I have not been to New York yet.

d) ... or which have happened and might happen again.
I have only been to New York once.

WATCHWORDS: ever, never, yet, up to now, so far , before, already, often ...

e) It is used to describe events within a time period which, for the speaker, is **not yet complete**.
(said before midday) I have spoken to him this morning. (it is still the morning)
BUT (said after midday) I spoke to him this morning. (morning is past)

WATCHWORDS: today, this afternoon, evening, week, weekend, month, year ...

f) It is used with "**since**" and "**for**" where the **present tense** is used in German.
They haven't spoken **since** 2002. We have lived here **for** ten years.

▶ Exercises

**Be5 As part of your training you have been observing a child in a play group.
From these notes write a report in the present perfect about the girl's behaviour so far:
It is eleven o'clock. Up to now this morning Mathilda …**

Example: do/two jigsaws ➔ Up to now this morning she has done two jigsaws.

- Talk/a lot/neighbours
- Share/biscuits/new boy
- Read/storybook/frequently
- Draw/picture/doll's house
- Play/swings and slide
- Go toilet (negative)
- Help/new boy/write/title
- Have a drink (negative)

Be6 Form sentences in the present perfect from these elements. (* Use the negative.)

1	I/visit/Greece	(up to now, only once)
2	We/eat*	(yet, today)
3	She/meet/new supervisor	(just)
4	I/ make/a mistake*	(so far)
5	She/broke/ three cups	(in the last five minutes)
6	You/see/this film?	(already)
7	They/live/in London	(for six years)
8	You/work/with young people?	(before)

➔ *NB:* The present perfect is practised with other past tenses on page 206.

Modal Verbs

In this section only those aspects of modal verbs which cause learners the most difficulty will be explained. Even good speakers of English make mistakes in these areas. You can really improve but you must pay attention and practise.

1 **Can/Be Able** (können)

a) Can I go out now, Dad? (Erlaubnis – darf ich?)
Yes, you can / No, you can't (cannot).

b) Can you (= are you able to) swim? (Fähigkeit)
Yes, I can / No, I can't.

2 **Could** (konnte)

a) I could run very fast. (Leistung)
b) I was able (I managed) to find a good restaurant. (Ich habe es geschafft.)

NB: ~~**I could find**~~ … Falsch, typischer Fehler!

c) I could **not** run very fast. (im negativen Zusammenhang)
I could **not** find a good restaurant.

Work with me ISBN 978-3-582-77856-7

3 **Could** (könnte)

a) I could run very fast … if … (wenn nur …)

b) I could catch the train. (Das ist nur eine Fahrmöglichkeit.)

4 **Could I?** (in Höflichkeitsfloskeln)
Could I come in? Could you tell me your name?

5 **The Verb in Five Tenses**

Past Perfect	I had (not) been able (to do …)
Present Perfect	I have (not) been able
Simple Past	I was (not) able; I could not
Simple Present	I can/can't/cannot; I am (not) able
Future	I will (not) be able

Note also: could have

I could have come earlier.	Ich hätte früher kommen können.
You could have flown to Stuttgart.	Du hättest nach Stuttgart fliegen können.

▶ Exercises

Be7 O or ö ? Simple past or conditional? Translate these sentences into German.

1 Could you come and listen to Jemima reading?
2 Could she understand the question?
3 Could they perhaps play outside for half-an-hour?
4 How much time could we perhaps spend on the storybook?
5 I couldn't find the magazine I wanted to bring.
6 It could be very cold tomorrow.
7 We managed to find her lunch in the end.
8 She couldn't find a policeman nearby.

Be8 Translate these sentences into English.

1 Ich konnte gestern Andreas überreden (to persuade), einen Satz vorzulesen.
2 Wir könnten vielleicht einen Ausflug zum Zoo machen.
3 Sie war so heiser, sie konnte nicht singen.
4 Konntest du letztendlich das albanische Kind verstehen?
5 Könnten Sie um elf Uhr zu mir kommen?
6 Er konnte endlich das neue Wort aussprechen.

Be9 Put the German translations of these English sentences into the correct order and add the correct form/tense of the missing verbs.

Example: We were able to find an interesting page on the Internet.
Seite Internet interessante wir im eine finden + … ?
➔ Im Internet **konnten** wir eine interessante Seite finden.

1 You could have asked Paul an easier question.
Paul Frage du einfachere stellen eine +…?
2 I was able to find a more colourful storybook.
Geschichte finden buntere ich eine +…?
3 Until we found the instructions we had not been able to understand the game.
das Anweisungen fanden Spiel verstehen die wir bis wir nicht +…?
4 I hope you will be able to read my writing.
Handschrift du hoffentlich meine lesen. +…?
5 She has not been able to eat a thing.
nichts essen gar sie +…?
6 They arrived so late, they weren't able to start until ten.
kamen erst zehn sie so sie um anfangen Uhr spät an +…?
7 Because you were naughty you can't go into the playground.
wart Spielplatz unartig ihr den weil auf gehen nicht +…?
8 If only we could buy a new TV set!
Nur einen kaufen Fernseher wir neuen wenn! +…?

6 Must/Have (got) to

a) I **must** go to the doctor's tomorrow!	(Entschluss)
I **have** (got) **to** go to the doctor's tomorrow.	(neutral; bin schon verabredet. Es kann aber auch betont werden: "I **have got to** go!")
b) You **must** not smoke.	(Es ist hier verboten.)
You **do not have/have not got to** smoke.	(Du kannst aufgeben, kannst wählen.)
c) You **do not have/have not got to** wear a tie.	(Du brauchst nicht; ohne Krawatte ist okay)
d) **Must** you smoke?	(Ton: Das ärgert mich. Ist es absolut nötig?)
Do you have/Have you got to smoke?	(Ton: wie oben, aber auch: Bist du so schwach?)

7 The Verb in Five Tenses

Past Perfect	I had (not) had to (work)
Present Perfect	I have (not) had to
Simple Past	I had to/I had got to
Simple Past negative	I did not have to/I had not got to
Simple Present	I must/I have to/I have got to
Simple Present negative	I must not/I do not have to/I have not got to
Future	I will have to

Work with me ISBN 978-3-582-77856-7

▶ Exercise

Be10 MÜSSEN. Make up sentences. Use these elements and the tense shown in brackets.
Any ~~verbs~~ should be written in the negative.

Example: you/~~let~~/Paul/climbing frame (present simple)
➔ You must not let Paul (play) on the climbing frame.

1	as part of our training/we/do/outward-bound course	(past simple)
2	she/contact/police	(present perfect)
3	the mother/explain/burn/on child	(future)
4	until Sanghita arrived from London/we/~~speak~~/any English/nursery	(past perfect)
5	the Indian girl/~~eat~~/any chicken soup/(vegetarian)!	(present simple)
6	I was so glad/I ~~speak~~/to that difficult parent!	(past simple)
7	We/tell/Jemima/today/about shouting	(present perfect)
8	I/contact/parent!/Little Peter/go/hospital	(present simple 2×)

8 May (altmodisch; begrenzt)

a) May I/we come in? (als Frage nur erste Person; sehr höflich)
(Antwort z. B.: Of course you may! Please do.)

b) No, you may not. (du darfst nicht; sehr streng)

c) I/he/she/we/they may come. (altmodisch: es kann sein, dass (er) kommt)

9 Might (ersetzt häufig "may")

She might not go on holiday this year. She might stay at home. (es ist möglich)

10 Should/Ought to

a) You should/ought to do your homework. (Ratschlag)

b) People should not eat/ought not to eat wild mushrooms. (Warnung)

Note also: should have
You should have been/ought to have been here at nine o'clock.
(Rüge; Du hättest um neun Uhr hier sein sollen!)

NB: "May", "might", "should" and "ought to" do not have other tense forms.
They are only used with these constructions:

With the infinitive	He may/might/should go/ought to **go**.
With to be + present participle	He may **be going**.
With to have + past participle	He may **have gone**.
With the present perfect progressive	He may **have been going**.

Work with me ISBN 978-3-582-77856-7

11 Is Supposed/Was Supposed

Supposed only has these two tense forms.

a) I am (was) supposed to wash the dishes and clean up.	(Aufgaben, die ich machen soll/sollte)
b) You are supposed to be the manager!	(ironisch, stellt Kompetenz des Gegenübers infrage)
He is supposed to be a good cook.	(neutral, kann aber auch ironisch sein)

▶ Exercise

Be11 MAY/MIGHT/SHOULD/SUPPOSED. Translate into German.

1 You are supposed to wash up today!
2 We should play outside now as it will rain later.
3 Jodie might not come tomorrow.
4 She might have caught a cold.
5 May I ask you a personal question?
6 Sebastian, you ought to let others play on the swing.
7 Katrina was supposed to go home with her father.
8 You should not have left the children unsupervised in the playground.

12 Will

Will has no other tense forms. It is often used in short form: 'll

• It is used with the infinitive to form **Future I**:	I will/won't go
• It is used with "be"+ present participle to form the **Future Progressive**:	I will be going
• It is used with the present perfect to form **Future II**:	I will have gone

a) I will/I'll see you on Saturday!	(Bestätigung einer Verabredung)
There will be a quiz next Tuesday.	(Bestätigung einer Veranstaltung)
b) She will (probably, surely etc.) be a star!	(Erwartung, Vorhersage)
c) In three years you will be earning a lot more.	(Versprechen)
d) I will learn proper English!	(betont, Vorsatz)
e) I will not/won't go!	(eigenwillig, Verweigerung)
f) You will not/won't go!	(als Verbot)

13 Shall

Shall has no other tense forms. It is only used to form **future tenses** but is used less often than "**will**". It does however have some very special uses:

a) Shall I?	(only in the first person singular)
Shall I open the window? Shall I close the door?	(sucht Zustimmung)
b) Shall we?	(only in the first person plural)
Shall we go home? Shall we get a takeaway?	(Vorschlag)
c) We shall never give in.	(rhetorisch; absolute Entschlossenheit)
They shall not pass.	
We shall overcome!	

Work with me ISBN 978-3-582-77856-7

14 Would (würde)

Would has no other tense forms. It is used (like the German "würde") to form the conditional.

I would not go.	Ich würde nicht hingehen.
I would not have gone.	Ich wäre nicht hingegangen.

15 Want (wollen)

The verb in five tenses	
Past Perfect	I had (not) wanted (to eat …)
Present Perfect	I have (not) wanted
Simple Past	I wanted/did not want
Simple Present	I want/I do not want*
Future	I will (not) want

*__NB__, falsch: ~~I want not~~

▶ Exercise

Be12 Role Play. An early-years teacher [A] is making suggestions to an unhappy child [B] and trying to get him/her to engage with an activity. Work with a partner.

A Shall we …?

Schaukeln 1	Bild malen 2	Geschichte lesen 3	Glas Milch trinken 4
KEKS ESSEN 5	Lied singen 6	Rutschen 7	Kuchen backen 8

B No, I don't want to …, I want to …

Spazieren gehen 1	Knetfigur basteln 2	Schlafen 3	Spiel spielen 4
Tanzen 5	Fernsehen 6	CD anhören 7	Heimgehen 8

C Comparisons

In this section only the more difficult aspects of comparisons are explained.

1 Irregular and More Difficult Forms of Comparative Adjectives (Steigerungsformen)

good – better – best	
bad (ill) – worse – worst	(krank)
much – more – most many – more – most	+ singular (much money etc.) + plural (many people etc.)
little – less – least few – fewer – fewest	+ singular (little money/wenig Geld) + plural (few people/wenige Leute)
old – older – oldest – elder – eldest	bei Verwandtschaft (my elder brother)
far – farther – farthest – further – furthest	(bei Strecken) übertragen, aber auch Strecken
near – nearer – nearest next	räumlich (The nearest petrol station is in Burbage.) Reihenfolge (Stop at the next garage!)

2 The … the … (je mehr … desto)
The more you speak the better your English will be.

3 More and more (immer mehr)
He gets louder and louder and his behaviour gets worse and worse.
He finds it more and more difficult to make friends.

▶ Exercise

Ce1 Translate the following sentences into English, using the correct forms of C1.

1. Meine ältere Schwester ist ein Jahr älter als mein Bruder.
2. Es waren heute weniger Kinder im Kindergarten als gestern.
3. Du solltest weniger Farbe und mehr Wasser anwenden. *(to use)*
4. Sophie liest am wenigsten.
5. Der nächste Jugendklub ist in Elmshorn. Die nächste Disko dort findet morgen statt.
6. Jetzt siehst du noch kränker aus und du hast so wenig gegessen.

Work with me ISBN 978-3-582-77856-7

D Gerunds

The gerund is a substantive formed from a verb. Of course the German language uses the infinitive to create nouns but English gerunds always end with -ing.
Danc**ing** is stupid! Tanz**en** ist doof!

1 Gerunds can be used stylishly with the verbs below as direct objects in sentences where clauses often have to be used in German.

Verbs:
(to) admit, avoid, begin, carry on, continue, deny, (dis)like, enjoy,
feel like, finish, give up, go on, hate, imagine, keep, mention, mind (missbilligen),
miss, practise, prefer, remember, risk, start, stop, suggest, try

He denied **eating** the cake. — Er leugnete, dass er den Kuchen gegessen hatte.
She admitted **stealing** the purse. — Sie gab zu, sie habe das Portemonnaie gestohlen.

▶ Exercise

De1 GROUP OR PAIR WORK. Take turns to make up sentences using (some of) the verbs and gerunds above. Score a point for every good one. Who can make up the funniest or strangest sentence?

Examples: I like swimming. — Well, I like listening to music.
I gave up smoking. — My dog hates smoking. He prefers biting postmen.

2 After verbs with prepositions English can use a gerund where German must use a noun or clause.

Verbs with prepositions:
(to) agree with, apologize for, believe in, blame (tadeln) for, dream about,
insist (bestehen) on, look forward to, object (dagegen sein) to, prevent from,
protect from, succeed in, talk about, thank for, think about/of, worry about

I look forward to our **meeting** again. — Ich freue mich auf unser **nächstes Treffen**.
I apologize for **coming** late. — Entschuldige, **dass ich zu spät komme**.

Work with me ISBN 978-3-582-77856-7

▶ Exercise

De2 COMPLETING SENTENCES. From the list of D2 choose suitable verbs, put them into any tense and combine them with these ideas.

Example: breaking the glass! ➔ I (must) apologize for breaking the glass!

1 being a millionaire
2 talking to the supervisor
3 finding the purse
4 going on holiday
5 paying the bill
6 me … the child falling off the swing. So unfair!
7 passing the test
8 you talking to me so impolitely!

3 To be + Adjective + Preposition + Gerund
I am good at painting.

Adjectives:
afraid of, bad at, famous for, fond of (mögen), interested in, keen on (sehr interessiert an), sorry about, sick of, tired of, used to, worried about

4 To have + Noun + Preposition + Gerund
She has a good chance of winning (a prize).

Nouns:
difficulty in, an interest in, pleasure in, a problem with, a reason for, a way of

Note also: to take advantage of her **being** away (Vorteil ziehen aus)
to take an interest in **drawing**
to take pleasure in **chatting** online

▶ Exercise

De3 YOUR PROFILES. Divide the adjectives in D3 into two columns, positive and negative. Write a sentence for each and pass your papers around the class (do not write your name on them). Take turns in reading them out aloud. Can the class guess who is who?

Example:

POSITIVE	NEGATIVE
I am famous for liking pizza.	I am afraid of touching spiders.

5 Prepositional phrases with **gerunds** are often translated into German …

a) by a clause

Prepositions:
apart from, by, in spite of, instead of, since (seit), without

By **singing** English songs the children were learning lots of new words.
Indem sie englische Lieder sangen, lernten die Kinder viele neue Wörter.

In spite of **eating** the whole cake he's still hungry.
Trotzdem/Obwohl er den ganzen Kuchen gegessen hat, hat er noch Hunger.

Work with me ISBN 978-3-582-77856-7

Apart from/Except for **saying** hello she did not speak
Außer dass sie Guten Tag gesagt hat, hat sie nicht gesprochen.

Since **living** in England I have drunk a lot of tea.
Seitdem ich in England lebe, trinke ich viel Tee.

b) by an infinitive construction
Instead of **painting** she sat and sulked. — Anstatt zu malen, saß sie und schmollte.
Without **speaking** we left the room. — Ohne zu sprechen, gingen wir aus dem Zimmer.

▶ Exercise

De4 Put the English translations of these German sentences into the correct order and add the missing gerund.

Example: Obwohl sie in London studiert hat, ist ihr Englisch nicht sehr gut.
not very good/in spite of/her English/in London/is
➔ In spite of **studying** in London her English is not very good.

1 Obwohl er fleißig arbeitete, fiel er durch.
hard/he/despite/failed

2 Indem sie gut aufpasste, lernte sie das Spiel schnell.
learnt/close attention/soon/she/by/the/game

3 Außer einem Gesicht zu zeichnen machte der Junge heute nichts.
a face/apart from/did nothing/the boy/today

4 Ohne ein Wort zu sagen, ging sie aus dem Zimmer.
went/room/without/a word/out of/she

5 Du hättest die rote Farbe und nicht die gelbe nehmen sollen.
the yellow/should have used/the red paint/you/instead of

6 Seitdem er Englisch gelernt hat, macht er mehr mit.
joins in/English/he/more

7 Die Mutter ist verschwunden, ohne die Gebühr zu zahlen.
the fee/disappeared/the mother/without

8 Du solltest mitmachen, statt bloß hier in der Ecke zu sitzen!
just/corner/join in/here/should/instead of/you/in the corner

Work with me ISBN 978-3-582-77856-7

E If-Clauses

The tense of the <u>if-clause</u> decides the tense of the main clause.

1 Present – Future I
(betrifft Ergebnisse eines möglichen Ereignisses, die wahrscheinlich/bestimmt sind)

A –	B	
If she **comes** today,	I **will be** surprised.	
If you **eat** too much,	you **will feel** sick.	(passiert A, wird dann B höchstwahrscheinlich die Folge sein)

However there are situations where the tenses of the if-clause and the main clause are **present – present**:

a) If (ever) she **eats** chocolate, she **becomes** hyperactive.
If (ever) I **say** "stop", you **must**. (anhaltende Situationen)
TEST: „**when**" kann „**if**" ersetzen

> **BUT:** If you ever do that again, I **will** tell your mother!! (Warnung)
> TEST: „**when**" kann „**if**" hier nicht ersetzen

b) Can – Can
If you **can** behave well for one day, then you **can** behave every day!
If I (**can**) pass my exams, I **can** get a good job.

c) If – Might
If you eat too much, you **might** get fat (weniger sicher)
If you smoke, you **might** get cancer.

▶ EXERCISE

Ee1 Complete these sentences using the correct tense of the verbs from the box and the words in brackets. (~~Verbs~~ should be used in the negative.) You do not need two of the verbs.

VERBS: ~~understand~~ – agree – play – phone – paint – affect – come – be – get – listen

1	If ever he does a picture, he	(house)
2	If you don't stop shouting, I	(father!)
3	If we can clear the glass from the swings, we	(outside)
4	If you don't listen now, you	(story)
5	If you touch the socket (Steckdose), you	(shock)
6	If ever I feel depressed,I	(music)
7	If kids watch too much TV, it	(their play)
8	If I say "don't scream", you	(quiet!)

2 Simple Past – Conditional I (betrifft Bedingungen, die eher unwahrscheinlich sind)

A –	B
If she **came** today,	I **would be** surprised.
If you **ate** too much,	you **would feel** sick. (passierte A, dann würde wohl B das Ergebnis sein)

Work with me ISBN 978-3-582-77856-7

Note also: simple past – might
If you **stopped** talking, you **might** hear me. (oft ironisch gemeint)

Note also: simple past – could
If we **went** to the park, we **could play** on the swings! (Vorschlag)

Note also: could – could (ö – ö)
A – B
If she **could** learn her lines, she **could** be in the play. (B hängt direkt von A ab. B ist aber nicht ganz sicher, auch wenn A passiert.)
BUT: If she **could** learn her lines, she **would** be in the play. (Wenn A geschähe, dann wäre B bestimmt der Fall.)

▶ Exercise

Ee2 Complete these sentences using the correct tense of the verbs from the box and the words in brackets. (~~Verbs~~ should be used in the negative.) You do not need two of the verbs.

VERBS: have – ~~dislike~~ – work – hang – arrive – go – see – call – ~~get~~ – understand

1 If I knew his number, I
2 If she could speak better English, she (London)
3 If we bought some cake and balloons, we (party!)
4 If Joshua finished his picture, I (wall)
5 If you listened, you (confused)
6 If we ate early, we (cinema!)
7 If you didn't keep hitting them, the others
8 If the mother came in, she (how Scarlet behaves)

3 **Past Perfect – Conditional II** (betrifft frühere Bedingungen, die jetzt unerfüllbar sind)
If she **had come** today, I **would have been** surprised. (Sie ist nicht gekommen, kein Wunder!)
If you **had eaten** too much, you **would have felt** sick. (Du warst vernünftig, hast nicht zu viel gegessen.)

▶ Exercise

Ee3 CHANGING TENSES. Make the sentences in Ee2 into past perfect – conditional II.

Work with me ISBN 978-3-582-77856-7

F Infinitive Constructions

English uses infinitive constructions where German uses a clause.

1 Verb + Pronoun/Noun + Infinitive

I want him/Paul to listen. (Ich will, dass er/Paul aufpasst.)

This pattern is used with these verbs:
(to) advise, allow, arrange for (abmachen), ask, cause, count on (rechnen mit/sich verlassen auf), enable (befähigen), encourage, expect, force (zwingen), get s. o.(hier: jem. veranlassen), help, invite, like, love, make s. o. (jem. zwingen), persuade (überreden), prefer, remind (erinnern), rely on, show … how (zeigen … wie) teach, tell, wait for, want, warn

▶ Exercise

Fe1 GROUP WORK. Make suggestions how to solve Vanessa's problems at the nursery, using verbs from the list above. Use these nouns: other children – Vanessa – her parents – her neighbour – the assistant (~~Verbs~~ should be made negative.)

Example: her breath smells (~~tease~~, clean) ➔ WE SHOULD **tell** the other children <u>not</u> to tease her and **help** her/**show** her **how** to clean her teeth (properly).

1 her hair is often dirty (wash)
2 she stole Paul's sandwich and hid it (~~steal~~, find)
3 she needs help with her laces (tie)
4 she spoilt Tim's painting (respect)
5 she threw a book at Jenny (~~throw~~, be kind)
6 she is often very sleepy (lie down)
7 she can't cut up paper (hold scissors)
8 her mother doesn't believe she misbehaves (come in, watch)

2 To be + <u>Adjective + Preposition</u> + Pronoun/Noun + Infinitive

It was <u>nice of</u> her/Libby to help.

Adjectives with prepositions:
clever of, crazy of, cruel of (grausam), dangerous for, easy for, difficult for, good of, important for, naughty of (unartig), necessary for, nice of, normal for, possible for, sensible of (vernünftig), silly of, stupid of, tactful of, tactless of, useful for, (un)usual for, (un)wise of

▶ Exercise

Fe2 Today Jamie has done some good things and some naughty things. Use praise (!) to encourage his good behaviour and criticism (x) to change his bad behaviour. Try to use a different adjective in every case.

Example: to wash up (!) ➔ It was (so/really/very) nice of you to wash up, Jamie! Good boy!

1 slap your neighbour (x)
2 pay more attention than normal (!)
3 help Lisa mix the paint (!)
4 throw clay at Connor (x)
5 look for Amy's shoe (!)
6 shout so loud? (x)
7 listen to Harriet read (!)
8 break Callum's mug (x)
9 work out the right answer (!)
10 mention Bryony's dead rabbit (x)

Work with me ISBN 978-3-582-77856-7

3	Noun + Preposition + Pronoun/Noun + Infinitive		
(It is) a chance	for	her/Kay	to improve.

Nouns with prepositions:
a chance for, an idea for, a mistake for, an opportunity for, a time for

▶ Exercise

Fe3 GROUP WORK. How many sentences can you make up from these patterns? Which group can invent the most?

- Carola is going to London. It will be a chance for her to …
- Harry is lazy. It is time for him to …
- Wayne has just come out of prison. It would be a mistake for him to …
- –2 °C! Today it is too cold for us to …
- The hall in the new club is enormous! It is big enough for us to …
- We're off camping in the mountains. It will be a wonderful opportunity for us to ...
- Roswitha has got a work placement in an American kindergarten. What a marvellous chance for her …

4	Too/Enough + Adjective/Adverb	+ Preposition	+ Pronoun/Noun	+ Infinitive
The writing is	too small	for	us	to see.
Am I speaking	loud enough	for	you	to hear?

▶ Exercises

Fe4 Decide which adjectives and infinitives are missing in these sentences. Variants are possible.

Example: This crossword is too ___ for me ___ ➔ This crossword is too difficult for me to do/to complete.

1. Raining again! Now it's far too ___ for us ___ tennis.
2. This soup is much too ___ for the children ___ yet. Let it cool down for 5 minutes.
3. Is my diagram ___ enough for people at the back of the room ___ clearly?
4. The mother is not ___ enough ___ that pram. She has been ill recently.
5. One biscuit at break is too ___ for Sunita ___ full. So she steals food from her friends.
6. Six o'clock is far too ___ for me ___. So I'm staying in bed till seven!
7. Your poor old car is not ___ enough ___ us as far as Berlin.
8. Simon is boring. He talks about himself and his own interests far too ___ for me ___ him.

Fe5 MIME GAME. In pairs – or better – in groups try to mime an adjectival/infinitive phrase for your partner(s) to guess. For example, too hot to handle could be mimed by juggling something and looking as if it is burning your hands. Before you begin, as a practice, see who can do the best mimes for these phrases.

1 too cold to go out – 2 too small to see – 3 too much to eat – 4 too hard to understand

G Participle Constructions

The Past Participle

➔ *(see page 207f. for list of irregular verbs)*

1 A past participle can sometimes be used like an adjective to replace one of two sentences, or one of two main clauses joined by "and". The participle must describe the first direct object.

It upset him. He closed the door.
It upset him AND (so) he closed the door. ➔ **Upset**, he closed the door.

2 A construction with a past participle can replace a subordinate clause whose direct object is the subject in the main clause. This is only possible with conjunctions "**but**", "**if**", "**when**" …

a) in the past tense

A	B
When I asked the new boy to be quiet,	he began to cry.
➔ (When) **Asked** to be quiet,	the new boy began to cry.

b) also in the present tense (notice the second verb must stay in the present tense)

A	B
When/If I tell the new girl to take her coat off,	she refuses.
➔ (When/If) **Told** to take her coat off,	the new girl refuses.

You can improve your style by using a participle construction instead of a clause.
It is used in formal English, for example in reports. It is safest for you to use it with these **"communication" verbs:**
(to) ask, interrogate, question, remind, shout at, tell, tell off, warn

➔ ***NB:*** *In the above examples "upset", "asked" and "told" are in the* ***passive voice****.*
The passive is explained in detail on page 199.

▶ EXERCISE

Ge1 Change the underlined clause into a past participle construction.

1 The story was so depressing and I closed the book.
2 If I tell the children off, they just laugh.
3 Whenever Paula asks the mother about her son's diet she gets angry.
4 If I warn Amy about taking her neighbour's crayon, she usually listens.
5 If you shout at small children, they will only be scared.
6 When we asked Tony why he was crying, he blamed Kirsty.
7 I questioned Lisa about the bruise but she refused to answer.
8 The assistant reminded Harry about washing his hands but he was rude (unhöflich) to her.

Work with me ISBN 978-3-582-77856-7

The Present Participle

Like a gerund, a present participle always ends with -ing. **But** it is a part of the verb and **never** a substantive.

1 It can replace "**and**" in simple sentences. The subject in both clauses must be the same.
She sits **and** draws elephants. → She sits **drawing** elephants.

2 It can stylishly replace subordinate clauses introduced by these prepositions:

after*** – before** – when** – while** – as* – because* – since* *(da, weil)*

****may be left out of the new sentence*
***must be kept in*
** must be left out*

As she came late she missed the story. → **Coming** late, she missed the story.
Before you go out to play can you please tidy up! → Before **going** out to play please tidy up!

Note also: negative expressions
As she did **not** come late she did not miss the story. → **Not coming** late, she did not miss the story.

▶ Exercise

Ge2 Translate these clauses, using present participles, and match them to the suitable English main clauses mixed up on the right. (There are two more than you need.)

1 Wenn er mit einem Kind spricht	... he suddenly starts to cry.
2 ..., weil er farbenblind ist.	... he laughed and ran to her.
3 Nachdem er drei Äpfel gegessen hat, ...	... he cannot buy a watch.
4 Während er dem Märchen zuhörte, ...	... he has painted his tree red.
5 Bevor er den Vater anrief, ...	... he should have someone with him.
6 Da er keine Uhr hatte, ...	... he fell asleep.
7 Als er seine Mutter sah, ...	... he was late for the interview.
8 Als er sich hinsetzt, ...	... he asked me if I knew his name.
	... he got stomach ache.
	... he telephoned the father.

3 Present participles can replace relative clauses (who, which, that).
I heard Libby **who was talking to Andrew**. (This is bad English!)
→ I heard Libby **talking to Andrew**. (This is stylish.)

▶ Exercise

Ge3 Imagine you have been observing different children's behaviour in the nursery as part of your training. Make up sentences like the one above with "I watched" or "I heard" and think of a suitable verb to use.

Example: Callum/jigsaw → I watched Callum **doing** a jigsaw.

1 Sean/picture	2 Bethan/song	3 Amy/slide
4 Colin/argument/Tim	5 Emma/laces	6 Wayne/ball
7 Beverley/cake	8 Kerry/birthday present	

4 Present participle + past participle (or perfect participle)

This is a stylish, very formal construction used in written English.

a) It can replace a sentence which has a clear link to the next one.
He used to be a youth worker. He understood the child's point of view.
→ **Having been a youth worker** he understood the child's point of view.

b) It also replaces the first of two clauses linked by "**and**".
She had seen many cases of abuse and could recognise the signs.
→ **Having seen many cases of abuse** she could recognise the signs.

c) It can also replace an **after-clause**.
After the mother had looked round the nursery she enrolled *(anmelden)* her child.
→ **Having looked around** (= **After looking around) the nursery** the mother enrolled her child.

▶ Exercises

Ge4 Make up sentences using two elements. The first element should be a present participle + past participle construction.

Example: **to eat** to pay the bill (I) → **Having eaten** I paid the bill.

1	to break the window	to run away	(the boys)
2	to work in Manchester	to speak English with a northern accent	(Pia)
3	to call the police	to wait in her office	(the supervisor)
4	to walk back from the zoo	to be very tired	(the children)
5	to read the report	to become very angry	(the father)
6	to lose the map	not to find the youth hostel	(we)
7	hot drink	bed	(they)
8	tin opener	soup	(I)

Ge5 Change these sentences into their original form, using conjunctions not participles.

Example: **Seeing** that Paul was upset I went over to him. → **As soon as I saw** that Paul was upset I went over to him.

1 **Hearing** a child **screaming** she ran outside.
2 While **playing** on the swings Bethan began to choke (würgen).
3 He came into the room **singing**.
4 I heard a car **driving** off.
5 Very **frightened** by the noise, I locked the door.
6 **Warned** (by me) to be careful **crossing** the road Harry stopped **chattering**.
7 **Having spent** three years in Birmingham I knew the city quite well.
8 **Not having tasted** pasta before Jemimah was a little nervous.

Work with me ISBN 978-3-582-77856-7

H The Passive Voice

Here is a list of the main tenses, active and passive, of a very common verb, (to) cook.

Active		Passive
I had cooked (it) subject object	**Past Perfect**	(It) had been cooked (by me) new subject agent
I have cooked	**Present Perfect**	has been cooked
I cooked	**Simple Past**	was cooked
I was cooking	**Past Perfect Continuous**	was being cooked
I cook	**Simple Present**	is cooked
I am cooking	**Present Continuous**	is being cooked
I will cook	**Future I**	will be cooked
I will have cooked	**Future II**	will have been cooked
I would cook	**Conditional I**	would be cooked
I would have cooked	**Conditional II**	would have been cooked

Active		→ Passive	
subject +	object	→ new subject +	agent

▶ Exercises

He1 Make these passive sentences active and bring in a suitable subject.

Example: The broken glass was cleared up → **The cleaner** cleared the broken glass up.

1 The injured child will be seen soon.
2 Joanne was collected at 3 p.m. and taken home.
3 Gary was being bullied at school.
4 I had been told that my car would be repaired by 5 p.m.!
5 The letter is just being typed.
6 The football hooligans were arrested.
7 The nursery kitchen is frequently checked to make sure it has been cleaned.
8 Little Sasha has been stung.

He2 AN ACT OF VANDALISM. Youths have broken into the youth club and vandalised it. Here is a list of the damage they caused. Make it into an official report in the passive voice.

Example: Youths broke into the youth club. → The youth club **was broken** into. (no agent needed)

1 They smashed five large windows.
2 They took all the basketballs.
3 They ruined some display work.
4 They wrote graffiti on a wall.
5 They made a hole in a wall.
6 They tore up bushes in the garden.
7 They ripped the fabric in a sofa.
8 They pulled out the TV cable.

He3 THE GOOD NEWS! The damage will be put right.
Using the verbs from the box, say in the passive what action will be/will have been taken by the time the club is reopened. (Two verbs are not needed.)

Example: They did a lot of damage. → The damage **will be put right/will have been put right** when the club reopens.

(to) fill in – mend – paint over – reconnect – redo – replace – replant – sew – tie – wash up

I Reflexive Verbs, Reflexive Pronouns and Reciprocal Pronouns

a) These verbs are not reflexive in English but are reflexive in German:

(to) apologise	sich entschuldigen	hide	sich verstecken
open	sich öffnen	argue	sich streiten
hurry	sich beeilen	refer to	sich beziehen auf
change	sich ändern	imagine	sich vorstellen
refuse	sich weigern	complain	sich beklagen
join	sich anschließen, sich zusammenschließen	relax	sich entspannen
differ from	sich unterschieden	lie down	sich hinlegen
remember	sich erinnern	feel	sich fühlen
meet	sich treffen	wonder	sich fragen
happen	sich ereignen	move	sich bewegen
worry	sich Sorgen machen		

b) If these verbs add a reflexive pronoun, they change their meaning:

(to) apply	sich bewerben um	apply oneself	sich anstrengen
control	kontrollieren	control oneself	sich beherrschen
help	helfen	help oneself	sich bedienen
occupy	besetzen	occupy oneself	sich beschäftigen

c) These are used when the subject and object of the verb are **the same**.

Reflexive pronouns:
myself – yourself – himself – herself – (oneself) – ourselves – yourselves – themselves

d) These are used when **different** people are the objects of the verb.

Reciprocal pronouns: each other – one another

Paula and Paul love each other.

Paula and Paul love themselves.

e) Emphasis (Betonung)
Where German uses "selbst"/"selber", English uses reflexive pronouns.
Carla tied her shoelaces **herself**. We worked out a route **ourselves**.

▶ Exercise

Ie1 GROUP WORK. Make up a fairy story to include all the verbs from the table in a). Then act the story out, with a narrator, for other groups.

Work with me ISBN 978-3-582-77856-7

J Reported Speech

a) The verb of direct speech usually* changes tense in reported (indirect) speech.

DIRECT	INDIRECT
Present "I am ill."	**→ Past** He said, he was ill.
Simple Past "I was ill."	**→ Simple Past/Past Perfect*** He said, he *was ill / had been ill.
Present Perfect "I have been ill."	**→ Past Perfect** He said, he had been ill.
Future 1 "I will be ill."	**→ Conditional I** He said, he would be ill.

***Note also:**
If the quotation verb ("to say", "to answer" …) is in the **present tense** and the direct speech is also **present tense**, then the indirect speech verb **stays in the present**.
After lunch Pat always **says**, "I **am** tired" → After lunch Pat always **says** he **is** tired.

b) Reporting Instructions (Befehle)
To **tell** + direct object + **infinitive**
"Michael, behave yourself!" I said. → I **told** Michael **to behave himself**.

Note also: negative instructions
"Michael, do not touch the kettle!" I said. → I **told** Michael **not to touch** the kettle.

c) When questions are reported, the verb goes at the end of the sentence.
"What is your name?" I asked. → I asked him what his name was.

d) If there is no question word then "**if**" or "**whether**" are used.
"Are you tired, Patrick?" I asked. → I asked Patrick **whether** he was tired.

e) The auxiliaries "**do/does/did**" must be left out in reported speech.
"**Do** you want to lie down?" → I asked him if he wanted to lie down. (~~**DO**~~)

f) Adverbial Changes in Reported Speech

DIRECT	INDIRECT
ago	→ before, previously
here	→ there
last (year)	→ the previous (year), the (year) before
next (week)	→ the following (week)
now	→ then
this	→ that
today	→ that day
tomorrow	→ the next day
yesterday	→ the previous day/the day before

Work with me ISBN 978-3-582-77856-7

g) Quotation Verbs
These verbs can be used with direct speech and can be followed by "**that**" to report speech. To improve your style try to use these less common verbs, rather than just "**to say**", "**to answer**" or "**to ask**"!

DIRECT	INDIRECT
"And I can speak French," she added.	➔ She added that she could also speak French.

Quotation Verbs

(to) acknow-ledge	zugeben	explain	erklären	think	meinen
add	hinzufügen	insist	bestehen auf	suggest	vorschlagen
admit	zugeben	joke	scherzen	stress	(etw.) betonen
advise	(jem.) raten	maintain	behaupten	demand (of)	verlangen
announce	bekannt-geben	promise	versprechen	exclaim	ausrufen
argue	die Ansicht vertreten	recommend	empfehlen	emphasize	betonen
assert	behaupten	reply	erwidern	declare	erklären
assure s. o.	(jem.) versichern	repeat	wiederholen	shout	ausrufen
claim	behaupten	report	berichten	confirm	bestätigen
complain	klagen	retort	scharf antworten		

Note also: to wonder

to ask/to wonder (sich fragen) + **if/whether**
"Is she going to come?" he wondered ➔ He wondered **if** she was going to come.

Note also: to demand

a) "Stop swearing Mark!" I demanded ➔ I demanded that Mark **stop** swearing (**subjunctive**).
b) "Must you swear, Mark?" I demanded. ➔ I demanded of Mark **whether** he had to swear.

Note also: to deny (leugnen)

This verb is used with reported speech but not with direct speech.
"I am not lying!" she said. ➔ She denied (that) she was lying.

Work with me ISBN 978-3-582-77856-7

Exercises

Je1 A DIFFICULT PARENT. Here is a recording of a telephone conversation between Inga and an angry parent. Write it up as a report from Inga's point of view, using reported speech and quotation verbs which properly match the tone of the remarks.

- Are you Inga?
- *Yes, I'm Inga. Can I help you?*
- Stop picking on my daughter! You told her off yesterday! She didn't do anything!
- *I'm sorry … who is your daughter? Is it Amy?*
- Yes, Amy Goss. You told her off and shouted at her.
- *I certainly did not! I would never shout at her.*
- Yes, you did! You told her off for leaving a mess in the washroom.
- *I told the whole group about being untidy. It was a general comment. Not in anger. Amy is exaggerating. I did tell her off – calmly – some time ago for telling a lie.*
- Amy does not lie! I want to come in and see the supervisor about you. You frighten Amy!
- *Amy is very timid. I am always very careful how I speak to her.*

Je2 Take this narrative and reconstruct the dialogue which took place between the two nursery workers, as A and B.

I informed Barbara that the toilet by the front door wasn't flushing but she retorted angrily that she knew and had been on the phone to the plumber twice and she asked me what more she could do if he wouldn't come out till the next day? She had told the children to use the other toilet near the kitchen, but I pointed out that Chloe and Zoe had either forgotten this or ignored her and had used the broken one anyway. She said that she was really going to lose her temper with them and I told her to calm down. She apologized and explained that she had been under a lot of stress since the day before because her cat had gone missing and her husband had sprained his ankle and lost his wallet looking for it. And upon opening the garage door that morning, she had found the cat fast asleep on the bonnet of her car. She would not tell her husband. I sympathised with her and offered to make her a cup of coffee.

Do you want to check the grammar exercises you did? On page 236 ff. you will find the solutions to these exercises. → Solutions: Working with Grammar

K Verbs in the Past Tenses

English is rich in tenses. It is important to know and understand tense rules and to practise them.

→ The ***present perfect*** is discussed above under ***B Auxiliaries (B4)*** on page 181.
→ To see the past forms of irregular verbs see the list on page 207f.

The Simple Past

a) The simple past is used for events which began in the past and finished in the past.
In 2006 I returned to Berlin.

> WATCHWORDS:
> (two days) ago, last (year), in 2008, when I was (six), after (the film), before (I left home)

b) It also used in narratives, for example, novels.
He flew to Heathrow, hailed a taxi and went straight to Westminster.

c) In questions and negatives (→ see B3 on page 180) "**did**" + **infinitive** is used, not the simple past.
When **did** you **see** Mrs Bates? On Tuesday? *simple past*
No, I **didn't** see her on Tuesday. (BUT: I **saw** her on Wednesday.)

The Past Continuous (was/were -ing)

a) This describes an action in the past at a time when it was not complete.
At three o'clock yesterday **I was** (still) writ**ing** the report.

b) It also describes an activity which was interrupted by another event.
I **was eating** a sandwich when the telephone rang.

The Present Perfect Continuous (has/have been -ing)

This tense is used to describe an activity which began in the past, which has lasted some time and which is still happening now. (→ see B4 on page 181)
Claudia **has been** work**ing** here for two years.
She **has been** read**ing** that book since lunchtime.
I **have been** try**ing** to understand this grammar (and I still am!)

> Where English uses the present perfect continuous, German uses "seit" + present tense.

Work with me ISBN 978-3-582-77856-7

The Past Perfect (had done)

This tense describes an event which happened *further* back in the past before another time or event in the more recent past.

a) On *Monday* we had **stayed** in because of the storm, but on Tuesday we went to the park.

b) The **past perfect** must be used with the conjunction "**once**" if both events are in the past.

2:55 (phone home) — 2:56 (coffee) — ***Once*** he **had phoned** home he made some coffee.

c) With the conjunction "**after**" the **simple past** is more often used than the past perfect.
After he (had) **phoned** home he made some coffee.

d) With the conjunction "**before**" both tenses are also possible.
Before he made some coffee he phoned home.
Before he made some coffee he had phoned home.

e) Using the conjunctions "**when**", "**as soon as**":

- If event 1 is already over when event 2 happens, past perfect must be used for event 1.

  When/As soon as he had read (1) the newspaper (event 1 is over) the phone rang (2).

Note also: He had just finished reading the newspaper when the phone rang.

- But if events 1 and 2 happen almost at the same time, then **simple past** is more common.
  When/As soon as he **opened** the newspaper he noticed the photo.

Past Perfect Continuous (had been -ing)

a) This tense stresses the process or the length of time of an earlier event.
We **had been** wait**ing** so long for a bus. Finally it came.

b) It is used if an event is incomplete at a certain time …
By three o'clock we had been waiting so long for a bus that we decided to walk.

… or if a second event interrupts the first.
We had been waiting for a bus for half-an-hour when it began to snow.

In German the past tense + „schon" is used: Wir warteten schon eine halbe Stunde, als …

Work with me ISBN 978-3-582-77856-7

▶ Past Tense Exercise 1

Write out these sentences with the correct past tense verbs. (Do not forget the present perfect!) A word in brackets tells you to think about word order. This gives you the chance to think carefully about which tense to use and to see if you need more practice.
Sometimes more than one answer is possible. You could do this as a group quiz or test yourselves individually.

SCORES:
18–20 points/excellent 15–17/very good 12–14/fair 11 or less/revise then do Exercise 2

1	We ___ Paul's mother while you were out shopping.	(to discuss)
2	I ___ (never) such a story! It's crazy.	(to hear)
3	___ (you) to Mrs Hurst yesterday?	(to speak)
4	He said he ___ (still not) up his mind.	(to make)
5	Once I ___ to Germany I went into youth work.	(to come back)
6	___ (she) the supervisor yet?	(to meet)
7	___ (you) here in Hamburg long?	(to live)
8	She ___ down, looked at me and started to cry.	(to sit)
9	I ___ her when I was in Berlin.	(to know)
10	He would ___ her letter if he had not lost her address.	(to answer)
11	We (not) ___ the youth hostel warden so far.	(to see)
12	We ___ (not) until eight p.m.	(to eat)
13	___ (she) at the nursery long before she retired?	(to work)
14	The parents ___ in the office since nine this morning.	(to wait)
15	Please hurry! The film will ___ by the time we get to the cinema!	(to finish)
16	The train ___ when we arrived at the station.	(to leave)
17	When ___ (the plane)?	(to land)
18	It ___ twenty minutes ago.	(to land)
19	The fire alarm sounded as I ___ ready for bed.	(to get)
20	I ___ for some time now about changing my job.	(to think)

▶ Past Tense Exercise 2

1	Once I ___ to the father I ___ the child's difficulty.	(to speak, to understand)
2	Not ___ the book I ___ (not) the story.	(to read, to know)
3	As I ___ home I __ I (not) the letter.	(to walk, to remember, to read)
4	Last year three clubs ___ into.	(to break; *passive*)
5	Our club ___ (never) into.	(to break; *passive*)
6	___ by the fire alarm, the children ___ playing.	(to frighten, to stop)
7	Last month the fire alarm ___ off twice.	(to go)
8	When I ___ in London I ___ with Iranian students.	(to be, to live)
9	Whenever I ___ to London the sun (always).	(to be, to shine)
10	The last time I ___ Paul he ___ long hair.	(to see, to have)
11	Until last night I ___ (never) lobster before.	(to eat)
12	___ (ever) (you) chess?	(to play)
13	What ___ (you) since two o'clock?	(to do)
14	Dear Libby, we ___ a great hotel! It has a sauna.	(to find)
15	In the last ten minutes Simon ___ three glasses of water.	(to drink)
16	I __ his mum on Monday whether he ___ by the doctor.	(to ask, to examine; *passive*)
17	Where ___ (you) English?	(to study)
18	She ___ ever since she ___ at nine.	(to cry, to arrive)
19	He finally ___ that he ___ Amy's purse.	(to admit, to steal)
20	As soon as we ___ the news report we ___ the police.	(to hear, to phone)

_______ of 30 points

Work with me ISBN 978-3-582-77856-7

Irregular Verbs

Infinitive	Past Tense	Past Participle	
(to) be	was (sg.), were (pl.)	been	sein
(to) beat	beat	beaten	schlagen
(to) become	became	become	werden
(to) begin	began	begun	beginnen, anfangen
(to) bite	bit	bitten	beißen
(to) bleed	bled	bled	bluten
(to) blow	blew	blown	blasen
(to) break	broke	broken	brechen, zerbrechen
(to) bring	brought	brought	bringen, mitbringen
(to) build	built	built	bauen
(to) burn	burnt	burnt	brennen
(to) buy	bought	bought	kaufen
(to) can	could	–	können
(to) catch	caught	caught	fangen, ergreifen
(to) choose	chose	chosen	wählen
(to) come	came	come	kommen
(to) cost	cost	cost	kosten
(to) cut	cut	cut	schneiden
(to) deal (with)	dealt	dealt	sich kümmern um, sich beschäftigen mit
(to) do	did	done	machen, tun
(to) draw	drew	drawn	zeichnen, malen
(to) dream	dreamt	dreamt	träumen
(to) drink	drank	drunk	trinken
(to) drive	drove	driven	(Auto) fahren
(to) eat	ate	eaten	essen
(to) fall	fell	fallen	fallen
(to) feel	felt	felt	fühlen
(to) fight	fought	fought	bekämpfen, kämpfen
(to) find	found	found	finden
(to) fly	flew	flown	fliegen
(to) forget	forgot	forgotten	vergessen
(to) forgive	forgave	forgiven	vergeben, verzeihen
(to) freeze	froze	frozen	frieren, gefrieren
(to) get	got	got	bekommen, kommen
(to) give	gave	given	geben
(to) go	went	gone	gehen, fahren
(to) grow	grew	grown	wachsen
(to) have	had	had	haben
(to) hear	heard	heard	hören
(to) hide	hid	hidden	(sich) verstecken
(to) hit	hit	hit	schlagen, stoßen
(to) hold	held	held	halten, abhalten
(to) hurt	hurt	hurt	(sich) verletzen
(to) keep	kept	kept	behalten, halten

Appendix *Irregular Verbs*

Infinitive	Past Tense	Past Participle	
(to) know	knew	known	wissen, kennen
(to) lead	led	led	führen
(to) learn	learnt	learnt	lernen
(to) leave	left	left	verlassen, abfahren
(to) lend	lent	lent	leihen, verleihen
(to) let	let	let	lassen
(to) lie	lay	lain	liegen
(to) lose	lost	lost	verlieren
(to) make	made	made	machen, anfertigen
(to) mean	meant	meant	bedeuten
(to) meet	met	met	treffen, begegnen
(to) pay	paid	paid	bezahlen
(to) put	put	put	setzen, legen, stellen
(to) read	read	read	lesen
(to) ride	rode	ridden	reiten, (Rad) fahren
(to) ring	rang	rung	klingeln, läuten
(to) rise	rose	risen	aufstehen (Sonne: aufgehen)
(to) run	ran	run	rennen, laufen
(to) say	said	said	sagen
(to) see	saw	seen	sehen
(to) seek	sought	sought	suchen
(to) sell	sold	sold	verkaufen
(to) send	sent	sent	senden, schicken
(to) shake	shook	shaken	schütteln
(to) show	showed	shown	zeigen
(to) shut	shut	shut	schließen
(to) sing	sang	sung	singen
(to) sit	sat	sat	sitzen
(to) sleep	slept	slept	schlafen
(to) smell	smelt	smelt	riechen
(to) speak	spoke	spoken	sprechen
(to) spend	spent	spent	verbringen, ausgeben
(to) stand	stood	stood	stehen
(to) steal	stole	stolen	stehlen
(to) swim	swam	swum	schwimmen
(to) take	took	taken	nehmen, mitnehmen
(to) teach	taught	taught	lehren, unterrichten
(to) tear	tore	torn	zerreißen
(to) tell	told	told	erzählen
(to) think	thought	thought	denken
(to) throw	threw	thrown	werfen
(to) wake (up)	woke	woken	aufwachen
(to) wear	wore	worn	(Kleidung) tragen
(to) win	won	won	gewinnen
(to) write	wrote	written	schreiben

Work with me ISBN 978-3-582-77856-7

Basic Vocabulary

Anleiter/-in	supervising tutor (Praktikum: practical instructor)
Ausbildung, Berufsausbildung	vocational training
Auszubildende/-r	trainee
Behinderung	disability
Betreuung	care
Bildung	education
Erzieher/-in	early-childhood teacher, - professional, - educator (staatl. anerkannt: qualified/certified educator), early-years teacher
Erzieher/in im Familienzentrum	family worker
Erzieher/-in in der Jugendarbeit	youth worker
Erziehung in Krippe, Kindertagesstätte	early-childhood education
Fachschule für Sozialpädagogik	vocational college for (social) education / for pedagogy
Förderbedürfnisse, besondere	special educational needs
Fortbildung	further education
frühkindliche Erziehung	early-childhood education
Grundschule, ca. 5–10 Jahre	primary school
Grundschule, die ersten Jahre	infant school
Heilerziehungspfleger/-in	educational therapist, special needs teacher
Heim	residential home
Heimerzieher/-in	residential childcare / youthcare worker
Hort, ca. 6–14 Jahre	day-care centre, after-school care centre / club
Kind mit Behinderung	child with special needs
Kinder- und Jugendhilfe	child and youth welfare
Kinderbetreuung	childcare
Kindergarten, ca. 3–5 Jahre	nursery school, nursery (US: preschool) (UK auch: nursery class)
Kinderpfleger/-in	nursery nurse, childcare worker
Kindertagesstätte, alle Altersstufen	childcare centre, day-care centre
Kleinkind, ca. 1–3 Jahre	toddler
Krippe, ca. 0–3 Jahre	crèche, crib
Lese- und Schreibfähigkeit	literacy
Oberschule, ab ca. 12 Jahre	secondary school, high school
Pflege-	foster
Praktikum	practical work experience, on-the-job training
Säugling, ca. 0–1 Jahr	infant
Sozialpädagogik	social education, pedagogy, social care
Spielgruppe	playgroup
Tagesmutter, -vater	childminder
Verhalten	behaviour
Vorschule	preschool

Alphabetical Vocabulary

[coll] (colloquial): umgangssprachlich
s.o.: someone
sth.: something
see also page III Basic Vocabulary

A

(to) abduct	entführen
ability	Fähigkeit
absentee	Abwesende/-r
absenteeism	Krankfeiern
absorbed	absorbiert, vertieft, auch: aufgesaugt, gedämpft
abuse	Missbrauch, Misshandlung
access	Zugang
(to) access sth.	Zugang zu etw. haben
(to) achieve sth.	etw. erreichen, leisten
(to) acquire	erwerben, annehmen
acquired	angeeignet, erlangt, erworben
(to) act out	ausleben
ADHD	Aufmerksamkeitsdefizit-Syndrom ADS
(to) adjourn	sich an anderen Ort begeben; auch: vertagen
adjuster; (to) adjust	jem. der angepasst ist; sich anpassen
(to) adopt	annehmen, übernehmen, adoptieren
adventure education	Abenteuerpädagogik
adventurous	abenteuerlich
advice	Rat(schlag)
affairs	Angelegenheiten, tägliche Arbeit
air traffic control	Flugsicherung
(to) alienate	verfremden
all sorts of stuff [coll]	allerlei Sachen
(to) allocate	(Mittel) zuteilen
amazing	erstaunlich
ambiguity	Mehrdeutigkeit, Ambiguität
ample	reichlich, umfänglich
analogy	Ähnlichkeit
anger management	Selbstbeherrschung
annual grant	jährlicher Zuschuss
(to) anticipate	erwarten, vorausahnen
anticipation	Vorannahme, Erwartung
anxiety	Angst, Ängstlichkeit
appearance	äußere Erscheinungsform
apposition	Anreihung, Apposition
approach	Herangehensweise, Vorstoß
appropriate	angebracht, angemessen
archery	Bogenschießen
ascribed to sth.	einer Sache zugeschrieben sein
Asperger's Syndrome	Asperger-Syndrom (Autismus)
(to) aspire to	streben nach
assault	Körperverletzung
at a (certain) rate	zu einem (bestimmten) Grad
(to) attend	besuchen, teilnehmen
at your earliest convenience	möglichst bald
ataxic	ataktisch, unsicher, ungeordnet, regellos
athetoid	athetoid
athetosis	Athetose, Hammond'sches Syndrom
attainment; (to) attain	Leistung; leisten
attendance	Anwesenheit
attention span	Aufmerksamkeitsspanne
audience	Publikum, Zuhörerschaft
auditory nerve	Gehörnerv
autism spectrum disorders	Bandbreite der autistischen Störungen
award	Auszeichnung
awareness	Bewusstsein

Work with me ISBN 978-3-582-77856-7

B

(to) back up	unterstützen
basics	Grundwissen
(to) become involved in	sich engagieren
(to) behave	sich verhalten
behavioural	Verhaltens-
benefit	Vorteil; Nutzen
(to) benefit	profitieren
bias	Einseitigkeit
bicycle tyres (BrE), tires (AmE)	Fahrradreifen
(to) blister	Blasen werfen
blueprint	Bauplan, Entwurf
(to) blur	verwischen
(to) boil down to sth. [coll]	auf etw. hinauslaufen
boisterously	heftig, ungestüm, wild
(to be) bookish	ein "Bücherwurm" sein
bossy	rechthaberisch, herrisch
(to) bounce back	rasch wieder auf die Beine kommen
Braille	Blindenschrift
brain	Gehirn
brainstem	Gehirnstamm
bricks	Ziegel, Bausteine
bureaucracy	Bürokratie
bushcraft	extension of "survival skills"
(to) button	aufknöpfen
by trial and error	durch Ausprobieren

C

(to) capture	erfassen, auch: erobern, einfangen
cardiovascular disease	Herz- und Gefäßkrankheit
carer	Fürsorger
caress, (to) caress	Liebkosung, liebkosen
(to) carry out	verrichten
catfishing	das Verführen mithilfe einer falschen Identität im Internet/sozialen Medien
case load	Belastung
celebrity	Berühmtheit, Star
cerebellum	Kleinhirn
cerebral	zerebral, vom Gehirn gesteuert
cerebral palsy	Zerebralparese, zerebrale Kinderlähmung
(to) characterise	kennzeichnen
(to) charge	anklagen
cheeky	frech
chief institution	Hauptinstitution
childcare	Kinderbetreuung
child minder	Tagesmutter, -vater
chores	Pflichten, Routinearbeiten
church elders	Kirchenälteste, Ältestenkreis
(to) claim	behaupten
climax	Höhepunkt
(to) coach	einarbeiten
combining	kombinierend
come off it [coll]	hör auf damit
command	Befehl, auch: Kontrolle
commerce	Handel, Kommerz
committed	pflichtbewusst
common interests	gemeinsame Interessen
competence	Können, Zuständigkeit
competition	Wettbewerb
completion	Vervollständigung
complexion	Teint
compulsory	obligatorisch, gesetzlich
confusing	verwirrend
(to) conjugate	konjugieren
conscious	bewusst, absichtlich
concise	präzise, kurzgefasst
consistent	konsistent, einheitlich
(to) console	jem. trösten
constraint	Bedingung
(to) consult	zu Rate ziehen; befragen
content	Inhalt
context	Zusammenhang
contextual	textabhängig
(to) continue	weitermachen, weiterführen

(to) contribute	beitragen
contrivances	Erfindungen
convictions	Vorstrafen
(to) convince	überzeugen
(to) coo	gurren
(to) cope	verkraften, bewältigen
cortex	Hirnrinde
'cos (because)	weil
counterpart	Gegenstück
court	(jur) Gericht
(to) crack	unterbrechen, aufbrechen
cramped	eng
(to) crawl	krabbeln, kriechen
crayon	Buntstift
crèche	Krippe
crucial	ausschlaggebend, entscheidend
crutch	Krücke
curious	neugierig, auch: ungewöhnlich, merkwürdig
currently	gegenwärtig
cut off	abgeschnitten, abgeschirmt

D

D'you	do you
dandelions	Löwenzahn
daily basis	täglich
deaf	taub, hörbehindert
(to) decay	verfaulen
decreased	reduziert, geschmälert
defender	(jur) Verteidiger/-in
degree	Grad
delinquent	kriminell
deprivation	Mangel
deprived	benachteiligt
descending	absteigend
detached	freistehend, getrennt
determined	festgelegt, entschlossen
(to be) determined to do something	entschlossen sein, etwas zu tun
(to) detract from	etw. beeinträchtigen
development	Entwicklung
development of motor skills	Entwicklung der motorischen Fähigkeiten
devoted to	gewidmet
dietary requirements	diätische Ansprüche
(to) differ from	sich unterscheiden von
(to) differentiate	unterscheiden; differenzieren
diplegia	Diplegie, doppelseitige Lähmung
disability	Behinderung
disaffected	unzufrieden, desillusioniert
disastrous	katastrophal
disguise	Verkleidung
(to) disintegrate	sich auflösen
(to) display sth.	ew. abbilden, ausstellen
dispute	Streit
(to) disrupt	stören
distinct	deutlich, ausgeprägt
distinguishable	erkennbar, unterscheidbar
distorted	verzerrt, entstellt
distraction	Ablenkung
distrustful	misstrauisch
diversity	Vielfältigkeit
diversity	Vielfalt
(to) divide	teilen
divisive	spalterisch
doable	machbar
dole [coll] BrE	Arbeitslosengeld
domestic abuse	häusliche Gewalt
drained	erschöpft
drug addiction	Drogenabhängigkeit
dunno [coll]	I don't know
dysfunctional	funktionsunfähig
dyskinetic	dyskinetisch, bewegungs(ablauf)gestört

E

E3	Electronic Entertainment Expo
early action [lit]	Spannungsbogen

Work with me ISBN 978-3-582-77856-7

early-childhood education	frühkindliche Erziehung
early-childhood teacher	Erzieher/-in
(to) ease	mildern, lindern
EBM	Musikstil: electronic body music
eccentric	exzentrisch
economic position	Wirtschaftslage
educational therapist	Heilerziehungspfleger/-in
educator	Erzieher/-in
effectively	wirkungsvoll
effort	Anstrengung
electronic retrieval systems	elektron. Datenabfrage-system
elevator (AmE), lift (BrE)	Fahrstuhl
elementary school	Grundschule
(to) eliminate	beseitigen
emergency folder	Notfallordner
emergency services	Rettungsdienst
emerging skills	neu entstehende, junge Fertigkeiten
emotional bonding	emotionale Bindung
(to) empathise	sich einfühlen
(to) emphasise	betonen, hervorheben
(to) empower	bemächtigen
(to) enable	befähigen
(to) encounter	begegnen, begegnet
(to) encourage	ermutigen
energy-dense foods	kalorienreiche Kost
(to) engage s.o.	jem. anstellen, engagieren
(to be) engaged in doing something	mit etwas beschäftigt sein
enormous	riesig
(to) enrol s.o.	jem. aufnehmen (in Schule)
(to) ensure	gewährleisten, sicherstellen
(to) entice	locken
environmental education	Umweltpädagogik
essential	notwendig, entscheidend
(to) establish	etablieren, aufbauen
estate	Wohnsiedlung
(to) estimate	schätzen
evidence	Beweise
(to) evoke	hervorrufen
(to) exacerbate	verschlechtern
(to) exaggerate	übertreiben
(to) exceed	übertreffen
exception	Ausnahme
excerpts	Auszüge
exclusion	Ausschluss, Zurückweisung
exclusively	ausschließlich
exhilarating	berauschend
expatriates	Nicht-Einheimische, Auswanderer
expectation	Erwartung
experiential education	Erlebnispädagogik
explicit	deutlich; auch: freizügig
(to) exploit	ausbeuten
exposure	Kontakt; das Ausgesetztsein
(to) extend	erweitern, verlängern, ausweiten, erstrecken
extremity	Extremitäten

F

(to) facilitate	ermöglichen; fördern
(to) falsify	fälschen
features	Eigenschaften
fictitious	fiktiv
fine-tuning	Feinabstimmung
fins or scales	Flossen oder Schuppen (vom Fisch)
fissure	Spalte, Bruch, Naht, Riss
fluent	fließend (sprechen)
flummoxed	verblüfft, verwirrt
FMV	full motion video
footwear	Schuhwerk
forebrain	Vorderhirn
(to) form	formen, bilden
(to) foster	fördern
foster	Pflege(-)
(to) found sth.	etw. gründen

fraction	Bruchteil
framework	Rahmen
frequency of tuition	Regelmäßigkeit des Unterrichts
frequently	häufig
frontal lobe	Frontallappen, Stirnlappen
(to) fuel	anheizen
full command	vollständige Kontrolle
further education course	Fortbildungs-veranstaltung

G

gadgets	Geräte
(to) gain sth.	etw. erlangen, etw. gewinnen
(to) gather	(ein)sammeln, versammeln
gearshift	Gangschaltung
genre	Gattung
Glial cells	Glia-Zellen (Neuron, Gehirn)
(to) go overboard [coll]	es übertreiben, überstrapazieren
goal	Tor, Ziel
good'un [coll]	a good one (in etwa: guter Witz)
gorge-walking	Marschieren in einer Schlucht
graduation	Schulabschluss
grain	Getreide
grasping, (to) grasp	Greifbewegung, etw. fassen
grateful	dankbar
(to) gratify	befriedigen, jem. gefällig sein
gratitude	Dankbarkeit
(to) groom	vorbereiten, auch: pfle-gen
growth	Wachstum
guidance	Führung, Leitung

H

hands-on	praktisch, spielerisch
happy slapping	Phänomen der Jugend-gewalt, "Aufmischen"
harassment	Belästigung, Mobbing
(to) have access to sth.	über etw. verfügen können, Zugang haben
hearing aid	Hörgerät
hemiplegia	Hemiplegie, komplette Halbseitenlähmung
(to) highlight	betonen
hiking	(Berg-)Wandern
(to) hinder	verhindern, behindern
(to) hiss	zischen
(to) hook	fesseln, auf sich ziehen
(to) hoover	staubsaugen
hops and skips	hüpft und springt
hut	Hütte

I

ICT	EDV
idiom	Redensart
imagination	Vorstellungskraft
(to) imitate	imitieren, nachmachen
immature	unreif
impact; (to) impact	Eindruck, beeinflussen
impairment	Beeinträchtigung
impartial	neutral, vorurteilslos, unbefangen
(to) implement	durchführen, anwenden
implied meanings	implizite Bedeutung
(to) imply	unterstellen, bedeuten, implizieren
improvement	Verbesserung
in addition to	neben, außer
(to be) in breach of	gegen etwas verstoßen
(to) incorporate	einbauen, enthalten
in passing	zwischen Tür und Angel
in similar fashion	in ähnlicher Weise
in terms of	im Hinblick auf
inappropriate	unangemessen
incident	Vorfall
(to) include	einbeziehen
increased	erhöht, gesteigert
increasingly	zunehmend
(to) indicate	andeuten

Work with me ISBN 978-3-582-77856-7

induction course	Einführungskurs
nursery school	Kindergarten
inferior	minderwertig
infinite	unendlich
(to) influence; influence	beeinflussen; der Einfluss
(to) infringe	übertreten, verstoßen
(to) inhibit	hemmen
initial	anfänglich
inquisitive	wissbegierig
insecurity	Unsicherheit
institute of higher education	Höhere Lehranstalt
(to) interact	interagieren
interpersonal	zwischenmenschlich
intrigued	fasziniert, interessiert
intuitively	instinktiv, intuitiv
invaluable	außerordentlich wichtig
investigation	Untersuchung
(to) involve	beteiligen, involvieren
issue	Frage, Belang
Ital	(Ernährungsgrundsatz der Rastafaris)

J

Jacob's ladder	spezielle Kletterleiter
jar	Glas/Gefäß
John Muir Award	Zertifikat bei Outdoor-Education-Veranstaltungen
judge	(jur) Richter/-in
judgement	Urteil
judgmental	wertend, kritisch, selbstgerecht

K

key elements	Schlüsselelemente
know-all	Alleswisser

L

(to) label	etikettieren
(to) lack	fehlen an, mangeln an
lacto-ovo vegetarian	Ovo-Lacto-Vegetarier/-in
lad [coll]	Bursche
language decoding skills	Sprach-Entschlüsselungs-mechanismen
latter	letztere
lawless	gesetzlos
lawyer	Anwalt/Anwältin
leaflet	Broschüre, Flyer
learning resources	Hilfsmittel zur Bildung
left to my own devices [coll]	auf mich allein gestellt
(to) lessen	verringern
liaison	Zusammenarbeit
limitless	ohne Grenzen
lingua franca	Welthandelssprache
linguist	Sprachwissen-schaftler/-in
linguistic features	sprachliche Merkmale
linkages	Verknüpfung, Verbindung
(to) lip-read	von den Lippen lesen
listening skills	Hörverstehen
literal translation	wörtliche Übersetzung
long-standing debate	langjährige Debate
loose-fitting clothes	locker sitzende Kleidung
(to) lose touch	Kontakt verlieren
loss	Verlust
lunatic asylum	psychiatrische Anstalt
(to) make an effort	sich bemühen
(to) make sth. up	sich etw. ausdenken, erfinden

M

(to) maintain	aufrechterhalten
(to) make up stories	Geschichten erfinden
manual	manuell
mardy [coll]	schlecht gelaunt, brummig
maritime	maritim, zur See gehörig
(to) master	beherrschen, meistern
master of ceremonies	Zeremonienmeister
mastered skills	"Meisterfertigkeiten"
maturity; (to be) mature	Reife/Laufzeit; reif, durchdacht
mentoring (peer)	Beratung (von seinesgleichen)
(to) migrate	einwandern
Minister of Cultural Affairs	Kultusminister

misbehaviour	schlechtes Betragen
misogyny	Frauenfeindlichkeit
mobility programme	Austauschprogramm
mock exams	Probeklausuren
mockery	Spott
modesty	Bescheidenheit
mother tongue	Muttersprache
mucky [coll]	schmutzig
multi-faith centre	Zentrum verschiedener Religionen
muscle tone	Muskeltonus
mysterious	rätselhaft, geheimnisvoll

N

native-like	wie ein Muttersprachler
(to) neglect; neglect	missachten, versäumen; Vernachlässigung
nollie, grind, double-sets, nosegrab	Tricks beim Skate-boarding
non-progressive	nicht fortschreitend
non-verbal	nicht-sprachlich
non-verbal clues	nicht-sprachliche Hin-weise
notification	Mitteilung
nursery nurse	Kinderpfleger/-in
nursery school	Kindergarten
nutrient	Nährstoffe
nutrition	Ernährung

O

obesity	Fettleibigkeit
objective	Ansatz, Ziel, Zielvorgabe
obsessed	besessen
obsession	Leidenschaft, Manie
(to) obtain	beschaffen, erlangen
obviously	offensichtlich
(to) occur	sich ereignen, eintreten
odds	Widrigkeiten
offender	Straftäter/-in
offspring	Nachkomme(n)
on behalf of	im Namen (von)
on the fringe	am Rande, in der Randzone
onset	Entstehung, Anfang
opportunity	Gelegenheit
orally	mündlich
orthography	Rechtschreibung
outcome	Ergebnis
outdoor education	(vergleichbar mit) Erlebnispädagogik
outstripped	übersteigen
(to) overcome	überwinden
overcrowding	Überfüllung
(to) overpower	übermannen, überwältigen
overprotective	überfürsorglich
(to) pace	hin- und hergehen, schreiten

P

paedodontist	Kinderzahnarzt, Kinder-zahnärztin
parents' council	Elternbeirat
participant	Teilnehmer/-in
pathway	Weg, Bahn
perception	Wahrnehmung
(to) perform	agieren, vorführen, funktionieren
perils	Gefahren
permission	Erlaubnis
personality disorder	Persönlichkeitsstörung
(to) pester	belästigen, nerven
phonemic awareness	phonemisches Bewusstsein
(to) pick up [police]	verhaften (durch die Polizei)
(to) play into the hands of s.o.	jmdm. einen Vorteil verschaffen
play-based	spielerisch
(to) play truant	schwänzen
plight	Notlage
plot	Geschichte, Handlung
plot-outline	Handlungsumriss
plot-twist	Wendung in der Handlung
point of the story	Ziel der Geschichte
point of view	Perspektive, Standpunkt

Work with me ISBN 978-3-582-77856-7

(to) pollute	verschmutzen
(to) portray	schildern, darstellen
(to) pose	etw. darstellen, posieren
posture	Körperhaltung
potty trained	Kind ist sauber/trocken/ trägt keine Windeln mehr
(to) praise	loben
precious	wertvoll
precisely	präzise
predominance	Vorherrschaft
pregnant	schwanger
premature	verfrüht, frühreif
preschool	Vorschule
(to) pressure	unter Druck setzen
presumably	vermutlich
(to) pretend	so tun als ob
preventive measures	Vorsichtsmaßnahmen
prime suspect	Hauptverdächtige/r
primer	Grundierung, Ausgangspunkt
printing press	Druckerpresse
problem-solving skills	Problemlösefähigkeiten
processed	behandelt, verarbeitet
profound	tiefgreifend, schwer
progression	Fortschritt, Entwicklung
prom queen	Gewinnerin beim Abschlussball der High School
(to) promote	fördern/unterstützen
pronunciation	Aussprache
properties	Requisiten
props (short for "properties")	Requisiten
prosecutor	(jur) Ankläger/-in
(to) provide	(an-)bieten, bereitstellen
pun	Wortspiel
purposes	Zwecke
pursuit	Streben
(to) put off	hinauszögern
(to) put pressure on	unter Druck setzen

Q

quadriplegia	Quadriplegie, Tetraplegie, Lähmung der vier Extremitäten
quantity	Anzahl, Menge
(to) quell	unterdrücken

R

raft-building	Floßbauen
rag	Lappen, Fetzen
randomly	wahllos, willkürlich
range	Umfang, Reihe
rapid	rapide
reader's letter	Leserbrief
(to) rebel	rebellieren
recently	kürzlich, neulich
reception class (UK)	(vergleichbar mit Kindergarten und Vorschule)
receptive	aufnahmefähig
reciprocity	Gegenseitigkeit, Austausch
(to) recite	auswendig aufsagen
Recognition Year	Anerkennungsjahr
(to) recommend	empfehlen
recommendation	Empfehlung
recovery	Genesung, Erholung
(to) reduce	reduzieren
reflection	Reflexion, Rückblick
regulations	Regelungen
(to) re-invent	neu erfinden
relationship phobia	Beziehungsangst
reliable	zuverlässig
reluctantly	nur ungern
rennet	Lab (Käseherstellung)
re-offending	Rückfälligkeit
repetition	Wiederholung
repetitive pattern	sich wiederholendes Muster
request	Anfrage, Ersuchen
(to) require	bedürfen, benötigen; auch: beanspruchen
research	(wissenschaftliche) Forschung
residential home	Heim

Work with me ISBN 978-3-582-77856-7

resilience	Resilienz (psych.), Strapazierfähigkeit
resolution	Lösung
(to) resolve conflicts	Konflikte beheben, lösen
(to) resort to sth.	zu etw. greifen
resourceful	einfallsreich, findig
(to) respond	erwidern, auf etw. eingehen
responsible	verantwortungsbewusst
responsive	ansprechbar, reagierend
restricted	begrenzt
retakes	Wiederholungen
(to) retaliate	rächen, vergelten
Reverend	Pfarrer/Pfarrerin
review	Rezension
(to) revise	üben
(to) revolutionise	grundlegend verändern, revolutionieren
rigid	rigide, unnachgiebig
risky	gewagt, riskant
rivalry	Konkurrenz, Rivalität
rock climbing	Felsenklettern
ropes course	Seilgarten, Abseiling
row	Streit
runaway	Ausreißer
(to) rush	hetzen

S

sacred animal	heiliges Tier
salary	Lohn, Gehalt
satellite broadcasting	Rundfunk über Satellit
saturated fats	gesättigte Fette
savvy	praktische Fertigkeiten, Intelligenz
scapegoat	Sündenbock
school curriculum	Lehrplan
scientific	wissenschaftlich
scientist	Wissenschaftler/-in
(to) score	erzielen (Punkte)
scouts	Pfadfinder
second language	Zweitsprache
seizure	Anfall (Epilepsie, Krampf)
self-adornment	Selbstverschönerung
self-assured	selbstsicher
self-conscious	gehemmt, auch: selbstbewusst
self-esteem	Selbstachtung
self-harm	Selbstverletzung
self-sufficient	unabhängig
sensitive	sensibel, empfindlich
(to) settle in	sich einleben
(to) sever	abbrechen, abtrennen
severe	schwer, heftig
sex	Geschlecht
sexualised	hier: zu früh geschlechtlich bewusst
shaping	Formung
(to) share	teilen
sheepish	verlegen
shelter	Unterschlupf, Schutz
(to) shoo them out [coll]	sie rausscheuchen
shortage	Engpass
shortfall	Defizit
siblings	Geschwister
sign language	Zeichensprache, Gebärdensprache
significant	von Bedeutung
(to be) situated	gelegen sein
skill	Fertigkeit, Geschick, Können
skull	Schädel
(to) snatch	wegschnappen
social education	Sozialpädagogik
solitary play	Einzelspiel
(to) span	umfassen
spastic	spastisch
spasticity	Spastik
spatial sense	räumliches Vorstellungsvermögen
special feature	Sonderbeitrag
special needs	spezielle Bedürfnisse, Behinderungen
spinal cord	Rückenmark
(to) split	trennen, teilen

Work with me ISBN 978-3-582-77856-7

(to) spoil	Spaß verderben; auch: verwöhnen; zerstören
(to) spread	sich ausbreiten, etw. auftragen
statutory	gesetzlich
steady	beständig, gleichbleibend
(to) steer	lenken, steuern
stereotyped	klischeehaft
(to) stimulate	anregen
stimuli	Anregung, Reiz
stockings (AmE)	Socken
(to) storm	(er-)stürmen
studious	lerneifrig
stuffed	gestopft/vollgestopft
subsequently	anschließend
substance abuse	Drogenmissbrauch
(to) suggest	andeuten, empfehlen, Anzeichen für
suitable	passend
(to) sum up	zusammenfassen, Fazit ziehen
sunscreen	Sonnenschutz(-mittel)
(to) supervise	beaufsichtigen
(to) suppress	unterdrücken
surge	Flut
surplus	Zugabe, Überschuss
survival skills	Überlebenstechniken
(to) sustain	aufrecht erhalten
(to) switch; switch	schalten, wechseln; (Aus-)Schalter

T

(to) tag	ticken
(to) tailor to	zuschneiden auf
target	Ziel
tax burden	Steuerlast
(to) tear s.o. down	jem. herunterziehen
tear jerker [coll]	Schnulze
(to) tease s.o.	jem. ärgern, aufziehen
tells	(Körpersprache) unbewusste Zeichen
template	Vorlage
tempting	verlockend
tension	Anspannung
term	Ausdruck, Begriff
territories	Gebiete
(to) testify	etwas bezeugen
text evidence	Textnachweis
theft	Diebstahl
thick [coll]; thicko	dumm, begriffsstutzig; „Dummkopf"
thoroughly	gründlich
(to) threaten	bedrohen
(to) thrive	aufblühen, Erfolg haben
tight	angespannt, eng
time-commitment	zeitlicher Einsatz
timely	rechtzeitig, zeitgemäß
toddler	1- bis 3-jähriges Kind, Kleinkind
tolerance of ambiguity	Ambiguitätstoleranz
tooth decay	Karies
town council	Stadtrat
(to) trace back	zurückführen auf
trade	Handel
transition	Übergang
travellers' camp	Travellers: Leute, die in Wohnwagen wohnen
tray	Tablett, Ablagekorb
treaty	Abkommen, Vertrag
tremendous	riesig
trial	(jur) Gerichtsverfahren
(to) trigger (off)	auslösen

U

unaided	ohne fremde Hilfe
unanimously acclaimed	einstimmig bejubelt
uncluttered	ordentlich
unconstrained	locker, zwanglos
(to) underachieve	unter erreichbarem Leistungsniveau bleiben
unimaginable	unvorstellbar
uninhibited	ungehemmt
unique achievement	einzigartige Leistung
unprecedented	beispiellos

Work with me ISBN 978-3-582-77856-7

unpredictable	unvorhersehbar
unsuitable	unangemessen, ungeeignet
untreated	unbehandelt
urge, (to) urge	Drang; drängen
(to) utter	etw. äußern

V

variant	verschiedene
varieties	Unterschiede
various	viele, verschiedene
ventriloquist	Bauchredner
(to) vie	konkurrieren, wetteifern
villain	Schurke, Ganove
visual acuity	Sehschärfe
(to) visualise (BrE)	veranschaulichen
vital	unbedingt notwendig, unerlässlich
vividly	plastisch, lebhaft
voluntary basis	freiwillige Basis
vulnerable	schutzlos, angreifbar

W

wage-earner	Lohnempfänger
walker	Gehwagen
wealth	Reichtum
(to) weigh up	abwägen
wellbeing	Wohlergehen
wholeheartedly	mit ganzem Herzen, ernsthaft
wide range	große Auswahl
window of opportunity	Fenster der Möglichkeiten (Entwicklungspsychologie)
(to) withdraw	sich zurückziehen
woofters [coll]	"Schwuchteln"
(to) worsen	(sich) verschlimmern
(to) writhe	sich winden

Y

youth offending	Jugendkriminalität
youth worker	Jugendbetreuer, Jugendarbeiter

Work with me ISBN 978-3-582-77856-7

Working with Me (Methods and Skills)

Modern English lessons at vocational colleges are based on improving the four skills (reading, writing, speaking, listening) which you need in order to interact and communicate in a foreign language. The following pages give some ideas on how to work to improve your skills according to the Common European Framework of Reference for Languages (Reception, Production, Interaction, Mediation).

Classroom Phrases

If you want to use these phrases, make a poster and hang it on the wall where everybody can see it. Refer to it as often as you can during the lesson.
If you have a prepared discussion that your classmates have to listen to, you can use this chart as an observation sheet so that you can mark which phrases are used. With that you can check your active knowledge of classroom phrases.

Discussion Phrases

Opinion
I think/believe
I'm sure that
In my opinion
Agreement
I agree
You are right, (but)
Disagreement
I don' t agree at all
I'm afraid you are wrong
I think you are wrong
Well, I don't think so,
Giving reasons
That's why I feel that
I think he/she is right, because
Asking for reasons
Why do you think that ... ?
Can you justify that?

Doubts
Okay, but
I'm not sure whether
Do you really mean to say that ... ?
Interrupting
Hold on, can't you see that
Excuse me, but don't you
Just a minute, please
It is generally believed that
Let's begin with the fact
First we must define
I didn't quite understand what you meant
A few minutes ago you said that
Every argument has two sides.
Could you repeat the argument/point you have just made?
There seems to be a contradiction here
If I understood you correctly, you said
On the one hand ... but on the other hand

Phrases for Talking About a Text

What is the text about?
The text I read is about
The text tells us about
The text describes the situation of
The text presents the situation

Interpretation
The text shows
The text analyses
The text reveals
Style
The style is informative
The style is formal/informal
The style is boring

Appendix *Working with Me (Methods and Skills)*

Conclusion
All in all
To summarize the text
Connectors
in order to
however
therefore
at this point
as a result
not only but also
on the one hand … on the other hand

Agreement
I firmly believe that
I'm convinced that
There is no question that
Disagreement
I don't agree with
I'm of a different opinion
I cannot really believe

Interpretation Phrases

To refer to something
In line XX it says for example
The first part is about
This story consists of
The action takes place in/during
The problem is that
With reference to
With regard to
Stating an opinion
I doubt whether
Well, according to what I read
In my opinion
I'm for/against it
On the one hand … on the other hand
I (don't) want to criticize this but
My point of view is that
I suppose
Unlike the writer
I think he is right/wrong
To add ideas
moreover
furthermore
besides
To express reasons
therefore
that's why
consequently
To compare ideas
In the same way that
In comparison with
As well as
In contrast to
In other words
that means
that is to say

To indicate order
To begin with
First/secondly
The author goes on to say that
To indicate a consequence
accordingly
it follows that
To express concession
though
although
even
admittedly
To express condition
if
unless
suppose that
In the event of
To limit a previous statement
but
however
nevertheless
otherwise
on the contrary
inspite of
Conclusion
as a result
all in all
to sum up
finally

Work with me ISBN 978-3-582-77856-7

To Promote Talking and Listening

Double Circle

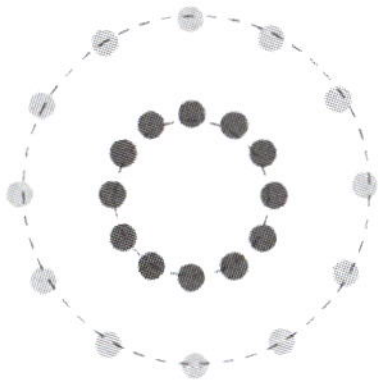

Aims:

To introduce a new topic (e.g. you can give your opinion on the topic or you can tell what you already know about the topic)
To talk about what you found out, e.g. during group work (you can either use notes which you have taken during group work or not, according to your speaking skills)

What You Need:

Space in the middle of the classroom
(Usually) three sentences/questions that deal with the topic you are working on
A signal to start/stop the talking

Method:

Divide the class into two groups. One group forms an inner circle and the other group an outer one so that everybody is facing a partner.
You either talk about your topic for a certain amount of time or you listen to your partner. After that you swap over. After finishing, those in the outer circle move to the left, so that everyone has a new partner fort the next question. After talking about all the questions you may go back to your seats.

Headstand

Aims:

The headstand technique teaches you how to think from a different viewpoint. It is often easier to name the negative aspects of a topic rather than the positive ones. This can be exploited in class brainstorming sessions where negative reactions and ideas are transformed into positive solutions.

What You Need:

Marker pens, metaplan-cards, metaplan-wall or black board

Method:

Instead of asking *"How can I be successful?"* the question is turned on its head (a headstand!) and becomes *"How can I be* ***un****successful?"*. This should produce a great number of responses, which can be written on the board or onto cards which students pin up on a display board. In the second stage negatives are turned into positives, e.g.: "LOOK UNTIDY" → "LOOK SMART". (If using a flipchart, the left-hand side could display the negatives and the right-hand side the positives.) Finally, solutions which the group has found can be evaluated and graded according to importance, possibly by another group.
This method is not only great fun but really can break down "blocks on thinking". Groups should be no smaller than six and no larger than twelve. The headstand technique is best used after a topic has been introduced by a lead-text or a case study.

Group Work

Aims:

To learn through cooperation
To give everyone an opportunity to communicate

What You Need:

Group tables
Worksheet with prepared tasks

Method:

Divide your class into several little groups (you can use puzzle pieces or cards) and take the tasks you have to work on. Tasks can be differentiated to suit the oral ability of the groups.

Work with me ISBN 978-3-582-77856-7

Appendix *Working with Me (Methods and Skills)*

Variation of Group Work: Jigsaw

Aims:

To split a difficult or complex topic into easier parts which are better to work on

What You Need:

An identification (cards, puzzle pieces) for "basic groups" and "expert groups"

Method:

First you work on your part of the topic in so called "expert groups". Each group has its own part to work on. After finishing your tasks go to "basic groups", consisting of other classmates. Thus you are the expert for your part and you tell the others about it. Everybody is an expert for his/her part of the topic. By listening to the others you gather the information of the whole complex topic. After finishing the "basic groups", go back to your "expert group". There you all compare your information and put it together.

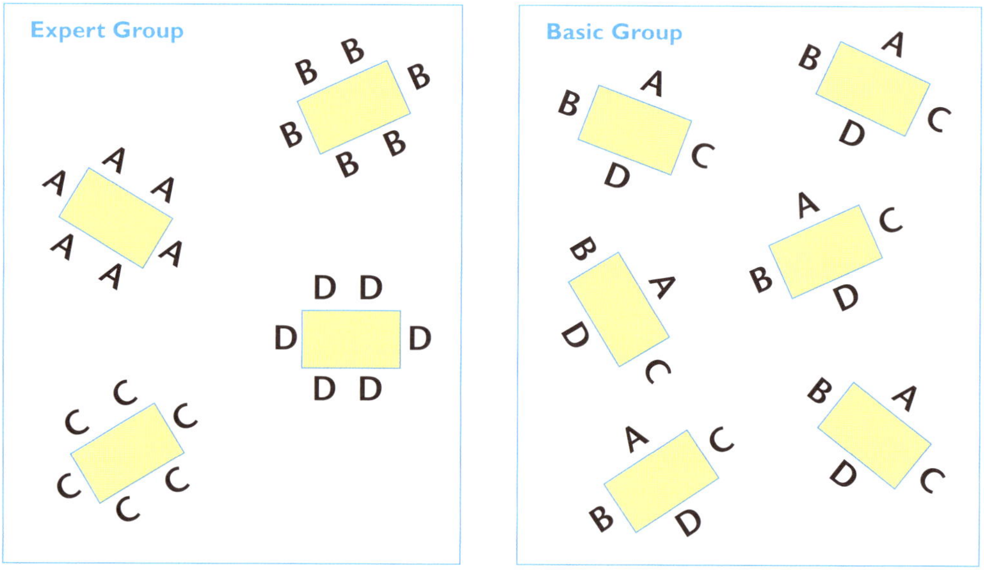

Evaluation of Group Work: Flashlight

Aims:

To collect feelings or statements either towards the group work itself or towards the given task

What You Need:

Circle of chairs

A symbol that shows which person is allowed to speak

Method:

You get the chance to say something either about

- how you feel
- how satisfied you are with results of your group work
- what you think about the given question/task

Everybody may say something but there is no obligation.

Only opinions are allowed.

Statements won't be commented on.

Just one person speaks at a time.

Work with me ISBN 978-3-582-77856-7

Project

Aims:

To have the opportunity to work on a topic based on your interests, using language you feel comfortable with. Remember to try to speak English all the time.

What You Need:

A longer period of time/lessons to develop your own ideas and structures

Method:

When you start a project you need a "frame" that you can work with. Here below is a suggestion on how to coordinate the project structure. Note that you do not have to follow all the steps in this order. You may skip a step or replace one step with another.

Suggested Guidelines for Project Work

Step 1: Collect ideas for topics in **small groups**.
Step 2: Discuss these ideas **in class**.
Step 3: Decide which are the main topics and which other ideas need to be included.
Step 4: Plan/organise the workload **together** answering the following questions:
What do we want to achieve?
What do we need?
What do we have to do?
To keep track of your progress you can keep a project diary (➔ see page 218) and write down your time-structure and workload (Work and Time Schedule ➔ page 219).
Step 5: Form **project groups**.
Step 6: Decide **together how** the results should be presented.
Step 7: Decide **together how** your work should be assessed.
Step 8: Work in groups.
Step 9: Present the results.

Role Play

Aims:

To work on a situation that is based on your own private life or on your job
To develop empathy for the characters of the role play
To develop different ways of handling a situation
To solve a given problem

What You Need:

A place for the "stage"
Properties

Method:

Depending on your aims, you could either act out the scenario several times in order to get used to the targeted language patterns or you could continue the scenario by introducing fresh ideas dealing with the situation.

ENGLISH	PROJECT:	PROJECT DIARY NUMBER:

PROJECT DIARY

NAME: ____________________

GROUP: ____________________

Date	Today I worked on …	Today, I …								My Intentions/ Personal Challenge
		talked a lot in English	listened to the others	did a good job	did okay	didn't do a good job	achieved my plan	achieved some of my plan	achieved non of my plan	

Work with me ISBN 978-3-582-77856-7

Work and Time Schedule

Working Group	
Topic	

1) What do we want to achieve?

2) What do we need?

3) What do we have to do?	WHO?	WHEN?	✔
PRESENTATION	Everybody		

To Practise Reading and Writing

Internet Research (Web Quest)

Aims:

To gather new information and knowledge from the Internet
Selection and integration of knowledge for presentation

What You Need:

Groups
Computers or laptops with Internet access

Method:

To use time efficiently working on the computer, the following steps should be considered:

1. You need an effective introduction to the topic.
2. Teacher: provide the students with a variety of websites (which you have thoroughly researched!) so that they can gather all necessary information to complete their tasks.
3. Teacher: outline the way students should work through their tasks and how to organise information for the presentation.
4. Conclude the Web Quest by reviewing and reflecting on what has been learned.

Mind Map

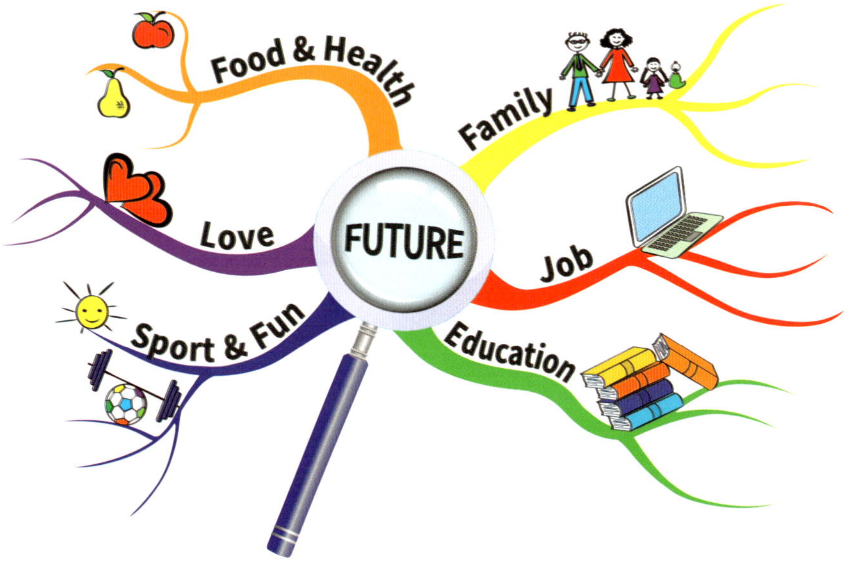

Aims:

To produce, to organise, to structure and to document thoughts and questions about a topic
To find out about already existing knowledge

What You Need:

Big posters or black board
Marker pens

Method:

The title of the main topic is written in the middle of the poster. Then write down the major aspects of the topic on main branches. Next, by drawing more lines, you subdivide the major aspects into minor aspects. It is important to write down your thoughts in key words only, otherwise the mind map might become overloaded. To clarify thoughts and to visualise the complexity of the topic, you may also use symbols, drawings and arrows.

Work with me ISBN 978-3-582-77856-7

Silent Written Discussion

"High-quality television for toddlers is very important"

How is high-quality TV defined anyway?

High-quality TV for babies should be just like a picture book (only with moving pictures)

There are several good childrens' shows out there ☺

Parents should watch TV together with their children, even if it's a special children's programme. And they should talk about it afterwards.

A no-no: commercials, violence, fast cuts, too much action

Toddlers don't learn by watching – they learn by doing it themselves. Therefore TV doesn't teach them anything!

Watching TV is part of our society!

Watching TV can be like a ritual (before bedtime etc.)

Not more than 30-60 minutes per day!

Children up to 3 years shouldn't watch TV at all (my opinion)

Kids take in television differently from adults – they have to "learn" first how to watch TV

Toddlers need simple structures (good, bad, cowardly). They do not understand complex characters yet.

CHILDREN TEND TO BELIEVE THAT TV IS REALITY, THEREFORE ONE HAS TO BE VERY CAREFUL …

It is useful to have the same animals or moderators lead through the show

SOME SAY: TV EVEN HELPS BABIES WITH THEIR BRAIN DEVELOPMENT …
– NO! WATCHING TV HINDERS THEIR CEREBRAL DEVELOPMENT!

Babies who watch TV regularly know 20 % fewer words than other babies!! ☹

Aims:

To join in, to warm up
To gather already existing knowledge
To discuss a topic
To argue and to persuade
To give feedback
To evaluate

What You Need:

Tables, flipchart, several posters or wallpaper, marker pens
Good writing skills

Method:

On each table there should be one poster (or piece of wallpaper) on which there is written a question, remark or keyword about the topic. Then walk around and write down your opinions, suggestions or answers on the posters without talking to each other. While walking around, read the remarks of other students and next to them write your own comments. As soon as everybody is finished you can talk about the different statements.

Appendix *Working with Me (Methods and Skills)*

Information Sheet

Aims:

To sum up the main information about a certain topic on one page (for more than **one** page → see "Brochure")

What You Need:

Resources (books, texts), computer

Method:

Collect the main facts/information about the given topic. First provide a short overview of the main theme. Divide your information into several aspects. Find headings for each one and make sure the sheet is well laid out so that the reader can easily see what the main points are. Also add the list of literature used.

Brochure

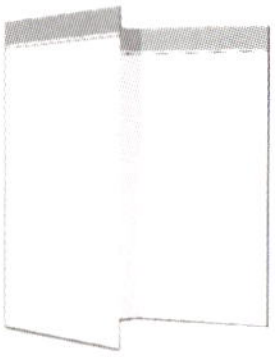

Aims:

To sum up the main information about a certain topic in a more detailed way (more than one page)
To analyse the problem from the expert's point of view
To present it to the public

What You Need:

Resources (Internet, books), computer

Method: Eight Helpful Steps in Writing a Brochure

1. Write the brochure with readers in mind. What are your readers' concerns? What do they want to know about the topic you are presenting to them?
2. Put helpful information in your brochure to encourage readers to keep it, refer to it often or pass it on to other people.
3. The first thing the reader will see is the front cover. It must be eye-catching to motivate the reader to look inside.
4. List the contents on the first page of your brochure and list the advantages of reading it.
5. Provide clear instructions and make sure each headline tells readers exactly what they can find out in each section.
6. Get straight to the point. Do not waste time on irrelevancies.
7. Make it personal. Write your brochure with an imaginary person in mind, as writing in a direct „I'm-talking-only-to-you" style will encourage a positive response.
8. Add atmosphere. Try to persuade your reader to share your feelings.

Poem "Elfin"

Aims:

An "elfin" (German "Elfchen") is a little poem which consists of eleven words. You can use it to give a short statement to a certain topic, e.g. at the end of a lesson.

What You Need:

Piece of paper with the following pattern of lines:

Method:

By using this poem you have to concentrate on the main facts. You have to find eleven words which describe your point of view or your statement and put them into the given pattern. It may be full sentences, it can also be just words in a certain order. You can use punctuation marks whenever you want.

Work with me ISBN 978-3-582-77856-7

Improving Your Skills

How to Analyse and Interpret Texts and Literature

How to Write a Summary

Before you start writing your summary you have to do some preparation.
Preparation:

First read the given text for overall content by "skimming through". Write one sentence that summarizes the whole text. Make sure to use the 3rd person and present tense.
Now reread the text thoroughly and highlight the main ideas. Divide the text into sections according to the writer's chain of reasoning. Try to sum up each section with one sentence.
Give a concise account of the main points and leave out minor facts. **Do not** include your own opinion and make sure you use your own words.

Writing the Summary:

In your opening statement include the title of the text, the name of the writer and your sentence summarizing the whole text, for example: *"This article, entitled XXX, by John Smith, discusses the dangers which the Internet poses for young children."*
Straightaway, the reader knows what the theme of the text is. Now you can link your other short sentences together to complete your summary. Finally: check for grammar and style.

How to Write a Characterisation

If you want to characterise a person, you have to gather the information given in the text and arrange them into different categories such as:

Situation/ Position	Outer Appearance	Behaviour	Thoughts	Feelings/ Attitudes	Reaction of Others Towards Him/Her
...	...	...	...	...	...

Make sure that you only describe the person and **do not** interpret their behaviour or thoughts. Ask yourself if the character changes during the development of the text and if so, how. Put the notes in the chart as well, so the development is visible. You can also compare two or more characters: just add more categories such as "Similarities" or "Differences".
Now write a short introduction where you present the character and their current situation.
Organise your notes into paragraphs and don't forget to quote from the text: *Christopher is an honest person ("I do not tell lies" page 24, line 1).*
At the end write a conclusion that sums up the result of your characterisation – here you may interpret behaviour.

Appendix *Working with Me (Methods and Skills)*

How to Write a Comment

When writing a comment you clearly state your opinion on a given topic, supporting your point of view by quoting arguments taken from the text or your own experience. To write a good comment keep four steps in mind:

Step 1 Preparation:
Read the task and make sure you understand the topic of the text. Collect and group the ideas (pros and cons) of the text and your own ideas.

Step 2 Introduction:
Start your comment with an introductory sentence, for example: *"Child poverty has recently been the subject of much media and public debate"*. This then leads on logically to the question you want to discuss, *"... and I wish to examine the arguments in the text and also state my own ideas."*

Step 3 Argumentation:
Devote one paragraph to each of the arguments you want to present and justify them by using quotations and examples. Link your ideas together and show possible consequences. Use expressions such as *however, on the other hand, in spite of that* if you are contrasting pros and cons (see Classroom Phrases, page 213). You should also anticipate points of view that other people could have.

Step 4 Conclusion:
After presenting all your pro and con arguments make a concluding statement, in which you sum up your arguments, giving a final thought.

Analysing Symbols in Literature

Symbols are an important key to understanding and analysing literature. A symbol has not only "literal" meaning, but also additional meanings beyond the literal (light, colour blue, dreams, signs ...). The more you read literature, the more you will come across words and objects that function symbolically. Symbols may have very narrow or quite wide ranges of meaning.
Because of the nature of symbols, literature has what is sometimes called "surplus meaning": one can never really *completely* state the meaning of a piece of literature. Another reader may produce new meanings. If you refer to symbols and their meaning try to convince the reader of your interpretation and even give proof of it.

How to Work on Your Application

→ *Please note that this letter of application is designed according to UK standards. If you want to send your application to a different country, check on the Internet for the appropriate design.*

Letter of Application

You usually write a letter of application when you want to respond to an advertised job offer which you may have found in the newspaper or on the Internet. You attach your CV to the letter of application. Your letter of application should contain the following aspects.

Recipient's Address: The address of the recipient is placed on the left-hand side. If you know the name and the position of the person whom you are writing to, put this with their address. The more precise you can make it the better, because this shows that you have really given your application a lot of thought.

Letterhead: The letterhead is usually placed on the right-hand side of the letter. It includes your address, telephone number and your e-mail address.

Work with me ISBN 978-3-582-77856-7

Date: The date is usually placed on the right-hand side under the letterhead. Make sure that you always use the actual date (in this format 24 April 2020).

Subject Line: The subject line is a key element in your letter of application. Here you give the main reason for writing. It is placed on the left-hand side again.

Salutation: If you know the person to whom you are writing, use their name in the salutation to make it more personal. If you do not know their name, use the formal "Dear Madam or Sir,".

Body: The aim of your letter is to describe your reasons for writing and your qualities as clearly and relevantly as possible. In a short opening paragraph state which post you are applying for and where you saw it advertised. In your next paragraph give your reasons for doing so and in a third describe those aspects of your education and work experience which are relevant to the job for which you are applying.

Complimentary Close: A closing paragraph sums up the letter and indicates the next steps you want to take. Write a short and factual sentence expressing your hopes. For example, *"I look forward to your reply/an offer of an interview at your earliest convenience."*

Ending and Signature: Make sure you use a standard ending, so that your letter is not too personal. Sign the letter by hand but also type your name underneath your signature.

Enclosed Documents: If you enclose documents such as your CV, it is essential to list them there.

Letter of application

Katja Deriks
Soltauer Str. 12
12345 Musterstadt
Tel. 01234-567899
k.deriks@gmx.de
Germany

Shoemaker Family
117 Arlington Road
Manchester
M2 5ND
UK

24 April 2025

Subject: Application for the Post of Nanny

Dear Mr and Mrs Shoemaker,

I wish to apply for the post of nanny which I saw advertised in (name of newspaper).

I enjoy working with children, toddlers and babies. At present, I look after a seven-month-old boy. My duties include feeding and bathing him and changing his diapers. But most of all I enjoy playing with him.

I am currently a trainee at the Vocational School for Early-Years Teachers in Lüneburg, Germany. I will take my final exams in June, 2025. My subjects at school include psychology, theory of education, childcare, handicrafts and English. My comprehension and my written English are good but my oral skills are less well developed. An opportunity to work in the UK would help me to improve them.

I would also love to get to know your wonderful country! I look forward to hearing from you at your earliest convenience.

Yours sincerely,

Katja Deriks
Katja Deriks

Enclosed documents:
CV

CV (Résumé)

General CV Guidelines

A Curriculum Vitae (lat., "course of life"), also known as a Résumé, is a summary of your relevant job experiences and education. You usually write a CV when you want to apply for a job. The purpose of a CV is to get you a job interview. The following guidelines give you some help of what to include in a good CV.

Length. A one-page CV works well if you want to start working after finishing your training as an early-childhood teacher. If you have two pages, make sure the most important information is stated on the first page.

Appearance. Direct the reader's eye with the format. Make sure it is well-organized and concise. Make sure there are no typographical, spelling or grammatical errors. Information that has been crossed out or handwritten is unacceptable.

Content. Design your CV with a particular objective in mind. Present information important to the objective first. List information in descending order of importance. Be selective about what you include in your CV, but never falsify or exaggerate information. Sell yourself – attract attention to your special abilities. Concentrate on the positive and use action verbs to describe your back-ground.

→ *You can also download a European CV. This so-called "Europass" is an initiative of the European Commission and helps people looking for experience abroad to make their skills/qualifications easily understood in Europe. See http://europass.cedefop.europa.eu*

CV Categories

The following categories are usually found in a CV. These are suggestions. You should adopt those that best fit your needs.

Personal Data. Make sure your name is the most obvious piece of information on your CV. Write down your marital status and the country you come from when you apply in a different state. Include your address and phone number, with ZIP and area codes. List a message phone number if you do not have an answering machine and give an e-mail address.

Objective. An objective gives your CV a "focus". It also gives credibility and direction to your CV and suggests commitment on your part. It should be specific enough to tell the employer the kind of work you seek, yet general enough to include the full range of jobs you will consider. This will take some thought! If the statement is so specific that it would eliminate you from consideration for other jobs in which you have interest, you might consider having a CV for each type of job (not necessarily each job). Some disciplines require objectives; others discourage their use.

Education. List your educational background in chronological order, starting with primary school up to your highest degree.

Work Experience. Sum up your work experience that shows your experience regarding the job you are applying for. Once again list it in chronological order.

Language Abilities. You can list this section separately, as a part of the qualifications statement, or in the additional information section if there is a likelihood that this ability will be used by employ-ers. Specify the language(s) you read, write and/or speak and your facility in each.

Additional Information. Skills, activities and hobbies or even language ability can be placed under this or a more specific category.

References. Generally, a reference sheet will consist of the name, title, business mailing address, phone number and the reference itself.

→ *Please note that in the UK the referee (= former employer) sends the reference to your future employer, after they have asked for it.*

Work with me ISBN 978-3-582-77856-7

Katja Deriks

Soltauer Str. 12
12345 Musterstadt
Tel. 01234-567899
k.deriks@gmx.de

Personal Data

• Marital Status:	Single
• Nationality:	German
• Age:	22 years
• Date of Birth:	23rd September 2003
• Place of Birth:	Bremen, Germany

Objective

Post of Nanny

Education

• 2009 – 2011	Primary School, Bremen
• 2011 – 2020	General Certificate of Secondary Education, Bremen
• 2021 – present	Vocational College of Further Education (Early-Childhood Teacher), Lüneburg

Work Experience

• February – April 2022 (10 weeks)	Practical training in residential home for children to the age of 8 years, Lüneburg
• July, 2023 – May, 2024 (2 days a week)	Practical training in crèche, Lüneburg
• August, 2024 – May 2025 (2 days a week)	Practical training in nursery school, Hamburg

Language Abilities

English
Comprehension and written skills good, oral skills less well-developed

• Summer (6 weeks) 2023	English teacher at EF-Summercamp, Malta
• June 2020 – May 2021	Nanny in Great Falls, Virginia, USA

Hobbies

- Running
- Mountainbiking
- Reading

Solutions: Working with Grammar

[Note: Other synonyms are of course sometimes acceptable.]

Ae1
1 perfect/good/excellent etc.
2 ill/poorly/unwell
3 unhappy
4 bad/dirty
5 angry
6 tired
7 cold
8 hoarse

Ae2
1 Have you **ever** met my brother?
2 You should do your homework **carefully**.
3 Rapidly **and greedily** she ate her hamburger.
4 It leaves **at six a.m. from platform 4.**
5 He came in … and **finally** sat down.
6 I did **quite** like the book but the film was **rather** boring.
7 The supervisor (**politely**) welcomed the parent **politely** who … **carefully** read the report.
8 The new boy can speak English **well** but cannot understand if you speak **fast** with an accent.

Ae3
1 Do we have to walk much **farther**?
2 He has been ill **lately**.
3 She has **hardly** slept four hours.
4 You speak too **fast.**
5 I was **highly** delighted.
6 They were **fairly** hungry.
7 He worked **hard**.
8 She was **ill** suited to work in a nursery

Be1
1 He is playing on the swings.
2 He is painting a clown.
3 He is riding a tricycle.
4 He is drinking milk.
5 He is arguing with Natasha.
6 He is building a tower out of bricks.
7 He is trying to do a jigsaw with a friend.
8 He is crying because he has hurt his finger/because his finger is hurting.

Be2
At the moment …
1 She is attending a conference.
2 She is bandaging a child's leg.
3 She is speaking with parents in her office.
4 She is taking/driving a child to hospital.

Tomorrow …
5 She is flying to London.
6 She is discussing the budget.
7 She is giving a lecture on environmental education at the university.
8 She is receiving/welcoming some Canadian students who are visiting Germany.

Be3
1 **Does** he ever **play** with Michael?
2 **Does** he **go** to the toilet very often?
3 **Does** he (occasionally) **steal** food from other children?
4 **Does** he (sometimes) **draw** violent pictures (sometimes)?
5 **Does** he usually **speak** much to his neighbours?
6 **Does** he ever **have** any marks or bruises?
7 **Did** he **arrive** late yesterday?
8 **Did** he **lose** his temper last week?

Be4
1 Do you think the child in the corner is ill?
2 The girl really does look sad.
3 Did she eat anything at break?
4 She did eat a banana …
5 … but didn't drink a thing.
6 She didn't come on time this morning …
7 … and her mother did look really grim (angry).
8 She does give me the impression that she is not exactly happy.

Be5
Up to now Mathilda **has talked (been talking)** a lot to/with her neighbours. She **has shared (been sharing)** her biscuits with the new boy. She **has read (been reading)** her storybook frequently. She **has drawn (been drawing)** a picture of the doll's house. She **has played (been playing)** on the swings and the slide. She **has not been/gone** to the toilet. She **has helped (been helping)** the new boy write a title. She **has not had** a drink.

Be6
1 I **have** only visit**ed** Greece once up to now.
2 We **have** not eat**en** yet today.
3 She **has** just **met** the new supervisor.
4 I **have** not **made** a mistake so far.

Work with me ISBN 978-3-582-77856-7

5 She **has broken** three cups in the last five minutes.
6 **Have** you already **seen** this film?
7 They **have** liv**ed** in London for six years.
8 **Have** you work**ed** with young people before?

Be7 1 Könntest du kommen, um Jemima beim Lesen zu hören?
2 Konnte sie die Frage verstehen?
3 Könnten sie vielleicht eine halbe Stunde draußen spielen?
4 Wie viel Zeit könnten wir beim Lesen der Geschichte verbringen?
5 Ich konnte die Zeitschrift nicht finden, die ich mitbringen wollte.
6 Es könnte morgen sehr kalt sein.
7 Letztendlich konnten wir ihr Lunchpaket finden.
8 Sie konnte keinen Polizisten in der Nähe finden.

Be8 1 Yesterday I was able to persuade Andreas to read a sentence aloud.
2 Maybe we could go on a trip to the zoo.
3 She was so hoarse she couldn't sing.
4 Were you able to understand the Albanian child in the end?
5 Could you come to me at eleven o'clock?
6 Finally he was able (managed) to pronounce the word.

Be9 1 Du **hättest** Paul eine einfachere Frage stellen **können**.
2 Ich **konnte** eine buntere Geschichte finden.
3 Bis wir die Anweisungen fanden, **hatten** wir das Spiel nicht verstehen **können.**
4 Hoffentlich **wirst** du meine Handschrift lesen **können.**
5 Sie **hat** gar nichts essen **können.**
6 Sie kamen so spät an, sie **konnten** erst um zehn Uhr anfangen.
7 Ihr dürft nicht auf den Spielplatz gehen, weil ihr unartig wart.
8 Wenn wir nur einen neuen Fernseher kaufen **könnten**!

Be10 1 As part of our training we **had to** do an outward-bound course.
2 She **has had to** contact the police.
3 The mother **will have to** explain the burn on her child.
4 Until Sanghita arrived from London we **had** not **had to** speak any English at the nursery.
5 The Indian girl **must** not eat any chicken soup as she is a vegetarian!
6 I was so glad I **did** not **have to** speak to that difficult parent.
7 We **have** not **had to** tell Jemima today about shouting.
8 I **must**/**have got to** contact a parent! Little Peter **<u>has got to</u>** *(~~must~~) go to hospital.

[*Obwohl es sich um einen Notfall handelt, wurde es nicht hier, sondern **vorher entschlossen**, dass Peter zum Krankenhaus musste. Es geht hier bloß um die Tatsache. Abgrenzung: "Peter must go to hospital!" würde man **in dem Moment sagen**, wenn der Ernst der Situation klar wird.]

Be11 1 Du sollst heute abwaschen!
2 Wir sollten jetzt draußen spielen, denn es wird später regnen.
3 Vielleicht wird Jodie morgen nicht kommen.
4 Es kann sein, dass sie sich erkältet hat.
5 Darf ich dir eine persönliche Frage stellen?
6 Sebastian, du solltest den anderen erlauben, auf der Schaukel zu spielen.
7 Katrina sollte mit ihrem Vater nach Hause gehen.
8 Du hättest die Kinder nicht ohne Aufsicht auf den Spielplatz lassen sollen.

Be12 SHALL WE
1 go on the swing
2 paint a picture
3 read a story
4 have a glass of milk
5 have a biscuit
6 sing a song
7 go on the slide
8 bake a cake?

NO, I DON'T WANT TO
1 go on the swing ... etc.

I WANT TO
1 go for a walk
2 make a clay figure
3 have a sleep
4 play a game
5 dance
6 watch television
7 listen to a CD
8 go home

Work with me ISBN 978-3-582-77856-7

Ce1
1. My **elder** sister is one year **older** than my brother.
2. Today there were **fewer** children at the nursery school than yesterday.
3. You should use **less** paint and **more** water.
4. Sophie reads (the) **least**.
5. The **nearest** youth club is in Elmshorn. The **next** disco is taking place there tomorrow.
6. Now you look **worse** and you have eaten so **little**.

De1 Open answers

De2 [Usually more than one answer is possible. Here are the most suitable ones.]
1. **I dream of** being a millionaire.
2. **I insist on** talking to the supervisor.
3. **She thanked me for** finding the purse.
4. **I am looking** forward to going on holiday.
5. **I worry about** paying the bill.
6. **He blamed** me for the child falling off the swing.
7. **I succeeded in** passing the test.
8. **I object to** you talking to me so impolitely!

De3 Open answers

De4
1. Despite **working** hard he failed.
2. By **paying** close attention she soon learnt the game.
3. Apart from **drawing** a face the boy did nothing today.
4. Without **saying** a word, she went out of the room.
5. You should have used the red paint instead of **using** the yellow.
6. Since **learning** English he joins in more.
7. The mother disappeared without **paying** the fee.
8. You should join in instead of just **sitting** here in the corner.

Ee1 [agree and come not needed]
1. If ever he does a picture, he **paints** a house.
2. If you don't stop shouting, I **will phone** your father!
3. If we can clear the glass from the swings, we/they **can play** outside.
4. If you don't listen now, you **won't/will not understand** the story.
5. If you touch the socket, you **will get** a shock. (*might get ist nicht streng genug*)
6. If ever I feel depressed, **I listen** to music.
7. If kids watch too much TV, it ***affects** their play OR **will affect** their play. (**when könnte if ersetzen)*
8. If I say "don't scream", you **must be** quiet OR you ***will be** quiet! (**betont, entschlossen wie B12)*

Ee2 [arrive and understand not needed]
1. If I knew his number, I **would/could call** him.
2. If she could speak better English, she **could work** in London.
3. If we bought some cake and balloons, we **could have** a party!
4. If Joshua finished his picture, I **would/could/might hang** it on the wall.
5. If you listened, you **would not/might not get** confused.
6. If we ate early, we **could go** to the cinema!
7. If you didn't keep hitting them, the others **might not/would not dislike** you.
8. If the mother came in, she **could/would see** how Scarlet behaves.

Ee3
1. If I **had known** his number, I **would/could have called** him.
2. If she **had spoken (could have spoken)** better English, she **could have worked** in London.
3. If we **had bought** some cake and balloons, we **could have had** a party!
4. If Joshua **had finished** his picture, I **would/could/might have hung** it on the wall.
5. If you **had listened**, you **would not/might not have gotten** confused.
6. If we **had eaten** early, we **could have gone** to the cinema!
7. If you **had not kept hitting** them, the others **might not/would not have disliked** you.
8. If the mother **had come** in, she **could/would have seen** how Scarlet behaves/behaved.

Fe1 [Many answers are possible]
We should …
1. … **ask/advise/remind/tell** her parents to wash her hair.
2. … **tell/warn** her not to steal and **make her find/tell** her to find the sandwich.
3. … **ask** the assistant to tie her laces OR **show/teach** Vanessa how to tie her laces.

Work with me ISBN 978-3-582-77856-7

4 … **encourage/remind/teach/tell** her to respect (other children's work).
5 … **warn** her not to throw and to be kind to others.
6 … **allow/get/persuade** her to lie down.
7 … **show** her/**get** her neighbour/the assistant to **show** her how to hold scissors.
8 … **arrange for/ask/get/invite** her mother to come in and watch her.

Fe2 [Many answers are possible]
It was …
1 … **crazy/naughty/cruel of** you to slap your neighbour.
2 … **good of/important for/sensible/wise of** you to pay more attention than normal.
3 … **good/kind of** you to help Lisa mix the paint.
4 … **naughty/silly/stupid of** you to throw clay at Connor.
5 … **good of** you to look for Amy's shoe.
6 Was it **necessary for/sensible/wise of** you to shout so loud?
7 … **kind of** you to listen to Harriet read.
8 … **stupid of** you to break Callum's mug.
9 … **clever of/important for** you to work out the right answer.
10 … **tactless/cruel of** you to mention Bryony's dead rabbit.

Fe3 Open answers

Fe4
1 wet; to play
2 hot; to eat
3 big/large; to see
4 strong/well; to push
5 little; to feel
6 early/soon; to get up
7 reliable/dependable; to get/to drive
8 much; to like

Fe5 Open answers

Ge1
1 **Depressed,** I closed the book.
2 **If told off**, the children just laugh.
3 **Whenever asked about her son's diet,** the mother gets angry.
4 **If warned about taking her neighbour's crayon,** Amy usually listens.
5 **If shouted at**, small children will only be scared.
6 **Asked why he was crying**, Tony blamed Kirsty.
7 **Questioned about the bruise,** Lisa refused to answer.
8 **Reminded about washing his hands,** Harry was rude to the assistant.

Ge2 [Not needed: He cannot buy a watch. He telephoned the father.]
1 **When speaking to a child** he should have someone with him.
2 **Being colour-blind** he has painted his tree red.
3 **After eating three apples** he got stomach ache.
4 **(While) Listening to the fairy story** he fell asleep.
5 **Before phoning the father** he made sure he had the right number.
6 **Having no watch** he was late for the interview.
7 **Seeing his mother** he laughed and ran to her.
8 **Sitting down** he suddenly starts to cry.

Ge3

I WATCHED…	I HEARD…
1 … Sean **painting/ drawing a** picture.	2 … Bethan **singing** a song.
3 … Amy **playing on/ sliding down** the slide.	4 … Colin **having** an argument with Tim.
5 … Emma **(un)tying** her laces.	
6 … Wayne **kicking/ throwing** a ball.	
7 … Beverley **making** a cake.	
8 … Kerry **(un)wrapping/ opening** a birthday present.	

Ge4
1 **Having broken the window** the boys ran away.
2 **Having worked in Manchester** Pia spoke English with a northern accent.
3 **Having called the police** the supervisor waited in her office.
4 **Having walked back from the zoo** the children were very tired.
5 **Not having read the report** the father become very angry.
6 **Having lost the map** we did not/could not find the youth hostel.
7 **Having had/made a hot drink** they went to bed.
8 **Having found a tin opener** I made some soup.

Ge5 [There is often more than one solution]
1 (When) She heard that a child was screaming (and) she ran outside.
2 Bethan was playing on the swings when she began to choke.
3 As he came into the room he was singing.
4 I heard a car drive off. *("I heard that/how a car was driving off" ist sehr linkisch.)*
5 The noise frightened me so I locked the door. *(Passiv: "I was very frightened by the noise so…")*
6 I warned Harry to be careful as/when he crossed the road and he ceased to chatter.
7 (After) I (had) spent three years in Birmingham I knew the city quite well.
8 Jemimah hadn't tasted pasta before and (so) (she) was a little nervous.

He1
1 The nurse/doctor will see the injured child soon.
2 The mother/father/parent collected Joanne at three p.m. and took her home.
3 A child/Children was/were bullying Gary at school.
4 The receptionist/the garage owner/mechanic had told me they would repair my car by five p.m.
5 The secretary is just typing the letter.
6 The police arrested the football hooligans.
7 The supervisor/we/the staff/the inspector frequently check(s) the kitchen to make sure that someone/staff has/have cleaned it.
8 A wasp/a bee/an insect/a nettle has stung little Sasha.

He2
1 Five large windows **were smashed**.
2 All the basketballs **were taken**.
3 Some display work **was ruined**.
4 Graffiti **was/were written** on a wall.
5 A hole **was made** in a wall.
6 Bushes **were torn up** in the garden.
7 The fabric in a sofa **was ripped**.
8 The TV cable **was pulled** out.

He3
1 The windows ***will be mended/replaced.** *(*or will have been mended/replaced, redone)*
2 The basketballs **will be replaced.**
3 The display work **will be redone**.
4 The graffiti/wall **will be painted over.**
5 The hole **will be filled in**.
6 The bushes **will be replanted**.
7 The sofa fabric **will be sewn.**
8 The TV cable **will be reconnected**.

Ie1 Open answers

Je1 [There are a number of possibilities]
The mother asked/demanded if I was Inga and I confirmed that I was. She demanded that I stop picking on her daughter/She shouted/declared/complained that I was picking on her daughter. She declared/complained that I had told her off the previous day/day before and asserted/maintained/insisted/exclaimed that she had not done anything (wrong).
I apologised/I replied/said/told her that I was sorry and asked who her daughter was. I wondered if it was Amy. She confirmed that it was. (Amy Goss). She repeated that I had told her off and added that I had shouted at her. I denied that I had/I asserted/maintained/ insisted that I had not and assured her/stressed that I would never shout at her. She retorted/insisted that I had and suggested/asserted that I had told her off for leaving a mess in the washroom. I confirmed/stressed that I had told off the whole group about being untidy and maintained/added/emphasized/explained that it had been a general comment and stressed that it had not been (said) in anger. I argued/suggested that Amy was exaggerating. I admitted/acknowledged that I had told her off calmly some time previously for telling a lie. The mother retorted that Amy did not lie/The mother denied that Amy lied. She announced that she wanted to come in and see the supervisor about me. She asserted/claimed/declared that I frightened her. I acknowledged that Amy was very timid but stressed that I was always careful how I spoke to her.

Je2
A: Barbara, the toilet by the front door isn't flushing.
B: I know! Listen, I've been on the phone twice to the plumber. What more can I do if he won't come out till tomorrow? I told the children to use the other toilet by the kitchen.
A: Chloe and Zoe either forgot or ignored you. They've used the broken one anyway.
B: I am really going to lose my temper with them.
A: Barbara, you should calm down.

Work with me ISBN 978-3-582-77856-7

B: I'm sorry ... I've been under a lot of stress since yesterday because my cat went missing and my hus-
band sprained his ankle and lost his wallet looking for it. And this morning, when I opened the garage door I found the cat fast asleep on the bonnet of my car. I won't tell my husband.

A: Oh, that's really sad. Shall I make you a cup of coffee?

PAST TENSE EXERCISE 1

1 We **discussed/were discussing/have been discussing** Paul's mother.
2 I **have** never **heard** such a story! It's crazy.
3 **Did** you **speak** to Mrs Hurst yesterday?
4 He said he **had** still not **made** up his mind.
5 Once I **had come** back to Germany I went into youth work.
6 **Has** she **met** the supervisor yet?
7 **Have** you **lived** here in Hamburg long?
8 She **sat** down, looked at me and started to cry.
9 I **knew** her when I was in Berlin.
10 He would **have answered** her letter if he had not lost her address.
11 We **have** not **seen** the youth hostel warden so far.
12 We **did** not **eat** until eight p.m.
13 **Did** she **work** at the nursery long before she retired?
14 The parents **have been waiting** in the office since nine this morning.
15 Please hurry! The film will **have finished** by the time we get to the cinema!
16 The train **was leaving/had left** when we arrived at the station.
17 When **did** the plane **land**?
18 It **landed** twenty minutes ago.
19 The fire alarm sounded as I **was getting** ready for bed.
20 I **have been thinking** for some time now about changing my job.

PAST TENSE EXERCISE 2

1 Once I **had spoken** to the father I **understood** the child's difficulty.
2 Not **having read** the book I **did** not **know** the story.
3 As I **was walking**/**(walked)** home I **remembered** I **had** not **read** the letter.
4 Last year three clubs **were broken** into.
5 Our club **has** never **been broken** into.
6 **Frightened** by the fire alarm, the children **stopp**ed playing.
7 Last month the fire alarm **went** off twice.
8 When I **was** in London I **lived** with Iranian students.
9 Whenever I **have been** to London the sun **has** always **shone**.
10 The last time I **saw** Paul he **had** long hair.
11 Until last night I **had** never **eaten** lobster before.
12 **Have** you ever **played** chess?
13 What **have you done/been doing** since two o'clock?
14 Dear Libby, we **have found** a great hotel! It has a sauna.
15 In the last ten minutes Simon **has drunk** three glasses of water.
16 I **asked** his mum on Monday whether he **had been examined** by the doctor.
17 Where **did** you **study** English?
18 She **has been crying** ever since she **arrived** at nine.
19 Kevin finally **admitted** that he **had stolen** Amy's purse.
20 As soon as we (**had**) ***heard** the news report we ***phoned** the police.
(* *gleichzeitig)*
OR: As soon as we **had listened** to the news report *(= ganze Sendung)* we phoned the police.

Appendix *Bildquellenverzeichnis, Textverzeichnis*

Bildquellenverzeichnis

akg-images GmbH, Berlin: S. 93/1 (akg-images); 152/1 (akg-images / Fototeca Gilardi); 152/3 (akg-images / Science Source)
Alamy Ltd., Oxon, Großbritannien: S. 164 (Jeffrey Blackler / Alamy Stock Foto)
Beyer foto.grafik, Berlin: S. 111
Depositphotos EU Limited, Limassol, Cyprus: S. 228 (Mind-Map)
dpa-Picture-Alliance GmbH, Frankfurt am Main: S. 2/1 (picture alliance / dpa); 26 (picture alliance/United Archives | 91070); 38 (picture-alliance/ dpa); 39 (picture-alliance/ dpa/dpaweb); 40 (picture alliance / Claudia Drescher/dpa-Zentralbild/ZB); 94 (picture alliance/The Advertising Archives); 95/1 (picture alliance / empics); 121 (picture-alliance/ dpa); 134/7 (picture-alliance/ dpa/dpaweb); 144/1 (picture-alliance/ dpa/dpaweb); 144/2 (picture-alliance / dpa); 152/2 (picture-alliance / dpa); 173 (picture-alliance/ dpa)
iStockphoto, Berlin: S. 7 (pawel.gaul); 11/1 (ljubaphoto); 33/2 (svetikd); 58 (GMVozd); 66/1 (South_agency); 80/1 (Yaroslav Olieinikov); 82 (SDI Productions); 90 (Gabriel Pevide); 96 (Johnny Greig); 98/1 (yacobchuk); 98/2 (blackwaterimages); 105 (kali9); 107 (duncan1890); 109 (Deagreez); 110 (FatCamera); 114 (SolStock); 115 (andreswd); 134/1 (FatCamera); 137 (SolStock); 146 (iStockphoto); 147 (gradyreese); 151 (vm); 157 (tatyana_tomsickova); 158 (stock_colors); 161 (kali9); 179/1 (Portra); 179/2 (sanse293); 183 (CreativaImages)
Köhn, Birte, Hamburg: S. 165/1; 200/1; 200/2
Meisterburg, Christina, Mainz: S. 88
Panther Media GmbH, München: S.47/1 (G.Grischa)
Shutterstock Images LLC, New York, USA: S. 2/2 (Undrey); 3/1 (CREATISTA); 3/2 (fizkes); 9/2 (Gabi Moisa); 11/2 (Pixel-Shot); 12 (Krakenimages.com); 18 (Oksana Kuzmina); 19/2 (Sebastian Kaulitzki); 22/1 (Anna Kraynova); 22/2 (Zabavna); 23/1 (Saran_Poroong); 23/2 (Vagengeim); 25 (Roman Samborskyi); 27 (Luzss); 32/1 (Krakenimages.com); 32/2 (Mala Iryna); 33/1 (stockfour); 35 (Gorlov-Studio); 44/1 (DI Studio); 44/2 (Roman Samborskyi); 44/3 (Roman Samborskyi); 44/4 (Roman Samborskyi); 44/5 (Roman Samborskyi); 44/6 (wedmoments.stoc); 45 (Andrii Spy_k); 52 (Zhuravlev Andrey); 54 (Yuriy Golub); 57/4 (Evan Lorne); 59/2 (margouillat photo); 60 (GraphicsRF); 62 (haveseen); 71 (Krakenimages.com); 78 (subarashii21); 80/2 (CroMary); 83 (Grégory Delattre); 85 (Halfpoint); 92/1 (Fordham Dabney); 92/2 (Hseena); 92/3 (Pixel-Shot); 92/4 (Aaron Amat); 93/2 (Ramona Heim); 95/2 (Marko Poplasen); 100 (LStockStudio); 101 (Giideon); 102 (Africa Studio); 103 (LumineImages); 108 (Dusan Petkovic); 113 (Juan Ci); 122,124,126,128,131 (Guillermo Sena Studio); 132/1 (aerogondo2); 132/2 (adriaticfoto); 134/8 (travelview); 134/9 (VIJAY SUNDAR SUVARNA); 139 (hanohiki); 155 (AYO Production); 156/2 (Monkey Business Images); 160 (Monstar Studio); 163/1 (conrado); 163/2 (Raggedstone); 163/3 (Kit8.net); 166/1 (Luis Molinero); 166/2 (Master1305); 167/1 (silvae); 167/1a (Luis Molinero); 168 (wallybird); 171 (Anatoliy Sadovskiy); 172/1 (vchal); 172/2 (Kiev.Victor); 185 (Ljupco Smokovski); 189 (Kabachki.photo)
stock.adobe.com: S. 9/1 (Nicolas Kelen); 14 (Gabees); 15 (Gabees); 19/1 (stoneman); 22/3 (Sport Moments); 24 (Alena Kovalenko); 31 (pictonaut); 47/2 (Katarzyna Leszczynsk); 51 (AboutLife); 55 (Reena); 57/1 (dinostock); 57/2 (volff); 57/3 (anaumenko); 57/5 (Paulista); 59/1 (volff); 68 (diego cervo); 73 (David); 74/1 (16to9foto); 74/2 (Klaus Eppele); 76 (Jack); 84 (Mikel Wohlschlegel); 86 (ollegn); 87/1 (Wenhao Zhu); 87/2 (Findus2000); 87/3 (sixmini); 106/1 (New Africa); 106/2 (pamela_d_mcadams); 112 (Karin Lau); 117 (Erika Kyte); 120 (Suzan); 134/2 (A. Jüttner_Lohmann); 134/3 (Hallgerd); 134/4 (Paul Moore); 134/5 (Irina Fischer); 134/6 (pzAxe); 142/1 (Kailash Kumar); 142/2 (Rui Vale de Sousa); 143 (Monkey Business); 149 (Klaus Eppele); 150 (Kaputtknie); 153 (VILevi); 156/1 (swmedia); 159 (Jürgen Fälchle); 170 (Patrick Hermans); Umschlag vorne innen: (dikobrazik); Umschlag hinten innen: (dikobrazik)
Verlag Handwerk und Technik GmbH: S. 34 (S.Bonik)

Textverzeichnis

S. 14	Greg, F.: Baby's Words, aus: www.netpoets.com, Colon, USA
S. 15	Fuchs, K. und J.: The Joy of Raising a Baby, aus: www.poemsource.com, Cocolalla, USA
S. 16	Child Development Institute, Child Development Chart, www.childdevelopmentinfo.com, Orange, USA
S. 19	Dr. Rosenzweig, M. http://faculty.washington.edu/chudler/neurok.html Brain development/K. A. Wesson http://www.sciencemaster.com/wesson/home.php Learning Brain Plasticity
S. 23	Brooks, R./Goldstein, S. http://familytlc.net/resilient_children_preteen.html;10 Ways to Make Your Children More Resilient
S. 26	Derman-Sparks, L.: Anti-Bias Curriculum, Washington, DC, USA 1989; Children are aware: www.teachingforchange.org
S. 31–33	The Foundation Stage Forum – www.foundation-stage.info, Lewes, UK
S. 34	Dr Hill, S.: Learning Stories, Magill, Australia
S. 39	Sooner or later, Spotlight 05/03, erschienen im Spotlight Verlag, www.spotlight-online.de, Planegg
S. 45	Wright, A/Betteridge, D./Buckby, M.: Games for Language Learning, Cambridge University Press, UK 1984
S. 46	Lutkat, S., Teaching English with Fairy Tales, Berlin 2004
S. 47	How can parents help their children, Spotlight 05/03, erschienen im Spotlight Verlag, www.spotlight-online.de, Planegg
S. 54	www.healthyfamilymag.com (2004); www.dw-world.de/dw/article/0,2144,2449356,00.html (2007)
S. 56	Five steps to a healthy lifestyle www.healthykids.nsw.gov.au Australien
S. 57	Tassoni, P.: Caring for Children (2001); Children's Care, Learning and Development Candidate Handbook (2005). Heinemann Educational Publishers, UK
S. 60	Sacristán, P.: The Toothy Toad, aus: freestoriesforkids.com
S. 62	ASDA Magazine, Juni 2003, UK
S. 76	Aston Business School, Birmingham, UK
S. 85	Gray, Kristi, eHow
S. 118	Moore, A. B. and Spencer Storch, S.: Family Portrait © 2001 by EMI April Music Inc/TVT Music/Left Handed Lover Music, Rechte für Deutschland, Österreich, Schweiz und Osteuropa (außer Baltikum): EMI Music Publishing Germany GmbH, Hamburg
S. 120	Burney, R. www.silcom.com/~joy2meu/joy_27.htm Roles in Dysfunctional Families; Wegscheider-Cruse, S.: Another Chance, Science and Behavior Books, USA 1989
S. 122 ff.	Skidmore, S./Barlow, S.: The Pressure Cooker, 1989 The Agency London Ltd., Erstausgabe bei Oxford University Press 1989, London, UK
S. 164	O'Bannon, M.: How to create a story, aus: www.shadowstargames.com, www.betterstorytelling.com
S. 168	Lawson, W., Interview, aus: www.mugsy.org/wendy, Warrnambool, Australien
S. 163	**Literaturtipp** (zu Literature Project): Breuer, U./Peters-Hilger, M.: EinFach Englisch Unterrichtsmodell – Mark Haddon 'The Curious Incident of the Dog in the Night-Time', Schöningh-Verlag, Paderborn 2007

Work with me ISBN 978-3-582-77856-7